Mindfulness

Mindfulness

An EIGHT-WEEK PLAN for

FINDING PEACE

in a FRANTIC WORLD

MARK WILLIAMS
and DANNY PENMAN

Foreword by Jon Kabat-Zinn

RODALE.

© 2011 by Mark Williams and Danny Penman
Foreword © 2011 by Jon Kabat-Zinn

Rodale books may be purchased for business or promotional use
or for special sales. For information, please write to:
Special Markets Department, Rodale, Inc., 733 Third Avenue,
New York, NY 10017

Printed in the United States of America
Rodale Inc. makes every effort to use acid-free ♾, recycled paper ♻.

"The Guest House" by Jalaluddin Rumi from *The Essential Rumi,* translated
by Coleman Barks with John Moyne, A. J. Arberry, and Reynold Nicholson
(Penguin, 1999) © Coleman Barks. Reproduced with permission.

Extract from *Here for Now: Living Well with Cancer through Mindfulness*
(2nd ed.) by Elana Rosenbaum (Satya House Publications, 2007)
© Elana Rosenbaum. Reproduced with permission.

Extract from Albert Einstein's letter to Norman Salit, 4 March 1950
© The Hebrew University of Jerusalem. Reproduced with permission.

"Hokusai Says" by Roger Keyes © Roger Keyes. Reproduced with permission.

The exhaustion funnel diagram on page 213 is reproduced with permission
from Marie Åsberg.

Library of Congress Cataloging-in-Publication Data
Williams, Mark.
    Mindfulness : an eight-week plan for finding peace in a frantic world / Mark
Williams and Danny Penman ; foreword by Jon Kabat-Zinn.
        p.   cm.
    Includes bibliographical references and index.
    ISBN 978–1–60961–198–9   hardcover
    1. Meditation—Therapeutic use.   2. Mindfulness-based cognitive therapy—
Popular works.   I. Penman, Danny, 1966–   II. Title.
RC489.M43W55 2011
616.89'1425—dc23   2011030548

Distributed to the trade by Macmillan
2   4   6   8   10   9   7   5   3   1   hardcover

We inspire and enable people to improve their lives and the world around them
www.rodalebooks.com

Contents

Acknowledgments   vii

Foreword by Jon Kabat-Zinn   ix

1. Chasing Your Tail   1

2. Why Do We Attack Ourselves?   15

3. Waking Up to the Life You Have   32

4. Introducing the Eight-Week
    Mindfulness Program   56

5. Mindfulness Week One: Waking Up
    to the Autopilot   67

6. Mindfulness Week Two: Keeping the
    Body in Mind   90

7. Mindfulness Week Three: The Mouse
    in the Maze   111

8. Mindfulness Week Four: Moving
    Beyond the Rumor Mill   136

9. Mindfulness Week Five: Turning
    Toward Difficulties   161

10. Mindfulness Week Six: Trapped in the
    Past or Living in the Present?   185

11. Mindfulness Week Seven: When Did
    You Stop Dancing?   211

12. Mindfulness Week Eight: Your Wild
     and Precious Life   238

     Notes   253
     Resources   265
     Index   270

Acknowledgments

This book would not have come together if it were not for the help and support of many people. We are enormously grateful to Sheila Crowley at Curtis Brown and to Anne Lawrance and her team at Piatkus.

Mark is grateful to the Wellcome Trust, not only for its generous financial support for the research that has sustained and extended the understanding of mindfulness, but also for the encouragement to take this work outside the academy.

We are also grateful to the many other individuals who have helped this project: Guinevere Webster, Gerry Byrne and the participants at the Boundary Brook training course, Oxford; Catherine Crane, Danielle Duggan, Thorsten Barnhofer, Melanie Fennell, Wendy Swift and other members of the Oxford Mindfulness Centre (an institution that remains a testimony to its founder, Geoffrey Bamford); Melanie Fennell and Phyllis Williams, who made many careful suggestions on an earlier draft of the text; Ferris Buck Urbanowski, Antonia Sumbundu and John Peacock, on whose wisdom Mark continues to draw; John Teasdale and Zindel Segal, codevelopers of MBCT, and close friends for so many years; and Jon Kabat-Zinn, not only for his original inspiration for this work, and his generosity in sharing it with us, but also for his continuing encouragement to bring its strong and compassionate wisdom to a frantic world.

Many of the ideas in this book and the words in which they are expressed come from the close collaboration over two decades between Mark Williams and Jon Kabat-Zinn, and Zindel Segal and John Teasdale. We are enormously grateful for their generosity in allowing us to once again share these ideas with people who are new to mindfulness, and with those who wish to renew their practice.

Danny would also like to thank Pat Field of Neston County Comprehensive School for having the courage and foresight to teach meditation to a group of belligerent teenagers (including him). In the early 1980s this was a radical educational step and one that transformed many lives. He is especially grateful to Pippa Stallworthy for her help and guidance.

Finally, each of us owes a tremendous debt to our families, and especially to our wives, Phyllis and Bella, for their loving support through our preoccupation with the inevitable challenges of writing.

Foreword by Jon Kabat-Zinn

The world is all abuzz nowadays about mindfulness. This is a wonderful thing because we are sorely lacking, if not starving for some elusive but necessary element in our lives. We might even have a strong intuition on occasion that what is really missing in some profound way is us—our willingness or ability to show up fully in our lives and live them as if they really mattered, in the only moment we ever get, which is this one—and that we are worthy of inhabiting life in this way and capable of it. This is a very brave intuition or insight, and it matters enormously. It could be world-transforming. It is certainly profoundly nurturing and life-transforming for those who undertake it.

That said, mindfulness is not merely a good idea: "Oh yes, I will just be more present in my life, and less judgmental, and everything will be better. Why didn't that occur to me before?" Such ideas are at best fleeting and hardly ever gain sustained traction. While it might very well be a good idea to be more present and less judgmental, you won't get very far with the idea alone. In fact, that thought might just make you feel more inadequate or out of control. To be effective, mindfulness requires an embodied engagement on the part of anyone hoping to derive some benefit from it. Another way to put it is that mindfulness, as Mark

Williams and Danny Penman point out, is actually a *practice*. It is a way of being, rather than merely a good idea or a clever technique, or a passing fad. Indeed, it is thousands of years old and is often spoken of as "the heart of Buddhist meditation," although its essence, being about attention and awareness, is universal.

The practice of mindfulness has been shown to exert a powerful influence on one's health, well-being and happiness, as attested to by the scientific and medical evidence presented in this book in a very accessible fashion. However, because it is a practice rather than merely a good idea, its cultivation is a process, one that of necessity unfolds and deepens over time. It is most beneficial if you take it on as a strong commitment to yourself, one that requires a degree of stick-to-it-ness and discipline, while at the same time being playful and bringing to each moment, as best you can, a certain ease and lightness of touch— a gesture of kindness and self-compassion, really. This lightness of touch, coupled with a steadfast and wholehearted engagement, is really a signature of mindfulness training and practice in all its various forms.

It is very important to have good guidance along this path, for the stakes are actually quite high. Ultimately, the quality of your very life and your relationships to others and to the world you inhabit is at stake, to say nothing of the degree of well-being, mental balance, happiness and integration in your life as it unfolds. You would do well to put yourself in the experienced hands of Mark Williams and Danny Penman, and give yourself over to their guidance and to the program that they map out. The program provides a coherent structure, an architecture if you will, within which you can observe your own mind and body and life unfolding, and a systematic and trustworthy approach for working with whatever arises. This architecture is strongly evidence-based, arising out of the curricula of mindfulness-based stress reduction (MBSR) and mindfulness-based cognitive therapy (MBCT), and fashioned into a coherent, compelling and commonsensical eight-week program for anyone caring about his or her own health and sanity, especially in this increasingly fast-paced and, as they refer to it, frantic world. I particularly like the simple yet radical habit-breaking suggestions, what they call "habit releasers," that they offer, which are meant to reveal and break open some of our most unaware life patterns of thought and behavior, patterns that unbeknownst to us, tend to imprison us in a smallness that is definitely not the full story of who we are.

And while you are putting yourself into the authors' hands for guidance, you are also, most importantly, putting yourself very much into your own hands by making the commitment to yourself to actually follow their suggestions, to engage in the various formal and informal practices and habit releasers, and put them to the test by seeing what happens when you begin to pay attention and act with kindness and compassion toward yourself and others, even if it feels a bit artificial at first. Such a commitment is ultimately a radical act of trust and faith in yourself. In concert with the inspiring program offered here, it could really be the opportunity of a lifetime, and a chance to reclaim and befriend that "lifetime" and live it more fully, moment by moment by moment.

I have known Mark Williams as a colleague, coauthor and good friend over many years. He is one of the premier researchers in the field of mindfulness worldwide, and has been a pioneer in its development and dissemination. He is a cofounder, along with John Teasdale and Zindel Segal, of MBCT, which has been shown in many studies to make a huge difference in the lives of people with the condition known as major depressive disorder by dramatically lowering their risk of relapsing back into depression. He is also the founder of the Oxford Mindfulness Center, and before that, the Center for Mindfulness Research and Practice at Bangor University, North Wales. Both centers are at the forefront of research and clinical training in mindfulness-based interventions. Now, with journalist Danny Penman, Mark has put together this very practical and pragmatic guide to mindfulness and its cultivation. May you derive great benefit from engaging in this program and its invitation to explore how you might be in a wiser and more fulfilling relationship to your "one wild and precious life."

Jon Kabat-Zinn
Boston, Massachusetts
December 2010

CHAPTER ONE

Chasing Your Tail

Can you remember the last time you lay in bed wrestling with your thoughts? You desperately wanted your mind to become calm, to just be *quiet*, so that you could get some sleep. But whatever you tried seemed to fail. Every time you forced yourself not to think, your thoughts exploded into life with renewed strength. You told yourself not to worry, but suddenly discovered countless new things to worry about. You tried fluffing up the pillow and rolling over to get more comfortable, but soon enough, you began thinking again. As the night ground ever onward, your strength progressively drained away, leaving you feeling fragile and broken. By the time the alarm went off, you were exhausted, bad-tempered and thoroughly miserable.

Throughout the next day you had the opposite problem—you wanted to be wide awake, but could hardly stop yawning. You stumbled into work, but weren't really present. You couldn't concentrate. Your eyes were red and puffy. Your whole body ached and your mind felt empty. You'd stare at the pile of papers on your desk for ages, hoping something, *anything*, would turn up so that you could gather enough momentum to do a day's work.

In meetings, you could barely keep your eyes open, let alone contribute anything intelligent. It seemed as though your life had begun to slip through your fingers . . . you felt ever more anxious, stressed and exhausted.

This is a book about how you can find peace and contentment in such troubled and frantic times as these. Or rather, this is a book about how you can *rediscover* them; for there are deep wellsprings of peace and contentment living inside us all, no matter how trapped and distraught we might feel. They're just waiting to be liberated from the cage that our frantic and relentless way of life has crafted for them.

We know this to be true because we—and our colleagues— have been studying anxiety, stress and depression for over thirty years at Oxford University, UMass, the University of Toronto, and other institutions around the world. This work has discovered the secret to sustained happiness and how you can successfully tackle anxiety, stress, exhaustion and even full-blown depression. It's the kind of happiness and peace that gets into your bones and promotes a deep-seated authentic love of life, seeping into everything you do and helping you to cope more skillfully with the worst that life throws at you.

It's a secret that was well understood in the ancient world and is kept alive in some cultures even today. But many of us in the Western world have largely forgotten how to live a good and joyful existence. And it's often even worse than this. We try *so* hard to be happy that we end up missing the most important parts of our lives and destroying the very peace that we were seeking.

We wrote this book to help you understand where true happiness, peace and contentment can be found and how you can rediscover them for yourself. It will teach you how to free yourself progressively from anxiety, stress, unhappiness and exhaustion. We're not promising eternal bliss; everyone experiences periods of pain and suffering, and it's naive and dangerous to pretend otherwise. And yet, *it is* possible to taste an alternative to the relentless struggle that pervades much of our daily lives.

In the following pages and in the accompanying downloads we offer a series of simple practices that you can incorporate into your daily life. They are based on mindfulness-based cognitive therapy (MBCT) that grew out of the inspiring work of Jon Kabat-Zinn at the UMass Medical Center in America. The MBCT program was originally developed by Professor Mark Williams (coauthor of this book), John Teasdale at Cambridge and Zindel Segal of the University of Toronto. It was designed to help people who had suffered repeated bouts of serious depression to overcome their illness. Clinical trials show that it works. It's been clinically proven to halve the risk of depression in those who have suffered the most debilitating forms of the illness. It's at least as effective as antidepressants, and has none of their downsides. In fact, it is so effective that it's now one of the preferred treatments recommended by the UK's National Institute for Health and Clinical Excellence.

The MBCT technique revolves around a form of meditation that was little known in the West until recently. Mindfulness meditation is so beautifully simple that it can be used by the rest of us to reveal our innate *joie de vivre*. Not only is this worthwhile in itself, but it can also prevent normal feelings of anxiety, stress and sadness from spiraling downwards into prolonged periods of unhappiness and exhaustion—or even serious clinical depression.

A one-minute meditation

1. Sit erect in a straight-backed chair. If possible, bring your back a little way from the rear of the chair so that your spine is self-supporting. Your feet can be flat on the floor. Close your eyes or lower your gaze.

2. Focus your attention on your breath as it flows in and out of your body. Stay in touch with the different sensations of each in-breath and each out-breath. Observe the breath without looking for anything special to happen. There is no need to alter your breathing in any way.

3. After a while your mind may wander. When you notice this, gently bring your attention back to your breath, without giving yourself a hard time—the act of realizing that your mind has wandered and bringing your attention back without criticizing yourself is central to the practice of mindfulness meditation.

4. Your mind may eventually become calm like a still pond—or it may not. Even if you get a sense of absolute stillness, it may only be fleeting. If you feel angry or exasperated, notice that this may be fleeting too. Whatever happens, just allow it to be as it is.

5. After a minute, let your eyes open and take in the room again.

A typical meditation consists of focusing your full attention on your breath as it flows in and out of your body (see "A one-minute meditation" on the opposite page). Focusing on each breath in this way allows you to observe your thoughts as they arise in your mind and, little by little, to let go of struggling with them. You come to realize that thoughts come and go of their own accord; that *you* are not your thoughts. You can watch as they appear in your mind, seemingly from thin air, and watch again as they disappear, like a soap bubble bursting. You come to the profound understanding that thoughts and feelings (including negative ones) are transient. They come and they go, and ultimately, you have a choice about whether to act on them or not.

Mindfulness is about observation without criticism; being compassionate with yourself. When unhappiness or stress hovers overhead, rather than taking it all personally, you learn to treat them as if they were black clouds in the sky, and to observe them with friendly curiosity as they drift past. In essence, mindfulness allows you to catch negative thought patterns before they tip you into a downward spiral. It begins the process of putting you back in control of your life.

Over time, mindfulness brings about long-term changes in mood and levels of happiness and well-being. Scientific studies have shown that mindfulness not only prevents depression, but that it also positively affects the brain patterns underlying day-to-day anxiety, stress, depression and irritability so that when they arise, they dissolve away again more easily. Other studies have shown that regular meditators see their doctors less often and spend fewer days in hospital. Memory improves, creativity increases and reaction times become faster (see "The benefits of mindfulness meditation" on the following page).

The benefits of mindfulness meditation

Numerous psychological studies have shown that regular meditators are happier and more contented than average.[1] These are not
just important results in themselves but have huge medical significance, as such positive emotions are linked to a longer and
healthier life.[2]

- Anxiety, depression and irritability all decrease with regular sessions of meditation.[3] Memory also improves, reaction times
  become faster and mental and physical stamina increase.[4]

- Regular meditators enjoy better and more fulfilling relationships.[5]

- Studies worldwide have found that meditation reduces the key
  indicators of chronic stress, including hypertension.[6]

- Meditation has also been found to be effective in reducing
  the impact of serious conditions, such as chronic pain[7] and
  cancer,[8] and can even help to relieve drug and alcohol
  dependence.[9]

- Studies have now shown that meditation bolsters the immune
  system and thus helps to fight off colds, flu and other diseases.[10]

Despite these *proven* benefits, however, many people are still
a little wary when they hear the word "meditation." So before
we proceed, it might be helpful to dispel some myths:

- Meditation is not a religion. Mindfulness is simply a method
  of mental training. Many people who practice meditation are

themselves religious, but then again, many atheists and agnostics are avid meditators too.

- You don't have to sit cross-legged on the floor (like the pictures you may have seen in magazines or on TV), but you can if you want to. Most people who come to our classes sit on chairs to meditate, but you can also practice bringing mindful awareness to whatever you are doing on planes, trains, or while walking to work. You can meditate more or less anywhere.

- Mindfulness practice does not take a lot of time, although some patience and persistence are required. Many people soon find that meditation liberates them from the pressures of time, so they have more of it to spend on other things.

- Meditation is not complicated. Nor is it about "success" or "failure." Even when meditation feels difficult, you'll have learned something valuable about the workings of the mind and thus will have benefited psychologically.

- It will not deaden your mind or prevent you from striving toward important career or lifestyle goals; nor will it trick you into falsely adopting a Pollyanna attitude to life. Meditation is not about accepting the unacceptable. It is about seeing the world with greater clarity so that you can take wiser and more considered action to change those things that need to be changed. Meditation helps cultivate a deep and compassionate awareness that allows you to assess your goals and find the optimum path towards realizing your deepest values.

Finding peace in a frantic world

If you have picked up this book, the chances are you've repeatedly asked yourself why the peace and happiness you yearn for so often slip through your fingers. Why is so much of life defined by frantic busyness, anxiety, stress and exhaustion? These are questions that puzzled us for many years too, and we think that science has finally found the answers. And, ironically, the principles underlying these answers were known to the ancient world: they are eternal truths.

Our moods naturally wax and wane. It's the way we're meant to be. But certain patterns of thinking can turn a short-term dip in vitality or emotional well-being into longer periods of anxiety, stress, unhappiness and exhaustion. A brief moment of sadness, anger or anxiety can end up tipping you into a "bad mood" that colors a whole day or far, far longer. Recent scientific discoveries have shown how these normal emotional fluxes can lead to long-term unhappiness, acute anxiety and even depression. But, more importantly, these discoveries have also revealed the path to becoming a happier and more "centered" person, by showing that:

- when you start to feel a little sad, anxious or irritable, it's not the mood that does the damage but how you react to it.

- the effort of trying to free yourself from a bad mood or bout of unhappiness—of working out why you're unhappy and what you can do about it—often makes things worse. It's like being trapped in quicksand—the more you struggle to be free, the deeper you sink.

As soon as we understand how the mind works, it becomes obvious why we all suffer from bouts of unhappiness, stress and irritability from time to time.

When you begin to feel a little unhappy, it's natural to try and think your way out of the *problem* of being unhappy. You try to establish what is making you unhappy and then find a solution. In the process, you can easily dredge up past regrets and conjure up future worries. This further lowers your mood. It doesn't take long before you start to feel bad for failing to discover a way of cheering yourself up. The "inner critic," which lives inside us all, begins to whisper that it's your fault, that you should try harder, whatever the cost. You soon start to feel separated from the deepest and wisest parts of yourself. You get lost in a seemingly endless cycle of recrimination and self-judgment; finding yourself at fault for not meeting your ideals, for not being the person you wish you could be.

We get drawn into this emotional quicksand because our state of mind is intimately connected with memory. The mind is constantly trawling through memories to find those that echo our current emotional state. For example, if you feel threatened, the mind instantly digs up memories of when you felt endangered in the past, so that you can spot similarities and find a way of escaping. It happens in an instant, before you're even aware of it. It's a basic survival skill honed by millions of years of evolution. It's incredibly powerful and almost impossible to stop.

The same is true with unhappiness, anxiety and stress. It is normal to feel a little unhappy from time to time, but sometimes a few sad thoughts can end up triggering a cascade of unhappy memories, negative emotions and harsh judgments. Before long, hours or even days can be colored by negative self-critical thoughts such as, *What's wrong with me? My life is a mess. What will happen when they discover how useless I really am?*

Such self-attacking thoughts are incredibly powerful, and once they gather momentum they are almost impossible to stop. One thought or feeling triggers the next, and then the next . . . Soon, the original thought—no matter how fleeting—has gathered up a raft of similar sadnesses, anxieties and fears and you've become enmeshed in your own sorrow.

In a sense, there is nothing surprising about this. Context has a huge effect on our memory. A few years ago, psychologists discovered that if deep-sea divers memorized a list of words on a beach, they tended to forget them when they were under water, but were able to remember them again when they were back on dry land. It worked the other way round too. Words memorized under water were more easily forgotten on the beach. The sea and the beach were powerful contexts for memory.[11]

You can see the same process working in your own mind too. Have you ever revisited a favorite childhood vacation destination? Before the visit you probably had only hazy memories of it. But once you got there—walking down the streets, taking in the sights, sounds and smells—the memories came flooding back. You may have felt excited, wistful or perhaps even a little bit in love. Returning to that context encouraged your mind to recall a host of related memories. But it's not just places that trigger memories. The world is full of such triggers. Has a song ever sparked a cascade of emotionally charged memories? Or the smell of flowers or freshly baked bread?

Similarly, our mood can act as an internal context that is every bit as powerful as a visit to an old vacation destination or the sound of a favorite tune. A flicker of sadness, frustration or anxiety can bring back unsettling memories, whether you want them or not. Soon you can be lost in gloomy thoughts and negative emotions. And often you don't know where they came from—they just appeared, seemingly from thin air. You can become bad-tempered, irritable or sad without really knowing why. You're left wondering, *Why am I in a bad mood?* Or, *Why do I feel so sad and tired today?*

You can't stop the triggering of unhappy memories, self-critical thoughts and judgmental ways of thinking—but you can stop what happens next. You can stop the spiral from feeding off itself and triggering the next cycle of negative thoughts. You can stop the cascade of destructive emotions that can end up making you unhappy, anxious, stressed, irritable or exhausted.

Mindfulness meditation teaches you to recognize memories and damaging thoughts as they arise. It reminds you that they are memories. They are like propaganda, *they are not real.* They are not *you.* You can learn to observe negative thoughts as they arise, let them stay a while and then simply watch them evaporate before your eyes. And when this occurs, an extraordinary thing can happen: a profound sense of happiness and peace fills the void.

Mindfulness meditation does this by harnessing an alternative way in which our minds can relate to the world. Most of us know only the analytical side of the mind; the process of thinking, judging, planning and trawling through past memories while searching for solutions. But the mind is also *aware.* We do not just *think* about things, we are also aware that we are thinking. And we don't need language to stand as an intermediary between us and the world; we can also experience it directly through our senses. We are capable of directly sensing things like the sounds of birds, the scent of beautiful flowers and the sight of a loved one's smile. And we know with the heart as well as the head. Thinking is not all there is to conscious experience. The mind is bigger and more encompassing than thought alone.

Meditation creates greater mental clarity; seeing things with pure open-hearted awareness. It's a place—a vantage point—

from which we can witness our own thoughts and feelings as they arise. It takes us off the hair trigger that compels us to react to things as soon as they happen. Our inner self—the part that is innately happy and at peace—is no longer drowned out by the noise of the mind crunching through problems.

Mindfulness meditation encourages us to become more patient and compassionate with ourselves and to cultivate open-mindedness and gentle persistence. These qualities help free us from the gravitational pull of anxiety, stress and unhappiness by reminding us what science has shown: that it's OK to stop treating sadness and other difficulties as problems that need to be solved. We shouldn't feel bad about "failing" to fix them. In fact, that's often the wisest course of action because our habitual ways of solving such difficulties often make them worse.

Mindfulness does not negate the brain's natural desire to solve problems. It simply gives us the time and space to choose the *best* ways of solving them. Some problems are best dealt with emotionally—we select the solution that "feels" best. Others need to be slogged through logically. Many are best dealt with intuitively, creatively. Some are best left alone for now.

Happiness awaits

Mindfulness operates on two levels. First and foremost is the core mindfulness meditation program. This is a series of simple daily meditations that can be done almost anywhere, though you'll find it most helpful to do them in a quiet spot at home. Some are as short as three minutes. Others may take twenty to thirty minutes.

Mindfulness also encourages you to break some of the unconscious habits of thinking and behaving that stop you from living life to the full. Many judgmental and self-critical thoughts arise out of habitual ways of thinking and acting. By breaking with some of your daily routines, you'll progressively dissolve some of these negative thinking patterns and become more mindful and aware. You may be astonished by how much more happiness and joy are attainable with even tiny changes to the way you live your life.

Habit breaking is straightforward. It's as simple as not sitting in the same chair at meetings, switching off the television for a while or taking a different route to work. You may also be asked to plant some seeds and watch them grow, or perhaps look after a friend's pet for a few days or go and watch a film at your local cinema. Such simple things—acting together with a short meditation each day—really can make your life more joyous and fulfilled.

You can do the program over as long or as short a period as you wish, but it's best to do it over the recommended eight weeks. It's as flexible as you want to make it, but it's worth remembering that it may take time for the practices to reveal their full potential. That's why they are called practices. Everything in this book is designed to help you along this path. And if you follow the path, you'll begin to find peace in a frantic world.

To start the program right away, we suggest you turn to Chapter Four. If you'd like to know more about the new scientific discoveries that reveal how and why we trap ourselves in negative ways of thinking and behaving—and how mindfulness meditation frees you—then Chapters Two and Three will help you with this. We really hope you will read these chapters, as they'll give you an understanding, at the deepest of levels, of why mindfulness is so powerful. They will greatly aid your progress and you'll also get the opportunity to try the Chocolate meditation. If you're anxious to get going now, however, there's no reason why you can't start the program immediately and read Chapters Two and Three as you go along.

At http://bit.ly/rodalemindfulness you will find eight tracks containing the meditations you will need to guide you through the program, narrated by Mark Williams. We suggest that you read through each meditation as you come to them in the book, and then do the meditation itself, following the guidance on the audio tracks.

CHAPTER TWO

Why Do We Attack Ourselves?

Lucy was outwardly a successful buyer for an international clothing chain. She was also stuck: she sat staring out of the window at three in the afternoon, stressed out, exhausted and thoroughly miserable:

> *Why can't I get on with this project?* she wondered. *I can usually do these figures in no time. Why can't I just come to a decision? What's wrong with me? I'm so tired—I can't even think straight . . .*

Lucy had been punishing herself with such self-critical thoughts for over an hour. Before that, she'd had a long, anxious chat with the kindergarten teacher about her daughter, Emily, who'd been crying when she'd left her earlier that morning. Then, in a bit of a rush, she'd phoned the plumber to find out why he hadn't been to look at the broken toilet in her house. Now she was staring at a spreadsheet, feeling drained of energy and munching on a chocolate muffin in lieu of lunch.

The demands and strains in Lucy's life had been growing steadily worse for months. Work was becoming ever more stressful and had started to drag on, way past her normal finishing time. Nights had become sleepless, days more drowsy. Her limbs had started to ache. Life had begun to lose its joy. It had become a struggle to keep going. She'd felt like this for brief periods before, when at college with exams looming, but those had been temporary. She'd never have guessed that they could become such a permanent feature of her life.

She kept asking herself repeatedly: *What's become of my life? Why do I feel so burned out? I should be happy. I used to be happy. Where did it all go?*

Lucy exists in a netherworld of overwork, general low-level unhappiness, dissatisfaction and stress. She's been sapped of her mental and physical energy and has begun to feel increasingly rudderless. She desperately wants to be happy and at peace with herself, but has no idea how to get there. Her unhappiness and dissatisfaction aren't severe enough to warrant a trip to the doctor, but enough to sap many of life's joys. She *exists*, rather than truly *lives*.

Lucy's story is hardly unique. She is one of countless millions who are neither depressed nor anxious in a medical sense—yet who are not truly happy either. We all go through life with rises and falls in mood and energy. Often these changes in mood come out of the blue. One moment we're happily bumbling through life, daydreaming, feeling content and unfussed, but then something subtle happens. Before we know it, we're

Unhappiness, stress and depression

Depression is taking a staggering toll on the modern world. Around 10 percent of the population can expect to become clinically depressed over the coming year. And things are likely to become worse. The World Health Organization[1] estimates that depression will impose the second-biggest health burden globally by 2020. Think about that for a moment. Depression will impose a bigger burden than heart disease, arthritis and many forms of cancer on both individuals and society in less than a decade.

Depression used to be an illness of the late middle-aged; now it strikes most people first when they are in their mid-twenties, and a substantial number of people suffer their first bout in their teens.[2] It can also persist, with around 15–39 percent of sufferers still depressed after one year. Around one-fifth remain depressed for two or more years—the definition of "chronic" depression.[3] But the scariest thing of all is that depression tends to return. If you've been depressed once, there is a 50 percent chance of a recurrence—even if you've made a full recovery.

Depression may be exacting a staggering toll, but its cousin—chronic anxiety—is becoming disturbingly common too, with *average* levels of anxiety in children and young people now at a point that would have been judged to be "clinical" in the 1950s.[4] It's not a great stretch of the imagination to assume that in a few decades unhappiness, depression and anxiety will have become the normal human condition, rather than happiness and contentment.

starting to feel a little stressed: there's too much to do and not enough time, and the pace of demands seems ever more relentless. We feel tired, but find that even after a good night's sleep we don't feel refreshed. And then we stop and ask ourselves: How did that happen? There may have been no big changes in life, we haven't lost any friends nor have our debts suddenly spiraled out of control. Nothing's changed, but the joy has somehow gone out of life and been replaced with a sort of generalized distress and listlessness.

Most people, most of the time, do snap out of these downward spirals. Such periods *do* generally pass. But sometimes they can tip us into a tailspin that persists for days. Or, as in the case of Lucy, they can persist for weeks and months with no apparent rhyme or reason. In severe cases, people can be tipped into a full-blown episode of clinical anxiety or depression (see box on the preceding page).

Although persistent periods of distress and exhaustion often seem to arrive from nowhere, there are underlying processes going on in the background of the mind that were only unraveled in the 1990s and early twenty-first century. And with this understanding has come the realization that we can "step outside" of our troubles and liberate ourselves from unhappiness, anxiety, stress, exhaustion and even depression.

Our troubled minds

If you'd asked Lucy how she felt when she was staring at her computer, she'd have said "exhausted" or "tense." At first glance these feelings seem like clear-cut statements of fact, but if she'd looked inside herself a little more closely she'd have realized that there wasn't one single thing that you could label as "exhaustion" or "tension." Both of these emotions were actually "bundles" of thoughts, raw feelings, bodily sensations and impulses (such as the desire to scream or storm out of the room). This is what emotions are; they're like a background color that's created when your mind fuses together all of your thoughts, feelings, impulses and bodily sensations to conjure up an overall guiding theme or state of mind (see diagram, "What makes an emotion?" p. 20). All of these different elements that make up an emotion play off each other and can end up enhancing (or tempering) overall mood. It's a phenomenally intricate dance full of subtle interactions that we're only now beginning to understand.

Take thoughts as an example. Several decades ago, it became apparent that thoughts could drive our moods and emotions, but it's only since the 1980s that it's become clear that the process can also run in reverse: moods can drive our thoughts. Think about that for a moment. Your moods can drive your thoughts. In practice, this means that even a few fleeting moments of sadness can end up feeding off themselves to create more unhappy thoughts by coloring how you see and interpret the world. Just as gloomy skies can make you feel, well, gloomy, momentary sadness can dredge up unsettling thoughts and memories, further deepening the mood. The same goes for other moods and emotions too. If you feel stressed, then this stress can feed off itself to create more stress. Likewise with anxiety, fear, anger and such "positive" emotions as love, happiness, compassion and empathy.

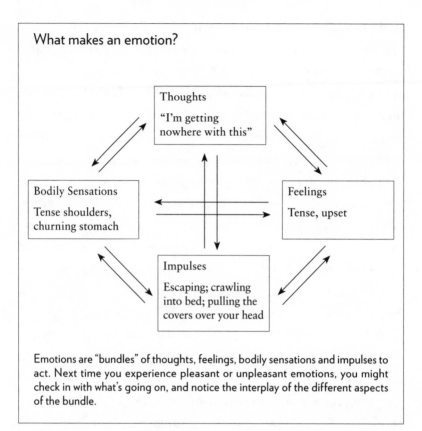

What makes an emotion?

Emotions are "bundles" of thoughts, feelings, bodily sensations and impulses to act. Next time you experience pleasant or unpleasant emotions, you might check in with what's going on, and notice the interplay of the different aspects of the bundle.

But it's not just thoughts and moods that feed off each other and end up wrecking well-being—the body also gets involved. This is because the mind does not exist in isolation; it's a fundamental part of the body and they both continuously share emotional information with each other. In fact, much of what the body feels is colored by our thoughts and emotions, and everything that we think is informed by what's going on in the body. It's a phenomenally complex process full of feedbacks, but research is showing us that our whole outlook on life can be shifted by tiny changes in the body. Something as subtle as frowning, smiling or altering posture can have a dramatic impact on mood and the types of

Depressed mood, depressed body

Have you noticed how low mood affects the body, such as the way you move?

Psychologist Johannes Michalak[5] and colleagues at the Ruhr-University at Bochum used an optical motion capture system to see how depressed people differ from non-depressed people as they walk: they invited depressed and non-depressed people to their lab and asked them to walk, choosing freely how to walk and at what speed. They tracked the walkers' three-dimensional movements using over forty small reflective markers attached to their bodies as they walked up and down.

They found that the depressed volunteers walked more slowly, swinging their arms less; the upper body did not move up and down very much when they walked, but was more likely to swing from side to side instead. Finally, they found that the depressed people walked with a slumped, forward-leaning posture.

It is not just that such slumped posture is the result of being depressed. If you try the experiment of sitting for a minute with your shoulders slumped forward and head down, notice how you feel at the end of it. If you feel your mood has worsened, perhaps finish the experiment by shifting to a posture in which you are sitting upright, with your head and neck balanced on your shoulders.

thoughts flickering across the mind (see box above).

To get a flavor of how powerful this feedback can be, the psychologists Fritz Strack, Leonard Martin and Sabine Stepper[6] asked a group of people to watch cartoons and then rate how funny they were. Some were asked to hold a pencil between their lips so that they were forced to purse them and mimic a scowl. Others watched the cartoons with the pencil between their teeth, simulating a smile. The results were striking: those who were forced to smile found the cartoons significantly funnier than those compelled to frown. It's obvious that smiling shows you are happy but it is, admittedly, a bit strange to realize that the act of smiling can itself *make* you happy. It's a perfect illustration of just how close the links are between the mind and body. Smiling is infectious too. When you see someone grin, you almost invariably smile back. You can't help it. Think about that for a moment: just the act of smiling can make you happy (even if it's forced); and if you smile, others will smile back at you, reinforcing your own happiness. It's a virtuous circle.

But there's an equal and opposite vicious circle too: when we sense a threat we tense up, ready to fight or run away. This so-called "fight-or-flight" response isn't conscious—it's controlled by one of the most "primeval" parts of the brain, which means it's often a bit simplistic in the way it interprets danger. In fact, it makes no distinction between an external threat, such as a tiger, and an internal one, such as a troubling memory or a future worry. It treats both as threats that either need to be fought off or run away from. When a threat is sensed—whether real or imagined—the body tenses and braces for action. This may manifest as a frown, the churning of the stomach, tension in the shoulders or the draining of blood from the skin. The mind then senses the tension in the body and interprets it as a threat (remember how a frown can make you feel sad?), which then makes the body tense up even further . . . A vicious circle has begun.

In practice, this means that if you're feeling a little stressed or vulnerable, a minor emotional shift can end up ruining your whole day—or even tip you into a prolonged period of dissatisfaction or worry. Such shifts often appear out of the blue, leaving you drained of energy and asking, Why am I so unhappy?

Oliver Burkeman recently discovered this for himself. He wrote in his column in the UK's *Guardian* newspaper about how minor bodily sensations sometimes seemed to feed back on themselves to tip him into an emotional spiral.

> I think of myself as generally happy, but every so often I'm struck by a fleeting mood of unhappiness or anxiety that quickly escalates. On a really bad day, I may spend hours stuck in angst-ridden maunderings, wondering if I need to make major changes in my life. It's usually then that I realize I've forgotten to eat lunch. One tuna sandwich later, the mood is gone. And yet, 'Am I hungry?' is never my first response to feeling bad: my brain, apparently, would prefer to distress itself with reflections on the ultimate meaninglessness of human existence than to direct my body to a nearby branch of Pret A Manger.

Of course, and as Oliver Burkeman has repeatedly found out for himself, most of the time such "angst-ridden maunderings" soon blow over. Something catches our eye and makes us smile—a friend calls and cheers us up or perhaps we'll watch a movie and go to bed early with a cup of hot chocolate. Virtually every time we're buffeted by life's ill winds, something crops up to redress the balance. But it's not always this way. Sometimes the weight of our own history intervenes to whip up an emotional squall because our memories can have a powerful impact on our thoughts, feelings, drives and, ultimately, our bodies too.

Take the case of Lucy. Although she describes herself as being "driven" and "mostly successful" she's acutely aware that something fundamental is missing from her life. She's achieved most of what she wanted, so finds it perplexing that she's not happy, contented and at peace with herself. She constantly tells herself, "I should be happy," as if saying this alone is enough to drive away unhappiness.

Lucy's bouts of unhappiness began when she was a teenager. Her parents split up when she was seventeen and the family home was sold, forcing both parents to move into apartments that were barely adequate. Lucy surprised herself, and her family, by toughing it out. Sure, she was initially devastated by her parents' divorce, but she soon learned to distract herself by working hard at school. This was her life-saver. She achieved good grades, went to college and got a decent diploma. She surprised herself again when she got her first job as a trainee buyer for an international clothing chain. She then spent most of her twenties climbing the promotion ladder until she was managing a small team of buyers.

Work gradually took over Lucy's life, leaving her with less and less time for herself. It happened so slowly that she hardly realized that life had begun passing her by. There were high points too, of course, like her marriage to Tom and the birth of their two daughters. She loved them all to bits, but she still couldn't quite shake the feeling that life was something that only happened to other people. She was walking "through slowly thickening syrup," she told us.

This "thickening syrup" was her current busyness and stress, together with the older patterns of thoughts and feelings from the past. Even though Lucy was outwardly successful, her thoughts were often dogged—deep down—by fears of failure. This ensured that when an entirely normal low mood appeared, her mind would spontaneously begin digging up memories of when she felt similarly in the past, while a harsh "inner critic" told her that it would be shameful to display any weaknesses. Vague feelings of fear or insecurity ended up triggering a cascade of painful feelings from the past that felt very real and visceral, and that quickly took on a life of their own, activating another wave of negative emotions. On the surface, these seemed to have little connection with each other; however, these emotions *were* connected because such feelings often come in constellations, with one part of a pattern triggering the rest.

As Lucy will testify, we rarely experience tension or sadness on their own—anger, irritability, bitterness, jealousy and hatred can all be bound up with them in an uncomfortable, spiky knot of pain. These feelings may be directed at others but, more often than not, they are aimed at ourselves, even if we're not consciously aware of it. Over a lifetime, these emotional constellations can become ever more closely coupled to thoughts, feelings, bodily sensations and even behavior. This is how the past can have an all-pervading effect in the present; if we trip one emotional switch, the others can follow behind (and likewise with bodily sensations such as an ache or a pain). All of these can trigger habitual patterns of thinking, behaving and feeling that we know are counterproductive, but somehow just can't seem to stop. And between them, they can create a very large net that will catch any slight emotional turbulence and whip it into a storm.

Gradually, the repeated triggering of negative thoughts and moods can begin wearing grooves in the mind; over time, these become deeper and deeper, making it easier to set off negative, self-critical thoughts and low or panicky moods—and more difficult to shake them off. After a while, prolonged periods of fragility can be triggered by the most innocuous of things, such as a momentary dip in mood or the slightest flux in energy levels. These triggers can be so small that you might not even be aware of them. To make matters worse, negative thoughts often come in the guise of harsh questions that beg answers. They nag. Grind away at your soul. Demand an immediate response: *Why am I unhappy? What's up with me today? Where have I gone wrong? Where will it end?*

The close links between the different aspects of emotion, stretching back into the past, can explain why a small trigger can have a significant effect on mood. Sometimes these moods come and go just as quickly as they arrive, like a squall blowing over; but at other times, the stress and fatigue, or the low mood, seem adhesive—they stick around and nothing seems to get rid of them. It's almost as if certain parts of the mind switch on, then get stuck and refuse to turn off again. As it turns out, this is what seems to be happening: sometimes the mind automatically switches to full alert, but then *does not switch off* again as it's meant to do.

A good way of illustrating this is to observe the ways in which many animals deal with danger as compared to humans. Cast your mind back to the last nature documentary you saw on TV. Perhaps it contained scenes of a herd of gazelles being chased by a leopard on the African savannah. Terrified, the animals ran like crazy until the leopard had either caught one or gave up the chase for the day. Once the danger had passed, the herd quickly settled back into grazing. Something in the gazelles' brains that gave the alarm when the leopard was noticed, switched off once the danger was past.

But the human mind is different, especially when it comes to the "intangible" threats that can trigger anxiety, stress, worry or irritability. When there is something to be scared or stressed about—whether real or imagined—our ancient "fight-or-flight" reactions kick in as they should. But then something else happens: the mind begins to trawl through memories to try and find something that will explain *why* we are feeling like this. So if we feel stressed or in danger, our minds dig up memories of when we felt threatened in the past, and then create scenarios of what might happen in the future if we cannot explain what is going on now. The result is that the brain's alarm signals start to be triggered not only by the *current* scare, but by *past* threats and *future* worries. This happens in an instant, before we're even aware of it. New evidence from brain scans confirms this: people who spend their days rushing around mindlessly, who find it difficult to stay present and get so focused on goals that they lose touch with the outside world, have an *amygdala* (the primeval part of the brain involved in fight-or-flight) that is on "high alert" all the time.[7] So when we humans bring to mind other threats and losses, as well as the current scenario, our bodies' fight-or-flight systems do not switch off when the danger is past. Unlike the gazelles, we don't stop running.

And so the way we react can transform temporary and nonproblematic emotions into persistent and troublesome ones. In short, the mind can end up making things far worse. This holds true for many other everyday feelings as well—take tiredness, for example:

As you sit here reading, see if you can tune in to any feelings of tiredness in your body right now. Spend a moment noticing how tired you are feeling. Once you have this tiredness in mind, ask yourself some questions about it. *Why am I feeling tired? What's gone wrong? What does this say about me that I'm feeling like this? What will happen if I can't shrug this off?*

Think about all these questions for a moment. Allow them to

swirl around in your mind: *Why? What's wrong? What does this tiredness mean? What will the consequences be? Why?*

Now how do you feel? You probably feel worse; virtually everyone does. This is because underlying these questions there is a desire to get rid of the tiredness, and to do so by trying to work out the reasons for it, its meaning and the possible consequences if you don't.[8] The understandable impulse to explain or banish the tiredness has made you feel more tired.

And this holds true for a panoply of human feelings and emotions including unhappiness, anxiety and stress. When we're unhappy, for example, it's natural to try to figure out why we're feeling this way and to find a way of solving the *problem* of unhappiness. But tension, unhappiness or exhaustion aren't "problems" that can be solved. They are emotions. They reflect states of mind and body. As such, they cannot be *solved*—only *felt*. Once you've felt them—that is, acknowledged their existence—and let go of the tendency to explain or get rid of them, they are much more likely to vanish naturally, like the mist on a spring morning.

Allow us to explain this seemingly heretical idea. Why do your best efforts to get rid of unpleasant feelings backfire so tragically?

When you try to solve the "problem" of unhappiness (or any other "negative" emotion) you deploy one of the mind's most powerful tools: rational critical thinking. It works like this: you see yourself in a place (unhappy) and know where you want to be (happy). Your mind then analyzes the gap between the two and tries to work out the best way of bridging it. To do so, it uses its "Doing" mode (so called because it performs well in solving problems and getting things done). The Doing mode works by progressively narrowing the gap between where you are and where you want to be. It does so by subconsciously breaking down the problem into pieces, each of which is solved in your mind's eye and the solution reanalyzed to see whether it's got you closer to your goal. It often happens in an instant and we're frequently not even aware of the process. It's a tremendously powerful way of solving problems. It's how we find our way across cities, drive cars and arrange hectic work schedules. In a more refined form, it's how the ancients built the pyramids and navigated the world in primitive sailing ships, and it is helping humanity to solve many of our most pressing problems.

It's perfectly natural, then, to apply this approach to solving the "problem" of unhappiness. But it's often the worst thing you can do because it requires you to focus on the gap between how you are and how you'd like to be: in doing so, you ask such critical questions as, *What's wrong with me? Where did I go wrong? Why do I always make these mistakes?* Such questions are not only harsh and self-destructive, but they also demand that the mind furnishes the evidence to explain its discontent. And the mind is truly brilliant at providing such evidence.

Imagine walking through a beautiful park on a spring day. You're happy, but then for some unknown reason a flicker of sadness ripples across your mind. It may be the result of hunger because you skipped lunch or perhaps you unwittingly triggered a troubling memory. After a few minutes you might start to feel a little down. As soon as you notice your lowered spirits you begin to probe yourself: *It's a lovely day. It's a beautiful park. I wish I were feeling happier than I am now.*

Think about that for a moment: *I wish I were feeling happier.*

How do you feel now? You probably feel worse. This is because you focused on the gap between how you feel and how you *want* to feel. And focusing on the gap *highlighted* it. The mind sees the gap as a problem to be solved. This approach is disastrous when it comes to your emotions because of the intricate interconnection between your thoughts, emotions and bodily sensations. They all feed into each other and, left unchecked, can drive your thinking in very distressing directions. Very quickly, you can become trapped inside your own thoughts. You begin to overthink; you begin to brood. You start to ask yourself endlessly the same pointed questions that demand immediate answers: *What's up with me today? I should be happy—why can't I just get a grip?*

Your spirits sink a little deeper. Your body may tense up, your mouth may frown and you may feel downhearted. A few aches and pains might appear. These sensations then feed back into your mind, which then feels even more threatened and a little more downbeat. If your spirits sink far enough, you'll start to become really preoccupied and miss the small, but beautiful things that would normally cheer you up: you might fail to notice daffodils beginning to bloom, the ducks playing on the lake, the innocent smiles of children.

Of course, nobody broods over problems because they believe it's a toxic way of thinking. People genuinely believe that if they worry enough over their unhappiness they will eventually find a solution. They just need to make one last heave—think a little more about the problem . . . But research shows the opposite: in fact, brooding reduces our ability to solve problems; and it's absolutely hopeless for dealing with emotional difficulties.

The evidence is clear: brooding is the problem,
not the solution.

Escaping the vicious circle

You can't stop the triggering of unhappy memories, negative self-talk and judgmental ways of thinking—but what you *can* stop is what happens next. You can stop the vicious circle from feeding off itself and triggering the next spiral of negative thoughts. And you can do this by harnessing an alternative way of relating to yourself and the world. The mind can do so much more than simply analyze problems with its Doing mode. The problem is that we use the Doing mode so much, we can't see that there is an alternative. Yet there is another way. If you stop and reflect for a moment, the mind doesn't just think. It can also be *aware* that it is thinking. This form of pure awareness allows you to experience the world directly. It's bigger than thinking. It's unclouded by your thoughts, feelings and emotions. It's like a high mountain—a vantage point—from which you can see everything for many miles around.

Pure awareness transcends thinking. It allows you to step outside the chattering negative self-talk and your reactive impulses and emotions. It allows you to look at the world once again with open eyes. And when you do so, a sense of wonder and quiet contentment begins to reappear in your life.

CHAPTER THREE

Waking Up to the Life You Have

The real voyage of discovery consists not in seeking out new landscapes but in having new eyes.

ATTRIB. MARCEL PROUST, 1871–1922

P icture yourself on a suburban hilltop in the rain and looking across a gray cityscape. It could be the town you grew up in or the one where you now live. In the rain it seems cold and inhospitable. The buildings look tattered and old. The streets are clogged with traffic and everyone seems miserable and bad-tempered. Then something miraculous happens. The clouds part and the sun comes streaming through. The whole world is transformed in an instant. The windows of the buildings turn to gold. Gray concrete changes to burnished bronze. The streets look shiny and clean. A rainbow appears. The mucky river becomes an exotic, glistening serpent threading its way through the city. For one fabulous moment, everything seems to stop; your breathing, your heart, your mind, the birds in the sky, the traffic in the streets, time itself. All seem to pause, to take in the transformation.

Such beautiful and unexpected changes in perspective have a dramatic effect—not only on what you see, but also on what you think and feel, and how you relate to the world. They can radically alter your whole outlook on life in the blink of an eye. But what's truly remarkable about them is that very little actually changes; the cityscape remains the same, but when the sun comes out you simply see the world in *a different light*. Nothing more.

Viewing your life from *a different place* can equally transform your feelings. Think back to a time when you were getting ready for a well-earned vacation. There was far too much to do and simply not enough time to cram it all in. You got home late from work after trying and failing to "clear the decks" before allowing yourself to take time off. You felt like a hamster trapped in a wheel going round and round and round. Even deciding what to take with you was fraught with difficulties. By the time the packing was complete, you felt exhausted and then had trouble sleeping because your mind was still churning through all of the things you'd been working on throughout the day. In the morning, you woke up, put all the bags in the car, locked up the house and drove away . . . And that was it.

A short while later you were lying on a beautiful beach, laughing and joking with your friends. Work and its priorities were suddenly a million miles away and you could hardly remember them at all. You felt refreshed and whole again because your entire world had shifted gear. Your work still existed, of course, but you were seeing it from *a different place*. Nothing more.

Time can also fundamentally alter your outlook on life. Think back to the last time you had an argument with a colleague or a stranger—perhaps with someone in a call center? At the time you were fuming. For hours afterwards you were thinking of all of the clever things you could have said, *should* have said, to put down your opponent. The aftereffects of the argument probably ruined your whole day. Yet a few weeks later, you didn't feel irritated by it any more. In fact, you hardly remembered it at all—the sting had gone out of your turbulent emotions. The event still happened, but you were remembering it from *a different point in time*. Nothing more.

Changing your perspective can transform your experience of life, as the above examples show. But they also expose a fundamental problem—they all occurred because something outside of you had changed: the sun came out, you went on vacation, time passed. And, the trouble is, if you rely *solely* on outside circumstances changing in order to feel happy and energized, you'll have to wait a *very* long time. And while you wait, constantly hoping that the sun will come out or wishing that you could travel to the peace and tranquility of an imagined future or an idealized past, your actual life will slip by unnoticed. Those moments might as well not exist at all.

But it doesn't have to be this way.

As we explained in Chapter Two, it's all too easy to become locked into a cycle of suffering and distress when you try to eliminate your feelings or become enmeshed in overthinking. Negative feelings persist when the mind's problem-solving *Doing* mode (see p. 28) volunteers to help, but instead ends up compounding the very difficulties you were seeking to overcome.

But there *is* an alternative. Our minds also have a different way of relating to the world—it's called the Being mode.[1] It's akin to—but far more than—a shift in perspective. It's a different way of knowing that allows you to see how your mind tends to distort "reality." It helps you to step outside of your mind's natural tendency to overthink, overanalyze and overjudge. You begin to experience the world directly, so you can see any distress you're feeling from a totally new angle and handle life's difficulties very differently. And you find that you can change your *internal landscape* (the *mindscape,* if you will[2]) irrespective of what's happening around you. You are no longer dependent on *external* circumstances for your happiness, contentment and poise. You are back in control of your life.

If Doing mode is a trap, then Being mode is freedom.

Throughout the ages, people have learned how to cultivate this way of being, and it's possible for any of us to do the same. Mindfulness meditation is the door through which you can enter this Being mode and, with a little practice, you can learn to open this door whenever you need to.

Mindful awareness—or mindfulness—spontaneously arises out of this Being mode when we learn to pay attention, on purpose, in the present moment, without judgment, to things as they actually are.

In mindfulness, we start to see the world as it is, not as we expect it to be, how we want it to be, or what we fear it might become.

These ideas may initially seem a little too nebulous to grasp fully. By their very nature they have to be experienced to be properly understood. So to ease this process along, the next section explains the "Mindful" (Being) mode of mind by contrasting it with the Doing mode, point for point. Although some of the definitions and explanations may remain a little unclear to you for a short while longer, the actual benefits of mindfulness are beyond question. In fact, it is possible to see the long-term benefits of mindfulness taking root in the brain using some of the world's most advanced brain-imaging technology (see pp. 46–9).

As you read the rest of this book, it will be helpful to remember that Doing mode is not an enemy to be defeated, but is often an ally. Doing mode only becomes a "problem" when it volunteers for a task that it cannot do, such as "solving" a troubling emotion. When this happens, it pays to "shift gear" into "Being" mode. This is what mindfulness gives us: the ability to shift gears as we need to, rather than being permanently stuck in the same one.

How to double your life expectancy

Being locked into the busyness of Doing mode erodes a vast chunk of your life by stealing your time. Take a moment to look at your own life:

- Do you find it difficult to stay focused on what's happening in the present?

- Do you tend to walk quickly to get to where you're going without paying attention to what you experience along the way?

- Does it seem as if you are "running on automatic," without much awareness of what you're doing?

- Do you rush through activities without being really attentive to them?

- Do you get so focused on the goal you want to achieve that you lose touch with what you are doing right now to get there?

- Do you find yourself preoccupied with the future or the past?[3]

In other words, are you driven by the daily routines that force you to live in your head rather than in your life?

Now extrapolate this to apply to the life you have left to you. If you are thirty years old, then with a life expectancy of around eighty, you have fifty years left. But if you are only truly conscious

The seven characteristics of "Doing" and "Being" modes of minds

1. Automatic pilot versus conscious choice

Doing mode is truly brilliant at automating our life using habits, and yet it's the feature that we notice the least. Without the mind's ability to learn from repetition, we'd still be trying to remember how to tie our shoelaces, but the downside comes

and aware of every moment for perhaps two out of sixteen hours a day (which is not unreasonable), your life expectancy is only another six years and three months. You'll probably spend more time in meetings with your boss! If a friend told you that they had just been diagnosed with a terminal disease that will kill them in six years, you would be filled with grief and try to comfort them. Yet without realizing it, you may be daydreaming along such a path yourself.

If you could double the number of hours that you were truly alive each day then, in effect, you would be doubling your life expectancy. It would be like living to 130. Now imagine tripling or quadrupling the time you are truly alive. People spend hundreds of thousands of dollars—literally—on expensive drugs and unproven vitamin cocktails to gain an extra few years of life; others are funding research in universities to try to expand radically the human lifespan. But you can achieve the same effect by learning to live mindfully—waking up to your life.

Quantity isn't everything, of course. But if it's true, as research suggests, that those who practice mindfulness are also less anxious and stressed, as well as more relaxed, fulfilled and energized, then life will not only seem longer as it slows down and you are really here for it, but happier too.

when you cede too much control to the autopilot. You can easily end up thinking, working, eating, walking or driving without clear awareness of what you are doing. The danger is that you miss much of your life in this way.

Mindfulness brings you back, again and again, to full conscious awareness: a place of choice and intention.

The mindful, or Being, mode allows you to become fully conscious of your life again. It provides you with an ability to "check in" with yourself from time to time so that you can make intentional choices. In Chapter One, we said that mindfulness meditation frees up more time than it takes to carry out the practices. This is the reason why. When you become more mindful, you bring your intentions and actions back into alignment, rather than being constantly sidetracked by your autopilot. You learn to stop wasting time pointlessly running through the same old habits of thinking and doing that have long since stopped serving any useful purpose. It also means that you are less likely to end up striving for too long toward goals that it might be wiser to let go of for a while. You become fully alive and aware again (see below).

2. Analyzing versus sensing

Doing mode needs to think. It analyzes, recalls, plans and compares. That's its role and many of us find we're very good at it. We spend a great deal of time "inside our heads" without noticing what's going on around us. The headlong rush of the world can absorb us so much that it erodes our sense of presence in the body, forcing us to live inside our thoughts, rather than experience the world directly. And, as we saw in the previous chapter, those thoughts can easily be shunted off in a toxic direction. It does not always happen—it's not inevitable—but it's an ever-present danger.

Mindfulness is a truly different way of knowing the world. It is not just thinking along a different track. To be mindful means to be back in touch with your senses, so you can see, hear, touch, smell and taste things as if for the first time. You become deeply curious about the world again. This direct sensory contact with the world may seem trivial at first. And yet, when you begin sensing the moments of ordinary life, you discover something *extra*-ordinary; you find that you gradually cultivate a direct, intuitive sense of what is going on in your inner and outer worlds, with profound effects on your ability to attend to people and the world in a new way, without taking anything for granted. This is the very foundation of mindful awareness: waking up to what's happening inside of you, and in the world, moment by moment.

3. Striving versus accepting

The Doing mode involves judging and comparing the "real" world with the world as we'd like it to be in our thoughts and dreams. It narrows attention down to the gap between the two, so that you can end up with a toxic variety of tunnel vision in which only perfection will do.

Being mode, on the other hand, invites you temporarily to suspend judgment. It means briefly standing aside and watching the world as it unfolds, while allowing it to be *just as it is* for a moment. It means approaching a problem or a situation without preconceptions, so that you are no longer compelled to draw only one preconceived conclusion. In this way, you are saved from closing down your creative options.

Mindful acceptance does not mean resignation to your fate. It's an acknowledgement that an experience is here, in this moment—but, instead of letting it seize control of your life, mindfulness allows you, simply and compassionately, to observe it rather than judge it, attack it, argue with it or try to disprove its validity. This radical acceptance allows you to stop a negative spiral from beginning; or if it already has begun, to reduce its momentum. It grants you the freedom to choose—to step outside your looming problems—and, in the process, it progressively liberates you from unhappiness, fear, anxiety and exhaustion. This gives you far greater control over your life. But most important of all, it allows you to deal with problems in the most effective way possible and at the most appropriate moment.

4. Seeing thoughts as solid and real versus treating them as mental events

When in Doing mode, the mind uses its own creations, its thoughts and images, as its raw material. Ideas are its currency and they acquire a value of their own. You can begin to mistake them for reality. In most circumstances, this makes sense. If you have set out to visit a friend, you need to hold your destination in mind. The planning, doing, thinking mind will get you there. It makes no sense to doubt the truth of your thinking: *Am I really going to see my friend?* In such situations, it's useful to take your thoughts to be true.

But this becomes a problem when you feel stressed. You might say to yourself: *I'm going to go mad if this goes on; I should be able to cope better than this.* You can take *these* thoughts to be true as well. Your mood plummets as your mind reacts in a way that is often very harsh: *I am weak; I'm no good.* So you strive harder and harder, ignoring the messages of your punished body and the advice of your friends. Your thoughts have ceased to be your servant and have become your master, and a very harsh and unforgiving master at that.

Mindfulness teaches us that thoughts are just thoughts; they are events in the mind. They are often valuable but they are not "you" or "reality." They are your internal running commentary on yourself and the world. This simple recognition frees you from the dislocated reality that we have all conjured up for ourselves through endless worrying, brooding and ruminating. You can see a clear path through life once again.

5. Avoidance versus approaching

Doing mode solves problems not only by bearing in mind your goals and destinations, but also by holding on to "anti-goals" and the places you *don't* want to go to. This makes sense when, for example, driving from A to B because it's useful to know which parts of town or the highway network to avoid. But it becomes a problem if you use the same strategy for those states of mind you're desperately trying to avoid. For example, if you try to solve the problem of feeling tired and stressed, you will also keep in mind the "places you don't want to visit" such as exhaustion, burnout and breakdown. So now, in addition to feeling tired and stressed, you begin conjuring up new fears for yourself, and this only enhances your anxieties and stresses, leading to even more exhaustion. Despite its best efforts, Doing mode, used in the wrong context, leads you step by step towards burnout and exhaustion.

Being mode, on the other hand, encourages you to "approach"

the very things that you feel like avoiding; it invites you to take a friendly interest in your most difficult states of mind. Mindfulness does not say "don't worry" or "don't be sad." Instead it acknowledges your fear and your sadness, your fatigue and exhaustion, and encourages you to "turn toward" these feelings and whatever emotions are threatening to engulf you. This compassionate approach gradually dissipates the power of your negative feelings.

6. Mental time travel versus remaining in the present moment

Both your memory and your ability to plan for the future are critical to the smooth running of your daily life, but they are also biased by your prevailing moods. When you are under stress, you tend to remember only the bad things that have happened to you and find it difficult to recall the good. A similar thing happens when you think about the future: stress makes you think that disaster is just around the corner, and when you feel unhappy or a creeping sense of hopelessness, you find it almost impossible to look to the future with optimism. By the time these feelings have bubbled through to your conscious mind, you're no longer aware that they are merely memories of the past or plans for the future, but have instead become lost in mental time travel.

We *re-live* past events and *re-feel* their pain, and we *pre-live* future disasters and so *pre-feel* their impact.

Meditation trains the mind so that you consciously "see" your own thoughts as they occur, so that you can live your life as it unfolds in the present moment. This does not mean that you are imprisoned in the present. You can still remember the past and plan for the future, but Being mode allows you to see them for what they are. You see memory *as* memory and planning *as* planning. Consciously knowing that you are remembering, and knowing that you are planning, helps free you from being a slave to mental time travel. You are able to avoid the extra pain that comes through re-living the past and pre-living the future.

7. Depleting versus nourishing activities

When you're locked into Doing mode, it's not just the autopilot that drives you—you also tend to get caught up in important career and life goals, and such demanding projects as homemaking, childcare and looking after elderly relatives. These goals are often worthwhile in themselves, but because they can be so demanding it's tempting to focus on them to the exclusion of everything else, including your own health and well-being. At first, you might tell yourself that such busyness is temporary and that you are, therefore, quite willing to forego the hobbies and pastimes that nourish your soul. But giving these things up can gradually deplete your inner resources and, eventually, leave you feeling drained, listless and exhausted.

Being mode restores the balance by helping you sense more clearly the things that nourish you and those that deplete your inner resources. It helps you sense the need for time to nourish your soul and gives you the space and courage to do so. It also helps you deal more skillfully with those unavoidable aspects of life that can drain away your energy and innate happiness.

Consciously shifting gear

Mindfulness meditation progressively teaches you to sense
the seven dimensions (as these points are known) outlined
above and, in so doing, it helps you to recognize which mode
your mind is operating in. It acts like a gentle alarm bell that
tells you, for example, when you are overthinking and
reminds you that there is an alternative: that you still have
choices, no matter how unhappy, stressed or frantic you
might feel. For example, if you sense that you are tying yourself in knots with overthinking and judgmentalism,
mindfulness helps you to become more accepting and allows
you to approach your difficulty with a sense of warmth and
curiosity.

Now we can let you into a secret: if you shift along *any* one
of these dimensions, the others shift as well. For example, during the mindfulness program you can practice letting go of
avoidance and find yourself being less judgmental as well; you
can work on "staying present" and you'll also find yourself taking your thoughts less literally; if you cultivate greater generosity toward yourself, you'll find that you also have more empathy
for others. And, as you do all of these things, a natural enthusiasm, energy and equanimity bubble up like a long-forgotten
spring of clear water.

Although the meditations in this book only take up twenty
to thirty minutes of "clock time" each day, the results can
have an impact across the whole spectrum of your life. You
will soon come to realize that while a certain degree of comparing and judging is necessary for daily life, our civilization
has raised them up to be gods. But many choices are false
choices—you simply do not need to make them. They are

driven by your thought stream. Nothing more. You don't need to compare yourself endlessly to others. There is no need to compare your life (or standard of living) with either a fictitious life in the future or some rose-tinted view of the past. You do not need to lie awake at night trying to judge the impact that a passing comment you made in a meeting will have on your career prospects. Nor do you need to concern yourself with a throwaway comment made by a friend. If you simply accept life as it is, you will be a lot more fulfilled and increasingly worry free. And if any action should need to be taken, then the wisest decision you can make will most likely pop into your mind when you are not brooding about it at all.

We must stress again that mindful acceptance is *not* resignation. It is not the acceptance of the unacceptable. Nor is mindful acceptance an excuse to be lazy or to do nothing with your life, your time and your innate talents and gifts. (Meaningful work, whether paid or unpaid, is a surefire way of boosting happiness.) Mindfulness is a "coming to your senses" that moves closer and closer to the fore, quite spontaneously, when you regularly set aside the time to practice. It allows you to experience the world—calmly and nonjudgmentally—directly through your senses. It gives you a tremendous sense of perspective. You can sense what is important and what is not.

In the long run, mindfulness encourages you to treat yourself and others with compassion. This sense of compassion liberates you from pain and worry, and in their place arises a true sense of happiness that spills over into daily life. It's not the kind of happiness that gradually dissipates as you become immune to its joys; rather, it's a flavor that soaks into the very fibers of your being.

Happiness taking root

One of the most astonishing features of mindfulness meditation is that you can see its profoundly positive effects actually changing the brain. Recent scientific advances allow us to see the parts of the brain associated with such positive emotions as happiness, empathy and compassion becoming stronger and more active as people meditate. The new science of brain imaging means that we can watch as critical networks in the brain become activated, almost as if they were glowing and humming with renewed life, and, as they do so, unhappiness, anxiety and stress begin to dissolve, leaving a profound sense of reinvigoration. And you don't need to spend years meditating to see the benefits. Every minute counts. Research has shown that committing yourself to daily practice over a period of eight weeks is sufficient for you to see the benefits for yourself.[4]

This realization is relatively recent. For many years it was assumed that we all have an emotional thermostat that determines how happy we are in life. Some people were presumed to have a happy disposition, while others had a miserable one. Although major life events, such as the death of a loved one or winning the lottery, can significantly alter mood, sometimes for many weeks or months on end, it was always assumed that there was a set-point to which we always return. This emotional set-point was presumed to be encoded in our genes or became set in stone during childhood. To put it bluntly, some people were born happy and others were not.

Several years ago, however, this assumption was shattered by Richard Davidson of the University of Wisconsin and Jon Kabat-Zinn of the University of Massachusetts Medical

School. They discovered that mindfulness training allowed people to escape the gravitational pull of their emotional set-point. Their work held out the extraordinary possibility that we can permanently alter our underlying level of happiness for the better.

This discovery has its roots in Dr. Davidson's work on indexing (or measuring) a person's happiness by looking at the electrical activity in different parts of their brain, using sensors on the scalp that measure activity or an fMRI brain scanner.[5] He found that when people are emotionally upset—whether angry, anxious or depressed—a part of the brain known as the right prefrontal cortex lights up more than the equivalent part of the brain on the left. When people are in a positive mood—happy, enthusiastic and bubbling with energy—the left prefrontal cortex lights up more than the right. This finding led Dr. Davidson to devise a "mood index" based on the ratio between the electrical activity in the left and right prefrontal cortices. This ratio can predict your daily moods with great accuracy. It's akin to taking a peek at your emotional thermostat—if the ratio shifts to the left, you are likely to be happy, contented and energized. This is the "approach" system. If it shifts to the right, you are more likely to be gloomy, despondent and lacking in energy and enthusiasm. This is the "avoidance" system.

Davidson and Kabat-Zinn decided to extend this work by examining the effect of mindfulness on the emotional thermostats of a group of biotech workers.[6] The workers were taught mindfulness meditation over a period of eight weeks. Something profound then happened. Not only did they become happier, less anxious, more energized and increasingly engaged with their work, but also Davidson's brain activation index had shifted to the left. Incredibly, this "approach" system continued to operate even when the participants were exposed to slow, depressing music and memories from their past that made them feel sad. Instead of this sadness being fought off or suppressed as an enemy, it was seen as something that could be approached, explored, befriended. It was clear not only that mindfulness boosted overall happiness (and reduced stress levels), but that this was reflected in the way their brains actually worked. This suggests that mindfulness has extremely deep-seated positive effects on the brain.

Another unexpected benefit of the mindfulness course was that the biotech workers' immune systems became significantly stronger. The researchers gave a flu shot to the participants, and later measured the concentration of disease-fighting antibodies that they had produced. Those who showed the greatest shift toward their brains' "approach" system also showed the greatest boost to their immune systems.

But even more interesting work was to follow. Dr. Sarah Lazar at the Massachusetts General Hospital found that as people continue to meditate over several years, these positive changes alter the *physical* structure of the brain itself.[7] The emotional thermostat is fundamentally reset—for the better. Given time, this means that you're more likely to feel happy, rather than sad, increasingly likely to live with ease, rather than be angry or aggressive, and be energized, rather than tired and listless. This change in the brain's circuitry is most pronounced in a part of the brain's surface known as the *insula*, which controls many of the features that we regard as central to our humanity (see the opposite page).[8]

The insula and empathy

Scientific research using brain imaging (fMRI) has shown that the insula becomes energized through meditation.[9] This is hugely significant because this part of the brain is integral to our sense of human connectedness as it helps to mediate empathy in a very real and visceral way. Empathy allows you to see into another's soul, as it were, helping you to understand their predicament "from the inside." With it comes true compassion, true loving-kindness. If you looked inside your brain using a scanner you would see this area buzz with life when you are feeling empathy for another person.[10] Meditation not only strengthens this area, but also helps it to grow and expand.

But why is this important? Apart from being good for society and all of humanity, empathy is good for *you*. Empathy and feeling genuine compassion and loving-kindness toward yourself and others have hugely beneficial effects on health and well-being. The longer a person has meditated, the more highly developed is the insula. But even eight weeks of mindfulness training is sufficient to show changes in the way in which this critical area of the brain functions.[11]

Numerous clinical trials have now shown that these hugely positive effects on the brain translate into benefits for our sense of happiness, well-being and physical health too. A few examples are shown in the box on page 50.

Other proven benefits of meditation

Research centers around the world are continuing to discover the benefits of mindfulness meditation on mental and physical health. Here are just a few:

Mindfulness, loving-kindness and positive mood

Professor Barbara Fredrickson and colleagues at the University of North Carolina at Chapel Hill have proved that meditation focusing on loving-kindness for the self and for others boosted positive emotions that then led to a sense of having a greater zest for life. After just nine weeks of training, meditators developed an increased sense of purpose and had fewer feelings of isolation and alienation, along with decreased symptoms of illnesses as diverse as headaches, chest pain, congestion and weakness.[12]

Different aspects of mindfulness affect different moods

Each of the meditations in this book produces different—but intimately connected—benefits. For example, research at the University Medical Center at Groningen, the Netherlands, shows that increases in positive mood and well-being are directly related to becoming more aware of routine daily activities, observing and attending to the ordinary experiences of life and acting less automatically. By contrast, decreases in negative mood are more closely related to accepting thoughts and emotions without judgment and learning to be open and curious about painful feelings.[13]

Mindfulness and autonomy

Kirk Brown and Richard Ryan at the University of Rochester, New York, have discovered that more mindful people engage in more autonomous activities. That is, they do not do things because others want them to or pressure them into doing them. Nor do they engage in tasks just to help them look good to others, or even to help them feel better about themselves. Rather, those who are more mindful spend more time doing things that they truly value, or that they simply find fun or interesting to do.[14]

Meditation and physical health

Numerous recent clinical trials have shown that meditation can have a profoundly positive effect on physical health.[14] One study, funded by the US National Institutes of Health and published in 2005, discovered that the form of meditation that has been practiced in the West since the 1960s (Transcendental Meditation) leads to a massive reduction in mortality. Compared with controls, the meditation group showed a 23 percent decrease in mortality over the nineteen-year period that the group was studied. There was a 30 percent decrease in the rate of cardiovascular mortality and also a large decrease in the rate of mortality due to cancer in the meditation group compared with combined controls.[15] This effect is equivalent to discovering an entirely new class of drugs (but without the inevitable side effects).

Meditation and depression

Research has shown that an eight-week mindfulness-based cognitive therapy (MBCT) course—which lies at the heart of the program in this book and was developed by Mark Williams and colleagues—significantly reduces the chances of suffering

(continued)

depression. In fact, it reduces the likelihood of relapse by about 40 to 50 percent in people who have suffered three or more previous episodes of depression.[16] This is the first demonstration that a psychological treatment for depression, taught while people are still well, can actually prevent relapse. In the UK, the government's National Institute for Health and Clinical Excellence (NICE) has now recommended MBCT for those with a history of three or more episodes of depression in their Guidelines for Management of Depression (2004, 2009). Research by Maura Kenny in Adelaide and Stuart Eisendrath in San Francisco has also suggested that MBCT may be an effective strategy for those whose depression is not responding to other approaches, such as antidepressant medication or cognitive therapy.[17]

Meditation versus antidepressants

We are often asked whether mindfulness can be used alongside antidepressants or instead of them. The answer to both questions is yes. Research from Professor Kees van Heeringen's clinic in Ghent, Belgium, suggests that mindfulness can be used while people are still on medication. It was found that mindfulness reduced the chances of relapse from 68 percent to 30 percent even though the majority (a similar proportion in both MBCT and control groups) were taking antidepressants.[18] With regard to the question of whether meditation can be an alternative to medication, Willem Kuyken and colleagues in Exeter and Zindel Segal and colleagues in Toronto[19] showed that people who came off their antidepressants and did an eight-week course of MBCT instead, did as well or better than those who stayed on their medication.

Mindfulness and resilience

Mindfulness has been found to boost resilience—that is, the ability to withstand life's knocks and setbacks—to quite a remarkable degree. Hardiness varies hugely from person to person. Some people thrive on stressful challenges that may daunt many others, whether these involve meeting ever increasing work performance targets, trekking to the South Pole or being able to cope with three kids, a stressful job and mortgage payments.

What is it that makes "hardy" people able to cope where others might wilt? Dr. Suzanne Kobasa at City University of New York narrowed the field down to three psychological traits that she termed *control, commitment* and *challenge*. Another eminent psychologist, Dr. Aaron Antonovsky, an Israeli medical sociologist, has also attempted to pin down the key psychological traits that allowed some to withstand extreme stress while others did not. He focused on Holocaust survivors and narrowed the search down to three traits that together add to having a *sense of coherence: comprehensibility, manageability* and *meaningfulness.* So "hardy" people have a belief that their situation has inherent *meaning* that they can commit themselves to, that they can *manage* their life and that their situation is *understandable*—that it is basically comprehensible, even if it seems chaotic and out of control.

To a large degree, all of the traits identified by both Kobasa and Antonovsky govern how resilient we are. Generally speaking, the higher you score on their scales the more able you are to cope with life's trials and tribulations.

As part of their ongoing evaluation of the impact of their eight-week mindfulness training course, Jon Kabat-Zinn's team at the University of Massachusetts Medical School decided to see whether meditation could boost these scores and thereby enhance hardiness. And the results were very clear cut. In general, not only did the participants feel happier, more energized and less stressed, they also felt that they had far more control over their lives. They found that their lives had more meaning and that challenges should be seen as opportunities rather than threats. Other studies have replicated this finding.[20]

But perhaps most intriguing of all is the realization that these "fundamental" character traits are not unchangeable after all. They can be changed for the better by just eight weeks of mindfulness training. And these transformations should not be underestimated because they can have huge significance for our day-to-day lives. While empathy, compassion and inner serenity are vital for overall well-being, a certain degree of hardiness is required too. And the cultivation of mindfulness can have a dramatic impact on these crucial aspects of our lives.

These hard-won findings of research from laboratories and clinics all over the world have profound implications. They are changing the way scientists think about the mind and allow us to have confidence in the experiences of the countless thousands of people who have discovered the benefits of mindfulness for themselves. Again and again, people tell us that mindful awareness greatly enhances the joys of daily life. In practice, even the smallest of things can suddenly become captivating again. For this reason, one of our favorite practices is the Chocolate meditation (see the opposite page). In this you are asked to attend actively to some chocolate as you eat it. Why not do this one right now, before you start the main eight-week program? You'll be astonished at what you discover.

The Chocolate meditation

Choose some chocolate—either a type that you've never tried before or one that you have not eaten recently. It might be dark and flavorsome, organic or fair-trade or whatever you choose. The important thing is to choose a type you wouldn't normally eat or that you consume only rarely. Here goes:

- Open the packet. Inhale the aroma. Let it sweep over you.

- Break off a piece and look at it. Really let your eyes drink in what it looks like, examining every nook and cranny.

- Pop it in your mouth. See if it's possible to hold it on your tongue and let it melt, noticing any tendency to suck at it. Chocolate has over three hundred different flavors. See if you can sense some of them.

- If you notice your mind wandering while you do this, simply notice where it went, then gently escort it back to the present moment.

- After the chocolate has completely melted, swallow it very slowly and deliberately. Let it trickle down your throat.

- Repeat this with the next piece.

How do you feel? Is it different from normal? Did the chocolate taste better than if you'd just eaten it at a normal breakneck pace?

CHAPTER FOUR

Introducing the Eight-Week Mindfulness Program

The remaining chapters of this book show you how to gradually settle your mind and enhance your natural happiness and
contentment using mindfulness meditation. It will take you along
a path that countless philosophers and practitioners have trodden in
the past; a path that the latest scientific advances show really does
dissipate anxiety, stress, unhappiness and feelings of exhaustion.

Each of the remaining eight chapters has two elements: the first
is a meditation (or series of shorter meditations) that you will be
asked to do for a total of around twenty to thirty minutes per day,
using the audio files found at http://bit.ly/rodalemindfulness; the
second is a "Habit Releaser," which gently breaks down ingrained
habits. These Habit Releasers are designed to reignite your innate
curiosity and are generally fun to do. They include such things as
going to the movies and choosing a film at random or changing
the chair you normally sit on at meetings. You'll be asked to do

these tasks mindfully, with your full attention. This may sound frivolous, but these things can be very effective at breaking down the habits that can trap you in negative ways of thinking. Habit Releasers snap you out of a rut and can give you new avenues of life to explore. You'll be asked to carry out one each week.

Each meditation practice should, ideally, be carried out on six days out of seven. If, for whatever reason, you can't manage six sessions in any given week, you can simply roll over the practice and carry it out for a further week. Alternatively, if you've only missed a few sessions you can move on to the next week's practice. The choice will be left up to you. It is not essential that you carry out the course in eight weeks, but it *is* important that you complete the program if you want to gain the maximum benefit and fully taste what mindfulness might offer you.

For clarity, in each chapter we have highlighted the "practices of the week" in a separate box. This makes it easy for you to read the whole book before embarking on the eight-week program should you choose to do so. If you take this approach, it would then be best if you reread the appropriate chapter when it's time for you to carry out the allotted meditation, so you can understand the aims and intentions of each practice.

For the first four weeks of the program, the emphasis is on learning to pay open-hearted attention to different aspects of the internal and external world. You'll also learn how to use the "Three-Minute Breathing Space" meditation (see p. 130) to ground yourself through the day, or whenever you feel that life is running away with you. It helps to consolidate the things that you learn during the longer formal practices. Many of those around the world who've completed our mindfulness courses say that it's the most important skill they've ever learned for regaining control over their lives.

A week-by-week summary of the program

Week One helps you to see the automatic pilot at work and encourages you to explore what happens when you "wake up." Central to this week is a *Body and Breath* meditation that stabilizes the mind and helps you to see what unfolds when you focus your full awareness on just one thing at a time. Another shorter meditation helps you to reconnect with your senses through mindful eating. Although both practices are very simple, they also provide the essential foundations on which all the other meditations are built.

Week Two uses a simple *Body Scan* meditation to help explore the difference between *thinking* about a sensation and *experiencing* it. Many of us spend so much of our time living "in our heads" that we almost forget about the world experienced directly through our senses. The Body Scan meditation helps to train your mind so that you can focus your attention directly on your bodily sensations without judging or analyzing what you find. This helps you to see, ever more clearly, when the mind has begun to wander away by itself, so that you gradually learn to "taste" the difference between the "thinking mind" and the "sensing mind."

Week Three builds on the previous sessions with some nonstrenuous Mindful Movement practices based on yoga. The movements, even though they are not difficult in themselves, allow you to see more clearly what your mental and physical limits are, and how you react when you reach them. They help the mind to continue the process of reintegrating with the body. You'll gradually learn that the body is exquisitely sensitive to emerging unsettling feelings when you are becoming too goal-focused—and this allows you to see how tense, angry or unhappy you become when things don't turn out the way you want. It's an early warning system of profound power and significance that allows you to head off problems before they gain unstoppable momentum.

Week Four introduces a *Sounds and Thoughts* meditation that progressively reveals how you can be sucked unwittingly into "overthinking." You'll learn to see your thoughts as mental events that come and go just like sounds. By meditating on the sounds around you, you'll come to learn that "the mind is to thought what the ear is to sound." This helps you to take a "decentered" stance to your thoughts and feelings, seeing them come and go in the space of awareness. This will enhance clarity of awareness and encourage you to take a different perspective on your busyness and troubles.

Week Five introduces a meditation—*Exploring Difficulty*—that helps you to face (rather than avoid) the difficulties that arise in your life from time to time. Many of life's problems can be left to resolve themselves, but some need to be faced with a spirit of openness, curiosity and compassion. If you don't embrace such difficulties, then they can increasingly blight your life.

Week Six develops this process even further, exploring how negative ways of thinking gradually dissipate when you actively cultivate loving-kindness and compassion through a *Befriending Meditation* and acts of generosity in daily life. Cultivating friendship towards yourself, including for what you see as your "failures" and "inadequacies," is the cornerstone of finding peace in a frantic world.

Week Seven explores the close connection between our daily routines, activities, behavior and moods. When we are stressed and exhausted, we often give up the things that "nourish" us to make time for the more "pressing" and "important" things. We try to

(continued)

clear the decks. Week Seven focuses on using meditation to help you make increasingly skillful choices, so that you can do more of the things that nourish you, and limit the downsides of those things that drain and deplete your inner resources. This will help you to enter a virtuous circle that leads to greater creativity, resilience and the ability to enjoy life spontaneously as it is, rather than how you wish it to be. Anxieties, stresses and worries will still come, but they are more likely to melt away as you learn to meet them with kindness.

Week Eight helps you to weave mindfulness into your daily life, so that it's always there when you need it the most.

The remaining four weeks of the program build on this work, giving you more practical ways to see thoughts as mental events—like clouds in the sky—and helping you to cultivate an attitude of acceptance, compassion and empathy toward yourself and others. And, from this state of mind, all else follows.

During the eight weeks of the program we deliberately place each dimension of the mindful Being mode (outlined in Chapter Three) in the foreground, so that you learn progressively, at the deepest of levels, what happens when you wake up to your life. Although it seems as if each week is teaching a different aspect of mindfulness, they are, in fact, all interrelated. As we said on p. 44, a shift in one dimension brings about a shift in the others as well. This is why you will be invited to do many different practices and to persist with each one for at least a week—for each of them provides a different gateway into awareness, and no one can say which, for you, at this point in your life, will be most helpful in helping you reconnect with what is deepest and wisest within you.

Habit Releasers

The Habit Releasers you'll be asked to carry out each week are based on beautifully simple practices that, as their name suggests, break down the habits that can trap you in negative ways of thinking. They snap you out of your old careworn ruts and give you exciting new avenues to explore. They exploit another understanding that you'll gain from meditation—that it's difficult to be curious and unhappy at the same time. Reigniting your innate human curiosity is a wonderful way of dealing skillfully with the frantic world in which we so often live. You'll soon discover that although you feel time-poor, you are actually moment-rich.

Setting up a time and space for meditation

Before you embark on the mindfulness program, spend a moment considering how to prepare yourself. The best way to approach the program is to set aside an eight-week period when you can commit yourself to spending some time each day doing the meditations and other practices. Each step of the program introduces new elements to the practice, so that over the eight weeks you are able to deepen your learning day by day.

It is important to take your time with the practices, and to follow the instructions as best you can, even if it feels difficult, boring or repetitive. In much of our lives, if we do not like something, we are tempted to rush on to something else, but this program is suggesting a different approach: to use your restless and churning mind as an opportunity to look more deeply into it, rather than as an immediate reason to conclude that the meditation is "not working." See if it's possible to keep in mind that the intention is not to strive for a goal. You are not even striving to relax, strange as this may sound. Relaxation, peace and contentment are the by-products of the work you are doing, not its goal.

So how can you put this time aside on a daily basis?

First, look on it as a time to *be* yourself and a time *for* yourself. You may find it difficult initially to find the time for your practice. One trick is to acknowledge that, in one sense, you do *not* have the spare time for this. You won't *find* the time, you'll have to *make* it. If you had a spare half hour each day, you'd have allocated it by now to other obligations. For these eight weeks, the commitment to this program may take some rearranging of your life. It can be very difficult to do this, even for two months, but it *will* need to be done or the practice will tend to get squeezed out by other, seemingly higher, priorities. You may find you have to rise a little earlier in the morning and, if you do so, you may then need to go to bed earlier, so that your practice is not done at the expense of your sleep. If you still feel that meditation will take up too much time, then try it as an experiment to see if you discover what others have reported—that it frees up more time than it uses—so that you find you are unexpectedly rewarded with *more* free time.

Secondly, we always remind those who participate in our classes that after they have settled on a time and a place for meditation, it's important to be warm and comfortable, and to tell whoever needs to know what you are doing, so that *they* can deal with interruptions by visitors or by the telephone. If the telephone *should* ring and no one else is there to answer it, see if it is possible to allow it to ring, or for the call to be taken by voicemail. Similar interruptions can also arise from "the inside," with thoughts of something you need to do—thoughts that seem to compel you to act now. If this happens, see if you can experiment with letting the ideas and plans come and go in your mind, rather than reacting instantly to them.

Lastly, it is important to remember that when you practice, you do not have to find it enjoyable (although many people do find it pleasant, but not in an obvious way). Follow the practices day by day, until this becomes a routine, although what you'll discover when you come to the practices is that they are never routine. You are only responsible for what you put into it. The outcome will be unique to you. None of us can tell in advance what there is to be discovered in the present moment, and what peace or freedom you will feel when it begins to reveal itself to you.

What will you need in the way of equipment?

You'll need an MP3 player, a room or place to sit where you will be undisturbed, a mat or a thick rug to lie on, a chair or stool or cushion for sitting, a blanket to keep you warm and a pencil or pen to keep a note of specific things from time to time.

A word of caution

Before you start, it's important to know that as you move through the program there will be countless occasions when you'll feel like you've failed. Your mind will refuse to settle. It will race off like a greyhound after a hare. No matter what you try, within seconds your mind may become a cauldron of bubbling thoughts. It may feel like you are wrestling a snake. You may even want to put your head in your hands in despair at ever achieving a calm state of mind. Or you may feel sleepy, and a deep drowsiness will begin undermining your intention to stay awake. You may find yourself thinking, *Nothing is working for me.*

But these moments are not signs of failure. They are profoundly important. Like trying anything new, whether it's learning to paint or to dance, it can be frustrating when the results do not correspond to the picture you have in your mind. In these moments, it pays to persist with commitment and kindness toward yourself. Apparent "failures" are where you will learn the most. The act of "seeing" that your mind has raced off, or that you are restless or drowsy, is a moment of great learning. You are coming to understand a profound truth: that your mind has a mind of its own and that a body has needs that many of us ignore for too long. You will gradually come to learn that your thoughts are not you—you do not have to take them so personally. You can simply watch these states of mind as they arise, stay a while, and then dissolve. It's tremendously liberating to realize that your thoughts are not "real" or "reality." They are simply mental events. They are not "you."

At the very moment when you realize this, the patterns of thoughts and feelings that gripped you may suddenly lose momentum and allow the mind to settle. A deep feeling of contentment may fill your body. But very soon your mind will race off again. After a while, you will once again become aware that you are thinking, comparing, judging. You may now feel disappointed. You might think: *I thought I really had it then—now I've lost it . . .* Once again, you will realize that your mind is like the sea. It is never still. Its waves rise up and down. Your mind may then once again settle . . . at least for a while. Gradually, the periods of calm tranquility will lengthen and the time it takes for you to realize that your mind has raced off will shorten. Even the disappointment can be recognized as another state of mind. Here now, then gone . . .

. . . until one is committed there is hesitancy, the chance to draw back, always ineffectiveness. Concerning all acts of initiative (and creation), there is one elementary truth, the ignorance of which kills countless ideas and splendid plans: that the moment one definitely commits oneself, then Providence moves too. All sorts of things occur to help one that would never otherwise have occurred. A whole stream of events issues from the decision, raising in one's favour all manner of unforeseen incidents, and meetings and material assistance, which no man could have dreamt would have come his way. I have learned a deep respect for one of Goethe's couplets:

"Whatever you can do, or dream you can, begin it.
Boldness has genius, power, and magic in it."
W. H. Murray, *The Scottish Himalayan Expedition*, 1951

Throughout the following eight chapters, it may sometimes feel as if the essence of what we are trying to convey is shrouded in mist. You may feel that you're not "getting it." This is because many of the concepts and much of the wisdom to be gained from meditation is simply inexpressible in any language. You simply have to do the practices and learn for yourself. If you do, then every now and again, you will have an "Aha" moment—a flicker of insight that is profoundly calming and enlightening. You will understand what other practitioners have been learning for thousands of years: that worries, stresses and anxieties can be held in a larger space, in which they emerge and dissolve, leaving you to rest in awareness itself—it's a sense of being complete and whole that is independent of your preconceptions. At the end of the eight-week program, many people report knowing, deep within themselves, that this feeling of profound stillness, of being happy, content and free, is always available to them—it is only ever a breath away.

We wish you well as you start along this path.

CHAPTER FIVE

Mindfulness Week One: Waking Up to the Autopilot

One evening, Alex trudged slowly up the stairs to his bedroom. He was still mulling over his day's work as he undressed and put on his nightclothes. His thoughts hopped from subject to subject. Soon, they'd latched on to a job he needed to do out of town the following afternoon, before dithering over the best way to get there by car to avoid the roadwork. The car! He remembered that his car insurance was due for renewal. He'd use his credit card tomorrow. The card! Had he remembered to pay his credit-card bill? He thought so. He remembered the printed bill with items reserving hotel rooms for next July's big event. Before he'd even realized it, he was thinking of his daughter's upcoming wedding.

"Alex," shouted his wife. "Are you ready yet? We're *all* waiting and it's time to go."

With a start, Alex realized he'd gone upstairs to change for a party, not for bed.

Alex isn't suffering from dementia, nor does he have a particularly poor memory. He'd simply been on "automatic pilot," his mind having been hijacked by his current concerns. It's a problem we're all familiar with. Have you ever set off for a friend's house, only to find yourself taking the road to work instead? Or started peeling potatoes, only to realize that you'd intended to cook rice this evening? Habits are frighteningly subtle, yet can be incredibly powerful. Without warning, they can seize control of your life and drive you in a direction totally different from that you'd intended. It's almost as if the mind is in one place and the body in another.

Psychologist Daniel Simons has done many experiments that illustrate the extent to which we miss seemingly obvious things through automatically paying attention elsewhere. In one study, he set up an experiment in which an actor stopped an ordinary person in the street and asked for directions.[1] As the person was giving the directions, two people carrying a door rudely barged between them. At the moment the person's view was blocked by the door, the actor asking for directions was switched with another. The new actor looked totally different. His jacket was of a different style and color. He wasn't wearing a sweater, nor did he have a crew cut. He even sounded completely different. Despite all this, only around half of the people questioned actually noticed the switch. This shows just how easily we can be absorbed in our busyness— and how powerful the side effects can be. It's almost as if our minds are purged of consciousness, leaving the autopilot in full control.

Our autopilot may be inconvenient, but it's not a mistake. Even though it can let us down at unexpected moments, it remains one of humanity's greatest evolutionary assets. It allows us to sidestep temporarily a shortcoming that all animals share—namely, that we can only truly concentrate on one thing at a time or, at best, pay intermittent attention to a small number of things. Our minds have a bottleneck in the so-called "working memory" that allows us to keep only a few simple things in them at any one time. That's one of the reasons why telephone numbers traditionally had only seven digits (plus the area code). As soon as you exceed this threshold, items tend to be forgotten. One thought seems to drive out another.

If there's too much information sloshing around in the mind, your working memory begins to overflow. You begin to feel stressed. Life starts to trickle through your fingers. You begin to feel powerless and your mind starts periodically "freezing," making you indecisive and increasingly unaware of what's going on around you. You become forgetful, exhausted and at your wits' end. It's similar to the way a computer gets slower and slower as you open more and more windows. At first, you don't notice the impact but, gradually, once you cross an invisible threshold, the computer becomes ever more sluggish, until it freezes—before finally crashing.

In the short term, the automatic pilot allows us to extend the working memory by creating habits. If we repeat something more than a couple of times, the mind links together all of the actions needed to complete a task in a brilliantly seamless manner. Many of the tasks we carry out each day are phenomenally complex, requiring the coordination of dozens of muscles and the firing of thousands of nerves. But they can all be linked together using a habit that consumes only a small part of your brainpower (and an even smaller proportion of your awareness). The brain can daisy-chain such habits together to carry out long, complex tasks with very little input from the conscious mind at all. For example, if you learned to drive in a car with manual gears, you probably found it very difficult to change gears at first, but now you can do it without thinking. As your driving abilities grew, you learned to carry out simultaneously many of the tricky tasks that you now take for granted. So you can now effortlessly change gears and hold a conversation at the same time. All are daisy chained habits coordinated by your autopilot.

Mindfulness and your autopilot

Have you ever turned on your computer to send an email, only to get lured into answering some others, and then turned your computer off again an hour later without sending the original message?

This is not what you had intended to do. But notice the consequence: when you next turn on your computer, you'll still have to send your original message, and you will also have to look at all the *new* messages in response to that one hour of unscheduled work.

When this happens, you may think you are doing a good job— just "clearing the decks"—but what you've actually done is to make the email system speed up a notch!

Mindfulness does not say, "Don't send emails," but it may remind you to check in with yourself and ask, "Is this what I had intended to be doing?"

If you are fully aware, then you maintain greater control of your automatic pilot and can use it to deploy habits as you need them. For example, come 5:30 p.m. you might engage in the "end-of-the-workday" habits, such as a final check of your emails, closing down the computer and a quick rummage through your bag to ensure that you've got your keys, phone and wallet or purse. At the same time, you might continue an engrossing conversation with a colleague, while thinking about what to have for dinner. But you can very easily lose conscious control of your automatic pilot. One habit can end up triggering the next, which triggers the next . . . and the next. For example, you might go home after work out of habit and forget to meet a friend for a drink. In so many seemingly small ways, habits can, surreptitiously, take control of your life.

As the years pass, this can become a huge problem as you cede more and more control of your life to the autopilot—including much of what you think. Habits trigger thoughts, which trigger more thoughts, which end up triggering yet more habitual thoughts. Fragments of negative thoughts and feelings can form themselves into patterns that amplify your emotions. Before you know it, you can become overwhelmed by deep-seated stresses, anxieties and sadnesses. And by the time you've noticed the unwanted thoughts and feelings, they'll have become too strong to contain. A "thoughtless" comment by a friend can leave you feeling unhappy and insecure. A driver who cuts in front of you can tip you over the edge into irritability and anger. You can be left feeling exhausted, frantic and cynically disconnected from the world. Then you might feel guilty about your loss of control. Another twist of the downward spiral has begun . . .

You may desperately try and head off the spiral of stress by trying to suppress it. You might try arguing with yourself, telling yourself: *I'm stupid for feeling like this*. But such thinking about thoughts, feelings and emotions simply makes them worse. Very soon the autopilot can become overloaded with too many thoughts, memories, anxieties and tasks—just like a computer with too many windows left open. Your mind slows down. You may become exhausted, anxious, frantic and chronically dissatisfied with life. And again, just like a computer, you may freeze—or even crash.

When you reach the point where such overload has seized up the conscious mind, it's very difficult to reverse the process simply by thinking your way out, for this is like opening yet another program on the computer, overlayering it with yet another window. Instead, you need to find a way of stepping outside the cycle almost as soon as you notice it's begun. This is the first step in learning to deal with life more skillfully. It involves training yourself to notice when your autopilot is taking over, so that you can then make a choice about what you want your mind to be focusing upon. You need to learn to close down some of the "programs" that have been left running in the background of your mind. The first stage of regaining your innate mindfulness involves returning to basics. You need to relearn how to focus your awareness on one thing at a time.

Do you remember the Chocolate meditation from Chapter Three (see p. 55)? Now you can explore this further by doing a similar exercise in mindful eating. The Raisin meditation (opposite page) is a more subtle version of eating chocolate mindfully. You may find that paying very close attention to what you're eating will change the experience in quite unexpected ways.

You only *need* do this practice once, but you can obviously do it as many times as you wish. It's a sampler, as it were. After you've carried it out, you have started the mindfulness meditation program.

The Raisin meditation[2]

Set aside five to ten minutes when you can be alone, in a place, and at a time, when you will not be disturbed by the phone, family or friends. Switch off your cell phone, so it doesn't play on your mind. You will need a few raisins (or other dried fruit or small nuts). You'll also need a piece of paper and a pen to record your reactions afterward. Your task will be to eat the fruit or nuts in a mindful way, much as you ate the chocolate earlier (see p. 55).

Read the instructions below to get an idea of what's required, and only reread them if you really need to. The spirit in which you do the meditation is more important than covering every instruction in minute detail. You should spend about twenty to thirty seconds on each of the following eight stages:

1. Holding

Take one of the raisins (or your choice of dried fruit or nuts) and hold it in the palm of your hand, or between your fingers and thumb. Focusing on it, approach it as if you have never seen anything like it before. Can you feel the weight of it in your hand? Is it casting a shadow on your palm?

2. Seeing

Take the time really to see the raisin. Imagine you have never seen one before. Look at it with great care and full attention. Let your eyes explore every part of it. Examine the highlights where the light shines; the darker hollows, the folds and ridges.

(continued)

3. Touching

Turn the raisin over between your fingers, exploring its texture. How does it feel between the forefinger and thumb of the other hand?

4. Smelling

Now, holding it beneath your nose, see what you notice with each in-breath. Does it have a scent? Let it fill your awareness. And if there is no scent, or very little, notice this as well.

5. Placing

Slowly take the object to your mouth and notice how your hand and arm know exactly where to put it. And then gently place it in your mouth, noticing what the tongue does to "receive" it. Without chewing, simply explore the sensations of having it on your tongue. Gradually begin to explore the object with your tongue, continuing for thirty seconds or more if you choose.

6. Chewing

When you're ready, consciously take a bite into the raisin and notice the effects on the object, and in your mouth. Notice any tastes that it releases. Feel the texture as your teeth bite into it. Continue slowly chewing it, but do not swallow it just yet. Notice what is happening in the mouth.

7. Swallowing

See if you can detect the first intention to swallow as it arises in your mind, experiencing it with full awareness before you actually swallow.

Notice what the tongue does to prepare it for swallowing. See if you can follow the sensations of swallowing the raisin. If you can, consciously sense it as it moves down into your stomach. And if you don't swallow it all at one time, consciously notice a second or even a third swallow, until it has all gone. Notice what the tongue does after you have swallowed.

8. Aftereffects

Finally, spend a few moments registering the aftermath of this eating. Is there an aftertaste? What does the absence of the raisin feel like? Is there an automatic tendency to look for another?

Now take a moment to write down anything that you noticed when you were doing the practice. Here's what some people who've attended our courses said:

"The smell for me was amazing; I'd never noticed that before."

"I felt pretty stupid, like I was in art school or something."

"I thought how ugly they looked . . . small and wrinkled, but the taste was very different from what I would normally have thought it tasted like. It was quite nice actually."

"I tasted this one raisin more than the twenty or so I usually stuff into my mouth without thinking."

Small fruit; big message

How many times in the past have you paid so much conscious attention to what you were doing? Did you notice how your experience of eating the raisin was transformed by the simple act of focusing on it? Many people say that they "got their money's worth" out of eating for the first time in years. What normally happens to all that taste? It just disappears. Unnoticed. Raisins are so insignificant; we tend to eat them

Routine activities we normally miss

Choose one of the following (or another of your own choosing), and each day for the next week, see if you can remember to pay attention while you are doing it. You do not have to slow it down, or even enjoy it. Simply do what you normally do, but see if you can be fully alive to it as you do so.

- Brushing your teeth
- Walking from one room to another at home or work
- Drinking tea, coffee, juice
- Taking out the garbage
- Loading the washing machine or dryer

Write your own choices here

. . . .

. . . .

Try this as an experiment with the same chosen activity each day for this week. See what you notice. The idea is not to make you feel by the handful, while doing something "more important." And if it was only the taste we were missing, this might not matter too much. But once you see the difference that paying full attention can make to the small things in life, you start to get an inkling of the cost of inattention. Just think of all the pleasures of seeing, hearing, tasting, smelling and touching that are drifting by you unnoticed. You may well be missing vast portions of your daily life. You only ever have a moment to live, *this* moment, and yet we all tend to live in the past or

different, but simply to allow a few more moments in the day when you are "awake." Go at your own pace when doing your chosen routine activity, for example:

Brushing your teeth: where is your mind when you are brushing your teeth? Pay careful attention to all the sensations—the toothbrush in relation to the teeth, the flavor of the toothpaste, moisture building up in the mouth, all the movements required to spit, etc.

Showering: pay attention to the sensations of the water on your body, the temperature and the pressure. Notice the movements of your hand as you wash and the movements of your body as you turn and bend, etc. If you decide to take some of your showering time to plan or reflect, do so intentionally, with awareness that this is where you have decided to focus your attention.

Next week, feel free to continue this experiment with a different activity.

in the future. We only rarely notice what is arising in the present moment.

The Raisin meditation is the first sample of the central tenet of the mindfulness program: that is, relearning how to bring awareness to everyday activities so that you can see life as it is, unfolding moment by moment. This sounds simple, but it takes a great deal of practice. After the raisin exercise, participants in our mindfulness classes are asked to choose one activity that they normally do each day without thinking, and to see if they can bring "raisin mind" to it for the next few days. Perhaps you'd like to choose one such activity and join them in this simple but profound journey of awakening to the ordinary moments of living (see the box on pages 76-7).

When Alex did the raisin exercise, he said that he suddenly realized just how much of his life was simply slipping by—both the good and the bad sides of life. Missing out on the good side meant that life simply wasn't as rich as it could be. "If a raisin tasted so much better when I focused on it," he mused, "what about everything else that I am eating and drinking?" He began to feel a little sad about all of the other opportunities to taste, see, smell, hear and touch in the world that he'd missed out on by rushing through his day—but then he stopped. Here was a choice: he could carry on rushing through his life *mindlessly*, or he could begin to practice "showing up" to his life. Many years later, he confided that eating that one raisin had changed his life and saved his marriage.

Hannah had a different experience with the raisin: "It made me really aware of all the thoughts and feelings going through my mind that were getting in the way of tasting it. I just wanted to stop thinking—just for a moment. It was a real battle—not pleasant at all." Hannah's experience is common. When you see more clearly how busy the mind is, even when you are doing something else, you can be appalled, and begin struggling to control it.

In mindfulness, you do not have to try and switch off your mind. Its restlessness is, itself, a gateway to mindfulness. Instead of trying to clear it, see if it's possible to allow yourself to acknowledge what is going on. Gradually, you will come to see that turning *toward* the chatter of the mind—becoming fully aware of it—grants you more choices and greater room for maneuver. And this gives you the freedom to engage with life more skillfully—dealing with looming difficulties before they seize control of the mind and your life.

Each of us must discover this for ourselves.

We can tell you this. And you can believe it. But that is not the same as truly knowing it. And the only way you can remember this point—when you really need it, when the world seems to be slipping through your fingers—is by discovering it for yourself. Time and time and time again.

So how can you take the message of the raisin practice and apply it? You need to learn to start paying full attention; but resolving to do this, even if you think it is a good idea, may not be enough. You need to do two things. First, you need to find a way to train the mind to focus. This takes practice, and we'll explain in a moment what this practice will entail. Secondly, you need to find ways of dissolving the habits that drive much of your routine behavior. We'll come to that later too.

Mindfulness meditation of the body and breath

Every meditation tradition begins with daily practices that help to focus a scattered mind. The most common way to start is by focusing on a single object that is always with you: the movement of the breath in the body. Why the breath?

First, the breath is something that you probably take for granted despite the fact that you cannot live without it. You can live without food for weeks, without water for days, but you cannot survive without the nourishment that the breath provides for more than a few tens of seconds. The breath really is life.

Secondly, there is an important way in which the breath does not need *us* to make it happen. The breath breathes itself. If it was up to us to remember to breathe, we'd have forgotten long ago. So tuning into the breath can be an important antidote to the natural tendency toward believing that we have to be in control. Attending to the breath reminds us that at the core of our being, something is happening that depends very little on who we are or what we want to achieve.

Thirdly, the breath provides a natural, gently moving target to focus on in your meditation; it grounds you in the here and now. You cannot take a breath for five minutes ago, or for five minutes' time. You can only take a breath for now.

Fourthly, the breath can be a sensitive monitor for your feelings. If you can sense more clearly when the breath is short or long, shallow or deep, rough or smooth, you can begin sensing your own internal weather patterns, and choose whether and how to take skillful action to look after yourself.

Finally, the breath provides an anchor for your attention, so that you can see more clearly when your mind has wandered, when it is bored or restless or when you are fearful or sad. During even the shortest meditation on the breath, you may become aware of how things are for you, and, returning to the breath, let go of the tendency to fix things right away. The breath opens up a different possibility, that of allowing life to live itself for a while, to see what wisdom emerges when you don't rush in to "put things right."

We suggest that you practice the meditation of the breath shown in the box on p. 83 for six out of the next seven days. The meditation takes just eight minutes and we recommend that you do it at least twice each day. You can do it sitting or lying, and feel free to experiment with whichever posture best supports your intention to stay awake for the period of the practice. You can also choose the times to do it. Many people find that the best times are in the morning and in the evening, but it's entirely up to you when you carry it out. At first, you might find it difficult to make the time, but as we've said, meditation ultimately liberates more time than it uses.

It's very important that you do make a commitment to yourself to carry out the meditation. It requires practice, but don't forget that these meditations have been proven in numerous studies around the world to help people. They do, however, work most fully if you put in the required time each day. They may not appear to have instant benefits; you have to practice. And to embed these benefits, you need to commit yourself to completing the eight-week course. However, some people do report feeling more relaxed and happy almost from day one.

There will be times when you will miss out on one of the practice sessions; since life can be busy and often frantic, it's not unusual for this to happen. If it does, there is no need to criticize yourself in any way. Likewise, you might be forced to miss out on a whole day. If you do, then don't chastise yourself—instead, see if you can make up the time later in the week. If you only manage to carry out the meditations on three or four days, try and begin Week One again. If you really don't want to repeat Week One, then move on to the next week.

You may wish to read the meditation through first. It's very detailed and gives you many pointers on what to become aware of when you're meditating. But see if it's possible to focus on the *spirit* of the meditation, rather than becoming hung up on the specifics. Even after you've read it through, it is best to do the meditation following along with the guidance found at http://bit.ly/rodalemindfulness, so that you are taken through the meditation on a moment-by-moment basis, and don't have to worry about when the time is up.

Hannah followed the instructions in the audio files at http://bit.ly/rodalemindfulness twice a day, every day, for a week. Given her reaction to the raisin, it did not surprise her that she found her mind-wandering during the practice almost unbearable: "On the first day, I sat for a few seconds, then found myself thinking: *I've got so much to do, this is just wasting time.* Then I argued with myself: *OK, I promised myself I would put this time aside. Fine. Sit. Breathe.* Then a few seconds later, I started to remember a report that I'd promised to get to a colleague by the next day. My stomach sank. *If I don't get it to him, what will he think?* Then I thought, *This meditation is making me feel worse!*"

Mindfulness of the Body and Breath

Track 1

This is a short body and breath meditation designed to settle and ground yourself in the present moment.

Start by finding a comfortable position. Either lie on a mat or a thick rug, or sit on a firm, straight-backed chair, a cushion or a meditation stool. If you're sitting on a chair, allow your feet to be flat on the floor with your legs uncrossed and your spine straight, so that your posture supports your intention to be awake and aware. In this way, the posture is dignified but comfortable—not stiff or tensed up. If you are lying down, allow your legs to be uncrossed, with your feet falling away from each other, and your arms lying alongside and slightly away from your body.

Now allow your eyes to close, if that feels comfortable, or lower your gaze. Bring your awareness to the sensations where the body is in contact with whatever you are sitting or lying on. Spend a few moments exploring these sensations.

At a certain point, gather your attention and move it to focus on your feet, so that the "spotlight of attention" takes in the toes, the soles of the feet, the heels, the top of the feet and the ankles. Attend to any and all of the physical sensations you can be aware of in your feet and ankles, moment by moment.

Notice how sensations arise and dissolve in awareness. If there are no sensations, simply register a blank. This is perfectly fine—we are not trying to make sensations happen—we are simply registering what is already here when we attend.

(continued)

Now expand your attention to take in the lower legs, the knees, then the rest of your legs. Hold both legs "center-stage" in awareness—notice whatever physical sensations there may be here in the legs.

Expand your attention up the body to the pelvis and hips, the lower back and the lower abdomen. Move up the torso to include the chest and the back—right up to the shoulders—noticing all the physical sensations in the torso.

Expand your attention again to include the left arm; then the right arm; then the neck and the face and head, until you are holding the whole body in awareness.

See if it is possible to allow the whole body and its sensations to be just as they are. There's no need to try to control anything. As best you can, allow sensations to be just as you find them.

At a certain point, bring your awareness to the center of the body—to the sensations in the abdomen as the breath moves in and out of the body. Become fully aware of the changing patterns of physical sensations in this region of the body. If you like, you can place your hand here for a few breaths and feel the abdomen rising and falling. There may be mild sensations of stretching as the abdomen gently rises with each in-breath, and there may be different sensations as the abdomen falls with each out-breath. For the full duration of each in-breath and the full duration of each out-breath, be fully alive to the sensations of breathing.

There is no need to try to control the breath in any way at all—simply let the breath breathe itself. Focus on the physical sensations, breath by breath and moment by moment.

Sooner or later, you'll probably find that the mind wanders away from the breath to thinking, planning, remembering or daydreaming. When this happens, and you notice that your attention is no longer on the breath, there is no need to judge yourself or criticize yourself in any way, and no need to "rush back" to the breath. Instead, taking your time, allow yourself to register where the mind had wandered to. Then, when you're ready, very gently but firmly bring your attention back to the breath.

Such mind-wandering will happen over and over again. Each time, remember that the aim is simply to notice where the mind has been, then to gently escort your attention back to the breath, seeing the mind-wandering as a chance to cultivate patience and compassion as you bring the attention back. Remind yourself that noticing that the mind has gone and bringing it back again and again and again *is* the meditation—this *is* the practice.

And now continue to practice this by yourself, coming back to the breath whenever the mind wanders; allowing the breath to be like an anchor, grounding you in the present moment.

Remember that the breath is always available to you to help bring you back into the present moment, when you find your mind scattered and dispersed by the rush and busyness of your life. It's always here as an anchor deep within you, a place of stillness and of peace.

We suggest that you do this practice at least twice a day for the first week of the mindfulness program.

Despite everything that she'd read, Hannah still assumed that the goal of mindfulness meditation was to clear the mind of thoughts. So when this did not happen, she became distressed, not only about what was going on in her mind—all the tasks she'd still not completed—but also about the fact that she could not shut these out. Secretly, she still believed that with the right trick, "mind clearing" could be accomplished and her stress would disappear.

For some reason, Hannah persisted with the practice twice a day. She found that there were some times when it felt as if a storm was raging. At other times, she found her mind wasn't so busy. Then, on the third day of her practice, something new happened. She began to think of her mind, its thoughts and its feelings, as a weather pattern, with her task simply being to observe the weather, even if it was stormy. At other times, she found it helpful to think of her mind as a lake, sometimes whipped up by winds, at other times quite still, so that it could reflect all the landscape around it.

Hannah was not trying to gain control over the "weather." Rather, she was becoming more interested in it, observing storms and the ensuing periods of tranquility with curiosity, but without self-criticism. She was slowly becoming aware of her thoughts *as thoughts* and the inner workings of her mind as passing mental events.

Seeing her mind as a lake, Hannah saw how often it had become disturbed by a passing storm. "Then," she said, "the water becomes murky and full of sediment. But if I am patient, I can see the weather changing. I can see the lake in all its beauty gradually becoming clear again. Not that this solves all my problems. I can still feel discouraged sometimes. But it helps if I see it as a process that I repeat time after time. I can see the point of practicing every day."

Hannah was discovering something profound: that none of us can control what thoughts rampage through our minds, or the "weather" they can create. But we *do* have some control over how we relate to it.

Our butterfly brains

As you practice day by day, see if your experiences are similar or different to Hannah's. You may discover that it's very easy to become distracted. Our minds tend to flit from thought to thought, so it can be very difficult to maintain concentration. This simple realization is a crucial step along the road to cultivating mindful awareness.

See if it is possible for you to be kind to yourself. When you practice, and your mind wanders, you may discover something of profound importance. You begin to "see" your thought stream in action. Like any stream, you will start to see all its bubblings and gurglings. For the briefest of moments, all of the thoughts, feelings and memories that flow incessantly across your mind will become apparent. Many of them will seem utterly random. It's almost as if your mind is digging around in the back room, offering up possibilities to gauge if *you*—your conscious awareness—like them or find them useful or interesting in some way. It's like a child holding up its toys to an approving adult. This is what your mind does—it offers up possibilities. You can then choose whether to accept these thoughts or not. But all too often we forget this. We confuse the mind's thoughts with reality and we identify ourselves far too closely with our minds.

After a moment or two of clear awareness, you may find that you've slipped back into the stream and become indistinguishable from it yet again. When this happens, the task is the same: just notice your thoughts as thoughts, and gently bring your awareness back to the breath, noticing any resistance to letting go, or a continuing wish to engage with them. You might like to acknowledge them by silently granting them names—"Ah, here's thinking," "here's planning" or "here's worrying'— before returning your awareness back to the breath. You have not failed. On the contrary—you've taken the first step back to full awareness.

Habit Releaser

Over the next week, we'd also like you to carry out a Habit Releaser. This is designed to help you start the process of loosening up your habits by adding a little randomness to your life.

Changing chairs

This week, see if you can notice which chairs you normally sit on at home, in a café or bar or at work (during meetings, for example). Make a deliberate choice to try another chair, or alter the position of the chair you use. It is extraordinary how much we are creatures of habit, and how we take comfort from such sameness. There is nothing wrong with this at all, but it can feed a sense of "taking things for granted" that allows the automatic pilot to thrive. You can easily stop noticing the sights, sounds, smells of everything around you, and even the feel of a chair supporting you can become over-familiar. Notice how your perspective can change just by changing chairs.

Practices for Week One

- The Raisin meditation (see p. 73).

- Mindful awareness of a routine daily activity (e.g. brushing teeth—see p. 76).

- Mindfulness of the Body and Breath meditation twice a day (track 1 at http://bit.ly/rodalemindfulness).

- Habit Releaser.

CHAPTER SIX

Mindfulness Week Two: Keeping the Body in Mind

"I used to call my job the silent killer," says Jason. "Being a driving instructor is probably the most stressful job in the world. Student drivers only seem to come in two types: those who think they're Formula One race car drivers or those who are timid little rabbits who are petrified of other cars and fearful of holding up other people. Neither is in control of the car and both can be disastrous on the road. I used to spend six to eight hours a day terrified that the student would lose control and wreck my car or kill us both.

"After seven years on the job I was diagnosed with a heart murmur. It was hardly surprising really. I'd spend the entire day trying to bottle up my terror and anger. I'd become hyperactive and sweat like a pig. I'd often sleep only fitfully at night and be exhausted the next day. Life was becoming awful."

If you watched Jason at work, you'd instantly see the distress painted across his face and understand why his life had become so unpleasant. His body was often rigid with tension, his movements were jerky and the furrows in his brow were a permanent fixture. He had become the very picture of misery and distress. In countless ways, he was trapped inside a vicious circle that was slowly eating away at his life.

Although he didn't know it, Jason was being driven as much by the fears and tensions locked into his body as by the thoughts and feelings in his mind. For as we saw earlier, thoughts, feelings and emotions can often be as much a product of the body as of the mind.

The body is acutely sensitive to even the tiniest flickerings of emotion that move constantly across the mind. The body often detects our thoughts almost before we've consciously registered them ourselves and frequently reacts as if they are solid and real, whether they *accurately* reflect the world or not. But the body does not just react to what the mind is thinking—it also feeds back emotional information into the brain that can then end up enhancing fears, worries and general overall angst and unhappiness. This feedback loop is a dance of phenomenal power and complexity that is only now beginning to be understood.

Many experiments show just how powerfully your body influences your thoughts—and your gestures and posture can affect even your most seemingly logical judgments too. In 1980, psychologists Gary Wells and Richard Petty conducted a groundbreaking (and oft repeated) experiment to show the impact of the body on the mind. Participants were asked to test some stereo headphones by rating the sound quality after they had listened to some music and a speech played over them. To simulate running, they were asked to move their heads while listening. Some volunteers were asked to move their heads from side to side, almost as if they were shaking their heads, some moved their heads up and down in a nodding sort of way and others were told not to move at all. You can probably guess which group rated the headphones most highly: the nodders, whose head movements suggested "yes," rated them higher than the group whose shaking heads suggested "no."

And if this wasn't suggestive and intriguing enough, the experimenters played a final trick on their human guinea pigs. As they were leaving the building, they were asked if they'd like to take part in a brief survey about college life. None of them knew that this was also part of the same experiment. Despite this, people's opinions were affected not only by what they had heard over the headphones, but also by their head movements. The voice they heard over the headphones had been discussing whether tuition fees should rise from $587 to $750. Strikingly, those who had kept their heads still, when asked afterwards what they thought the fees should be, gave an average recommendation of $582—close to the actual fee. The average fee suggested by those who had been shaking their heads was much lower at $467. And the nodders? Well, they believed that the fees should be increased to $646.[1] And none of them was aware that the movement of their heads had affected their judgment in any way.

It's clear—far more so than any of us would like to admit—that the judgments we make from moment to moment can be significantly affected by the state of our bodies at the time that we make them. For some, this will make disturbing reading, but it's also heartening because it means that simply altering your relationship to your body can profoundly improve your life. But there's just one catch: most of us are barely aware of our bodies at all. It's almost as if we're flying blind through huge parts of our lives.

We can easily spend so much time "in our head" that we almost forget we have a body at all. We can spend ages planning, remembering, analyzing, judging, brooding and comparing. None of these things is "wrong" in itself, but they can easily end up undermining our physical and mental well-being. We forget about our bodies and their influence on how we think, feel and behave and don't notice, as T. S. Eliot put it, our "strained time-ridden faces, distracted from distraction by distraction."[2]

This tendency to ignore the body can be reinforced by a sense that many of us have; that we do not like ours very much—they might not be as tall or as thin or as attractive as we'd like. Or perhaps they don't work as well as they used to. And, for some of us, there is a whisper at the back of our minds that one day they will let us down catastrophically; there will come a time when our bodies will grow old and die, whether we're ready for it or not.

This can mean we end up ignoring or mistreating our bodies. We might not treat them as enemies, but we certainly don't care for them as we would a friend. The body becomes something of a stranger. We tune out the messages it sends to us, creating more distress than we could ever imagine. For if mind and body are one, then to treat the body as somehow separate from us is to perpetuate a profound sense of dislocation, right at the heart of our being. If there is one thing that we need to learn in order to bring peace and "ease of being" into our lives in the midst of a frantic world, it is how to "come home" to this part of ourselves that we have ignored for too long.

To cultivate mindfulness truly,
we need to become fully integrated with
our body once more.

This is something that Jason, the driving instructor, learned: "I knew that I had to find a way of staying calm through the day and relaxing at the end of it. I tried various sports but none really grabbed me. I tried yoga and knew that the exercises and the mindfulness meditations at the end were just what I needed. I realized that I was completely disconnected from my body. I could barely sense it at all.

"It took a few weeks for me to feel the full effects, but gradually, inch by inch, I started to regain some control over my life. It's given me renewed perspective, which is incredibly useful in my job. I can now anticipate my students' mistakes a few moments before they happen. I've also gained a surprising amount of empathy, which helps me to deal more effectively with their fears and worries.

"Last week, one of my pupils reversed into a post. A year ago, I would have gone ballistic, but this time, I breathed deeply a few times and said to myself, *That's why I have insurance.*"

Whole again

The first week of the mindfulness program (Chapter Five) began the process of building a capacity for sustained mindful concentration and awareness. It may have given you a glimpse into the mind's inner workings and its tendency to "chatter." Gradually, moment by moment, you may have come to realize that although you can't stop the unsettling thoughts from arising in your mind, you *can* stop what happens next. You can stop the vicious circle from feeding off itself.

The next step is to deepen your capacity to see the mind's reactivity by learning to pay mindful attention to the body. Here, you can feel the first stirrings of emotionally charged thoughts. Instead of your body acting as an amplifier, it can become a sensitive emotional radar; an early warning system that alerts you to unhappiness, anxiety and stress almost before they arise. But if you are to learn to "read" and understand the messages from your body, you first have to learn how to pay attention, in detail, to those parts of the body that are the source of the signals. So which parts of the body are these? As you will soon discover, these signals can arise *anywhere* in the body. This means you need to use a meditation practice that includes every region of the body, ignoring nothing, befriending everything. And for this, we use the Body Scan.[3]

The Body Scan

The Body Scan meditation is beautifully simple and reintegrates your mind and body into a powerful and seamless whole. It does so by inviting you to move your attention around the body, holding each region center-stage in nonjudgmental awareness for a while, before disengaging that attention and shifting the spotlight on to the next region, until you've "scanned" the whole body. As you do this, you are developing your capacity to pay sustained attention. You are also discovering a special flavor of awareness—one that's characterized by a sense of gentleness and curiosity.

It's important to set the stage for this meditation, so it might be worth rereading the section from pages 61 to 64 on the practicalities of meditation. During Week One, you will have discovered which times of day suit you best for meditation. It is best to set aside fifteen minutes a day at two of these times and dedicate them solely to the Body Scan, aiming to meditate on six days out of the next seven, so that by the end of the week you will have completed twelve Body Scans. Remember that this is *your* time, set aside to replenish the inner you— your soul, as it were. You will find it most helpful to support your meditation by finding a place and time that excludes as much of the busyness of the outside world as you can, by switching off your phone, for example, and finding a quiet spot at home or at work.

There will be times when you'll feel that it's impossible to allocate the time for this. You'll simply feel too tired or busy. This is understandable, but you should remember that meditation is here to nourish you, so those days when it feels as though there is simply no time to squeeze in a fifteen-minute Body Scan may be just the ones when it's most important to persist with the practice as best you can. This is your investment in yourself. And this investment will reap ample rewards; as the days pass, you may come to realize that you are becoming progressively more efficient at home and at work. This is because old habits of thinking and feeling consume large chunks of time and produce few, if any, beneficial returns. They can make you dither and run over the same ground time and time again. They are like a dog frantically chewing on a dry bone with no nourishment in it. If you are able to dissolve these habits by becoming more mindful, then this time is liberated for other uses.

Body Scan meditation

Lie down on a mat, or a thick rug or bed. If it feels comfortable, allow the eyes to close. Let the hands lie alongside the body. The feet, uncrossed, can fall away from each other.

Notice the sense of the body as a whole and the contact between the body and whatever is supporting you.

Remind yourself that you're not trying to get anywhere, or striving to achieve any special state. The intention of this practice is to spend time with each region of the body in turn, cultivating awareness of what's already here. So you're not looking for anything special to happen, but are allowing things to be just as you find them. See if it is possible to let go of the tendency to want things to be a certain way, or to judge how you're doing. Simply follow along with the instructions as best you can, and, whenever the mind wanders away, as it will tend to do, bring it back, without giving yourself a hard time.

Now bring your attention to the sensations of the breath in the abdomen. Notice the stretching of the abdomen wall on the in-breath, and the falling away on the out-breath. Allow your attention to remain here for a short while, resting on the sensations of the breath.

When you're ready, gather the attention, and move it like a spotlight down the body to the feet. Notice the sensations in both feet when the attention arrives. Notice the sensations in the toes, the soles of the feet, the heels, the top of the feet. What's here right now?

If there are no sensations, then simply register a blank. If they are very subtle, then simply notice this. This is your experience right now; there's no *right* way to feel. Simply allow the attention to remain here for a few breaths.

(continued)

Now, taking a deeper breath, let go of the feet on the out-breath. Let them "dissolve" in awareness. Shift the attention to the ankles. What sensations are here?

Again, taking a deeper breath, let go of the ankles on the out-breath and shift the attention to the lower legs. Stay here for a few moments. Notice any sense of contact with whatever you're lying on. Be fully alive to any and all sensations, from the surface of the skin to inside the lower legs.

Now, taking a deeper breath, on the out-breath release the attention from the lower legs, and shift to the knees, letting the attention rest here. Don't *think about* the knees, but sense what's here right now. Notice which sensations change and which stay the same. See what's true for you, right now.

At a certain point, take another deeper breath. On the out-breath let go of the knees and shift the attention to the thighs. What do you notice? There may be sensations of contact between clothes and the skin, sensations of heaviness or lightness, pulsing, vibration. Notice these and any other sensations.

And now, when you're ready, on an in-breath imagine the breath coming into the body, flowing all the way into the legs, right down to the feet. Imagine it flowing back again on the out-breath up and out of the body. You're imagining, or sensing, what it would feel like if the breath could fill the legs as you breathe in, and empty from the legs as you breathe out. If you choose, just play with this sensation for the next few breaths.

Take a deeper breath, and as you breathe out let go of the legs. Allow them to dissolve in awareness, and shift the attention to the hips and pelvis. Notice sensations in the right hip, the left hip and the whole basin of the pelvis and the organs in this region. Imagine, if you wish, that the breath could flow into this region on the in-breath and out again on the out-breath.

Now, taking a deeper breath, on the out-breath let go of the hips and pelvis and shift the spotlight of attention to the back. Start with the lower back for a few breaths. Then, on an in-breath, expand the field of awareness to take in the middle of the back. Do the same to take in the upper back including the shoulder blades. You are now holding the whole of the back in awareness, "breathing with" the back.

Now take a deeper breath into the back. As you let go of the breath, let go of the back as well. Move your attention to the front of the body, to the lower abdomen, observing what sensations are waiting for you, as your attention moves into this region. Feel the changing sensations as you breathe.

From time to time, you may find yourself getting distracted by thoughts, daydreams, worries or the feeling of wanting to hurry up—to move on. Feelings of boredom or restlessness may come, sometimes pulling quite strongly. When this happens, it's not a mistake. Nothing's gone wrong. Simply take the opportunity to notice these feelings and distractions. Acknowledge them, perhaps noticing how they are affecting the body. Then, without judging yourself in any way, bring the attention back to where you had intended it to be—in the lower abdomen, breathing.

Take a deeper breath. On the out-breath let go of the abdomen and shift the attention to the chest. What sensations are here, moment by moment, as you cradle this part of the body in awareness?

Take a deeper, more intentional breath into the chest. When you're ready, as you let go of the breath, let go of the chest as well, and shift the attention to the hands and arms. Hold them "center stage"

(continued)

in awareness for a few breaths, fully alive to all the sensations in your arms and hands.

Take a deeper breath, and on the out-breath let go of the hands and arms. Shift attention to the shoulders and neck—what sensations are here? Be here for them, whatever they are. Breathe with them, reminding yourself that you don't have to control anything. Simply allow things to be just as they are.

Then take another deep breath. On the out-breath let go of the shoulders and neck. Move the attention to the head and face. Start with the lower jaw and chin, then the mouth and lips, the nostrils, the surface of the nose, the cheeks, the sides of the face, the ears, the eyes, the eyelids, the eyebrows, the space between the eyebrows, the forehead, the sides of the forehead and the scalp.

Now see if it is possible to imagine that the breath could fill the whole head, that you could feel the breath on the back of the face as it comes in, refreshing and renewing with each in-breath.

If you wish, you can extend this to imagine that the breath could fill the whole body, breathing in to the whole body, and out from the whole body, for one or two minutes.

Finally, let go of any intentions for the breath. Simply lie here. With a sense of coming home to the body, allow the body to be just as it is. Allow yourself to be just as you are—complete and whole, resting in awareness, moment by moment.

As you bring this period of meditation to an end, perhaps congratulate yourself for taking this time to nourish yourself in this way. Remind yourself that this practice—to be more fully in the body—is a gesture of deep healing for yourself, available to you at any time. It is a way for you to find peace and wholeness, as your life unfolds from moment to moment and from day to day.

Expectations and reality

Many people get to the second week of our course expecting to be able to clear their minds miraculously of all thoughts (still believing that this is the ultimate "aim" of meditation). They desperately want meditation to calm their troubled thoughts and soothe their frayed edges. Take Benjamin, who found that he could not focus. "My mind would not shut off," he said. "I didn't enjoy it at all." Fran agreed: "I was so restless; I found it difficult to lie still. It was better when I moved past my legs, but I couldn't really get relaxed until we were nearly finished. I thought of everything: work, shopping, paying the bills, difficulties I'd been having with a colleague."

These experiences are perfectly normal. Many of us find an endless stream of thoughts competing for our attention. At times, it may feel as if it is doing us no good at all. After all, surely if it was doing us any good, we'd be able to enjoy it. Isn't that what meditation is all about?

Once again, it is important to keep in mind that there isn't necessarily a connection between how much you are enjoying the practice and its longer-term benefits. It can take time for the mind to reconnect fully with the body as countless networks in the brain have to rewire and strengthen themselves. This process doesn't have to be difficult, but it often is. Why? Here is one way of looking at it:

When you are training your attention, it's like going to the gym after a long time away. It's as if you are exercising a muscle that has been underused. As with resistance training in the gym, in which you push your arms or legs against a carefully chosen weight so the muscles can redevelop their strength, so in the Body Scan you are asking your attention to focus for longer periods than usual on something that you usually ignore—your body. So if you become restless or bored, you can welcome these feelings because they are providing the very "resistance training" you need to enhance your concentration and awareness. If it does not feel a little strange or uncomfortable to focus your attention for such long periods, then it's quite possible that you're not exercising it enough. Any mind-wandering, restlessness or boredom that arises can be acknowledged as allies of your attention training. So when these distractions crop up, as best you can, gently acknowledge that your mind has wandered, perhaps by silently giving them such names as "thinking, thinking," "worrying, worrying" or whatever seems appropriate; or you might like to acknowledge feelings by mentally saying to yourself, "Ah, here's restlessness," or "Boredom is here." After you've acknowledged your wandering mind, gently shepherd your attention back to the part of the body you drifted away from.

There will be some days when you'll find it difficult to meditate—when you'll feel angry or frustrated with yourself. When this happens, there is no need to be harsh on yourself. See if it is possible to let go of such ideas as "success" and "failure," or such abstract notions as "trying to purify the body." It is easy to think, *This is not the way it should be*—as if there is a *right* way for you to feel. Then you may notice tension in the shoulders, neck or back, which will seem to confirm that the meditation "isn't working." On the contrary, these signs are indications that the Body Scan *is* revealing something important. For maybe the first time in years, you're noticing in *real time* how the mind creates tension in the body. Soon you'll notice that the body also creates tension in the mind in a self-sustaining loop. Awareness of this is a major discovery. As you spend more time observing these tensions, you will gradually realize that the simple act of awareness helps to diffuse them. You'll have to do nothing more than observe with friendly curiosity. All else follows.

Some people are genuinely incapable of feeling any sensations from some parts—or even most—of their bodies, at least initially. This comes as quite a shock, as it's often the first time they've noticed this. They can feel pain and their sense of touch remains intact, but the normal, "run-of-the-mill" gentle humming sensations of a body that's fully alive eludes them. If this is the case with you, then continue following the meditation on the website, doing what it says to do. Perhaps it will be helpful to imagine yourself as a naturalist, patiently waiting for a shy animal to appear, keeping the camera rolling even though nothing seems to be happening. Remember that you are not looking for anything special to happen. Eventually, you may find that some part of your body suddenly flickers with sensations, even if only fleetingly. Once you've found it, feel free to stay with it a little longer than the audio online suggests and explore its qualities a little more deeply. Then continue with the Body Scan. Over the course of this week, you may come to sense more and more of your body and progressively reconnect with it.

Ailsa found that there were some days when her mind was particularly unruly. Gradually, however, she came to accept this as part of an old habit of seeing everything as a threat or a challenge. She found that repeated practice with the Body Scan taught her that trying to wrestle with a restless mind meant that she'd go round in self-defeating circles. Eventually, she came to see, deep within, that meditation was not a competition. It was not a complex skill that she needed to perfect. The only discipline involved was regular and frequent practice. She learned how to "be with" agitation—to explore it, rather than chase it away as if it was an unwelcome visitor. She learned to do the practice with a spirit of openness and curiosity.

Sometimes, especially early on, she kept falling asleep while doing the Body Scan. At first, she found this frustrating, but gradually realized that if you're working long hours and not getting enough sleep at night, you're going to be tired, so this was entirely natural. When she awoke again, she simply carried on where she left off. But sometimes, she'd just enjoy the nap without giving herself a hard time. Not criticizing herself or feeling guilty about it meant that she felt more enthusiastic about coming back to the meditation another time.

Such befriending of the body and mind is central to meditation. So when you feel that you are "failing" in your meditation, you can use even these feelings as a gateway to awareness, and to nonjudgmental acceptance of yourself as you already are, making space for these feelings of "failure"; seeing how such familiar judgments come and go as bundles of thoughts, feelings and bodily sensations. See how they bring tendencies to act in certain ways. See if it's possible to watch as they arise and dissolve in the mind and body.

The Body Scan reveals the Doing mode

Listing all the things that you might experience when practicing the Body Scan, especially all of the possible difficulties, may make it seem like a hard slog. It isn't always like this though. Many people find it the most relaxing experience they've had in a long time. One participant said it was like having a spa, floating in warm water—and cheaper too! Another said that it felt like getting reacquainted with an old friend she had not been in touch with for decades. She felt a sense of profound connection to the deepest part of herself, and the tears that came were tears of joy.

So why mention all the difficulties? First, we don't want you to be disappointed if the Body Scan does not immediately seem to be liberating you from stress. But there is also a second reason, and it is this reason that makes the Body Scan one of the most important practices you'll be asked to do.

Remember the "Doing" mode of mind—the mode that never seems to let you off the hook—that gets you stuck in relentless and frantic busyness? If you look back to p. 28, you'll be reminded of the characteristics of "Doing" mode. They include judging everything, comparing the way things are with the way you want them to be and striving to make them different from how they actually are. They include being on automatic pilot much of the time, getting lost in thoughts that you take too literally and personally. Doing mode includes living in the past or future, and avoiding what you don't like. Finally, the Doing mode sees the world indirectly, through a veil of concepts that short-circuit your senses so that you no longer directly experience yourself and the world.

Do you recognize these aspects of the Doing mode?

Each of these can be regular visitors during the Body Scan. But this means, equally, that each can be used as a teacher—helping you to recognize when the Doing mode of mind is showing up and trying to reassert its authority, trying its best to intervene to help you out in the only way it knows. So if you find yourself feeling restless, agitated, bored, sleepy or avoiding a part of the body that you do not like, here is an opportunity to recognize this for what it is, and to begin, gradually, turning toward it rather than away from it. Or, if you find yourself on autopilot, as your mind wanders to the past or future, you can acknowledge this, seeing where your mind went and coming home again . . . and again . . . The going away and the coming back can turn out to be wonderful practice at making the elegant shift from Doing to Being. Then there will be times when you find yourself thinking *about* a part of the body and realize that you are not actually feeling it "from the inside" at all; when you have become lost in concepts, analyzing rather than sensing. So, when you notice this, you may begin to smile at the way the mind works so cleverly to get back to its own agenda! And in the smile is the awakening, the coming back to a direct sense of what it is like to be fully alive in this moment.

Now, if you have not already done so, pause for a few moments and decide when you will start the Body Scan. Once you've done so, you may wish to read through the guidance in the box on p. 97. Then when the time for practicing comes, follow along with the guidance on track 2 found at http://bit.ly/rodalemindfulness.

Habit Releaser: going for a walk

Walking is one of the finest exercises and an excellent stress reliever and mood booster. A good walk can put the world in perspective and soothe your frayed nerves. If you really want to feel *alive*, go for a walk in the wind or rain!

Over the next week, we suggest you arrange to go for at least one fifteen- to thirty-minute walk (or longer, if you wish). You don't have to go anywhere special. A walk around your neighborhood, taken in an open frame of mind, can be just as interesting as a hike through the mountains.

There's no need to feel that you have to rush anywhere; the aim is to walk as mindfully as you can, focusing your awareness on your feet as they land on the ground, and feeling the fluid movements of all the muscles and tendons in your feet and legs. You might even notice that your whole body moves as you walk, not just your legs. Pay attention to all of the sights, sounds and smells. If you're in a city you'll still see and hear a surprising number of birds and animals flapping and scurrying about. Notice how they react when they realize that you've seen them.

See if it is possible to be open to all your senses: smell the scent of flowers, the aroma of freshly cut grass, the mustiness of winter leaves or, perhaps, the smell of exhaust fumes and fast food; see if you can feel the breeze on your face or the rain on your head or hands; listen to the air as it moves; see how the patterns of light and shade can shift unexpectedly. Every moment of every season has a host of sensory delights—regardless of where you live.

Try stopping and looking upward too. If you are in a city, you'll be surprised by how many beautiful architectural features are just above natural eye level. You might also see tufts of grass or even trees growing out of roofs and guttering. If you are in a park or in the countryside, you'll see all manner of things, from birds' nests to bees' nests hidden in trees and bushes. If you're feeling more ambitious, you could tag along with your local walking group. It could be the start of a life-long hobby.

Appreciation here and now[4]

Happiness is looking at the same things with different eyes.

Life only happens here—at this very moment. Tomorrow and yesterday are no more than a thought. So make the best of it. You do not know how long you have got. This is a positive message. It helps to give appreciative attention to what is here now. How much appreciative attention do you have for the here and now? Become still and look around. How is the "now" for you?

You do not have to wait for the future to be an improvement on the present. You can find it here.

In Week One, you may have already discovered how easily we miss the beautiful things and how little attention they are given. Take time to pause for simple things, daily things. Maybe you can give a few of these activities or spontaneous events in your life extra attention.

Which activities, things or people in your life make you feel good? Can you give additional appreciative attention and time to these activities?

- ....

- ....

- ....

- ....

Can you pause for a moment when pleasant moments occur?

Help yourself pause by noticing:

- what *body sensations* do you feel at these moments?

- what *thoughts* are around?

- what *feelings* are here?

The ten-finger gratitude exercise

To come to a positive appreciation for the small things in your life, you can try the gratitude exercise. It simply means that once a day you bring to mind ten things that you are grateful for, counting them on your fingers. It is important to get to ten things, even when it becomes increasingly harder after three or four! This is exactly what the exercise is for—intentionally bringing into awareness the tiny, previously unnoticed elements of the day.

It's difficult to overestimate the transformative power of such simple acts as a gentle walk. Janie's experiences, for example, are not unusual: "The other morning I was walking along the river in the center of the city. It was a lovely morning. Then I noticed my mood take a dip. I suddenly thought what would happen to my partner and family if I should become seriously ill. It came from nowhere! I didn't try to argue with the negative thoughts. I stopped and gently told myself: That hasn't happened; worrying, worrying. A moment later, I noticed a seagull sitting on top of a post. Then I realized that every post along the river had a seagull sitting on top of it. They were all looking in slightly different directions. It was so comical to watch that I chuckled to myself. It cheered me up for hours afterward."

Practices for Week Two

- Body Scan practice (track 2 at http://bit.ly/rodalemindfulness) at least twice a day, six out of seven days.

- Carry out another routine activity *mindfully* (see box, p. 76)—choose a different one from last week.

- Habit Releaser—go for a walk for at least fifteen minutes at least once this week.

CHAPTER SEVEN

Mindfulness Week Three: The Mouse in the Maze

This planet has—or rather had—a problem, which was this: most of the people living on it were unhappy for pretty much most of the time. Many solutions were suggested for this problem, but most of these were largely concerned with the movements of small green pieces of paper, which is odd because on the whole it wasn't the small green pieces of paper that were unhappy.

DOUGLAS ADAMS[1]

A traveler to a small Greek island once watched as a young boy tried to persuade the family donkey to move. The boy had vegetables to deliver and he'd carefully loaded up the animal's panniers. But the donkey wasn't in the mood for moving. The boy became more and more agitated and started to raise his voice at the donkey, standing in front of him and pulling hard on the rope. The donkey dug in its hooves firmly. Very firmly.

This tug of war might have gone on a long time if it wasn't for the boy's grandfather. Hearing the commotion, he came out of the house and took in the familiar scene at a glance—the unequal battle between donkey and human. Gently, he took the rope from his grandson. Smiling, he said, "When he's in this mood, try it this way: take the rope loosely in your hand like this, then stand very close beside him, and look down the track in the direction you want to go. Then wait."

The boy did as his grandfather had bade him, and after a few moments, the donkey started to walk forward. The boy giggled with delight, and the traveler watched as animal and boy trotted off happily, side by side, down the track and round the far bend.

How often in your life have you behaved like the small boy tugging on the donkey's bridle? When things aren't working out as we'd like them to, it's tempting to try a little harder, to keep pushing and pulling in the direction we want to go. But is it always sensible to keep relentlessly pushing in one direction? Or should we follow the advice of the old man in the story and pause, simply waiting for things to pan out as they will, spotting opportunities as they arise?

For most of us, this attitude is almost a cardinal sin because it suggests passivity—and yet, often as not, it might be the best course of action. Pushing too hard at a problem, at a stubborn donkey, might just make things far worse. It can close down the mind and prevent us from thinking creatively, instead driving us round in ever decreasing and exhausting circles. Clear creative awareness thrives more readily in a mind that is open and playful.

In an experiment done by psychologists at the University of

Maryland and published in 2001,[2] a group of students were asked to play a simple game where they had to solve a maze puzzle. You'll probably recall these from your childhood; the idea is to draw a line with a pencil from the middle of the maze to the exit without taking the pencil off the page. Two groups of students were asked to solve the puzzles in which the goal was to help a cartoon mouse get safely to its mouse hole. But there was a twist. One group of students was working on a version of the maze that had a piece of delicious-looking cheese in front of the mouse hole near the exit of the maze. In technical parlance, this is known as a positive, or approach-orientated, puzzle. On the other group's version there was no cheese, but instead a picture of an owl that was poised to swoop and capture the mouse in its claws at any moment. This is known as a negative, or avoidance-orientated, puzzle.

The mazes were simple to do and all of the students completed them in around two minutes. But the aftereffects of the puzzles on the students were poles apart. For after completing the maze, all the students were asked to do a different, apparently unrelated test that measured creativity. When they did these, those who'd avoided the owl did 50 percent *worse* than those who'd helped the mouse find the cheese. It turned out that avoidance "closed down" options in the students' minds. It triggered their minds' "aversion" pathways, leaving them with a lingering sense of fear and an enhanced sense of vigilance and caution. This state of mind both weakened their creativity and reduced their flexibility.

This outlook couldn't have been more different from that of those students who'd helped the mouse find the cheese. They became open to new experiences, were more playful and carefree, less cautious and were happy to experiment. In short, the experience opened their minds. This experiment and others like it show that:

> *The spirit in which you do something is often*
> *as important as the act itself.*

Think about the significance of this for a moment. If you do something in a negative or critical way, if you overthink or worry or carry out a task through gritted teeth, then you will activate your mind's aversion system. This will narrow the focus of your life. You will become like a mouse with an owl complex: more anxious, less flexible, less creative. If, however, you do exactly the same thing in an open-hearted, welcoming manner, you thereby activate the mind's "approach" system: your life has a chance to become richer, warmer, more flexible and more creative.

And nothing activates the mind's avoidance system (and depresses the approach system) quite like the feeling of being *trapped*. This sense of being trapped is also central to extreme feelings of exhaustion and helplessness. Many people who work too hard, or for too long, end up being trapped by their own perfectionism and sense of responsibility—they feel, deep down, that there is "no escape." It might be that, some time in the past, they had to prove something to themselves or to others because they felt bullied into it at home or at school, but over the years this has turned into a script that keeps them locked into old habits. This bullying script may once have helped them get what they wanted in life, but now it simply exhausts them. In this way, it's all too easy to cede all the power to the "self-attacking" aspect of yourself, and over time, you can come to feel, deep down, that the only possible response is to submit to the pressure. Trapped, your world seems to present fewer and fewer alternatives for action, whatever the reality. The result is long-term "demobilization." Your playfulness becomes paved over with concrete.

Feelings of exhaustion ensure that you stop taking risks—you want to hide away in the corner, you want the world to go away and leave you alone, or at least stop noticing you. These behavior patterns are common to all animals, not just humans, but they can inflict an intolerable psychological burden on people. They drive depression, chronic stress and exhaustion, especially in those who are conscientious. And if the very effort of trying to free yourself from these patterns backfires, leading to ever greater anxiety, stress and fatigue, this then brings its own sense of defeat—a sense of being trapped in your own burnout, and your malaise is soon all-pervading.

Although these negative spirals are incredibly powerful, you can begin to dissipate them just by becoming aware of them. The simple act of turning toward and observing them helps to dissolve such patterns because they are maintained by the mind's Doing mode (which has volunteered to help, even though it's precisely the wrong tool for the job). The Doing mode entangles you even more in your own *ideas* of freedom, adding a sense of deep aversion and the demand that things should be different from how they are. So you become caught in a *fantasy* of freedom and miss the *actuality* of freedom available to you.

Week Three of the Mindfulness program brings *true* freedom a step closer by further enhancing your awareness of the body and mind.

Building and refining

By now you may have begun to realize the power of mindfulness for enhancing your life. Many of the changes will be quite subtle. You might have started to sleep better and begun to feel a little more energized the next day. You might be slower to anger and quicker to laugh. The momentum behind your negative thoughts might have begun to lessen. You might also have begun to notice such unexpected joys as the delicate beauty of the flowers in the park, or the way that birds sing to each other through the treetops. Other benefits might have crept up on you and only revealed themselves at unexpected times.

Freddy discovered this. He told us, "I've just filed my tax return. It was an unusually untraumatic experience. Normally, I climb the walls with stress and anger, as it's just about the most awful day of the year. This year, I did what was required in about half the normal time. I then went for a drink with a friend and it suddenly dawned on me that I wasn't stressed at all. That was odd and a blessed relief. I'm sure it's down to my daily practice."

Mindfulness is about reorienting your life, so you can enjoy it to the full. This does not mean that tiredness and suffering disappear. You will feel periods of sadness too. But there is a greater chance that when it comes, it arises as an empathic sadness, not as a corrosive emotion tinged with bitterness and anger that so many associate with unhappiness. So when you see people stuck in traffic with their stressed and angry faces, you might feel a little sad for them. When you look into the worried faces on the bus, or at work, you might share a little of their pain. This is normal. For some people, this sharing of other people's emotional burdens can be a bit tough. It might even be overpowering at times, particularly if you've spent decades suppressing your own emotions.

Opening yourself up to empathy is important because out of this sad-sweet emotion will arise compassion for yourself and for others. Compassion—particularly for yourself—is of overwhelming importance. It takes the fuel away from your endless, driving self-criticism. You will eventually be able to see more clearly that some things in life are less important than you had thought, and find it easier to let go of over-caring about them. You will find that the energy that they have been consuming can be used to treat yourself and the world more generously.

Steve Jobs, the chief executive of Apple and a keen meditator, learned this after a brush with cancer: "Remembering that I'll be dead soon is the most important tool I've ever encountered to help me make the big choices in life because almost everything— all external expectations, all pride, all fear of embarrassment or failure—all these things just fall away in the face of death, leaving only what is truly important."[3]

Weaving mindfulness into daily life

How can you build these insights into your daily life? The previous two weeks of formal meditations have introduced ways in which you can stabilize the mind and focus your attention. They, together with the informal practice of waking up to routine activities, have been laying the groundwork for everyday mindfulness—the type of awareness that tiptoes into your daily life and helps you become fully conscious of the world as it is, rather than how you wish it could be. We have begun the process of revealing how the mind works and raised the possibility that your thoughts are not you. This, in itself, can be phenomenally liberating. It helps you shake off some of the toxic thinking habits that periodically seize control of the mind when you are stressed and exhausted and sap your enthusiasm for living.

Week Three takes this enhanced awareness and begins to weave it even more closely into daily life. It uses three short meditations that we suggest you use six days out of the next seven (see box, below).

Practices for Week Three[4]

- Eight minutes of Mindful Movement meditation *followed* by an eight-minute Breath and Body meditation (see pp. 120 and 127).

- A Three-Minute Breathing Space meditation, to be practiced twice a day (see p. 132).

- A Habit Releaser—valuing the television (see p. 134).

Stretching without striving: the Mindful Movement meditation

Movement can have as profound and soothing an impact on the mind as the Body Scan. In its purest form, this is simply a meditation that involves anchoring awareness in the moving body. It provides an extended laboratory (or playground) to explore your mind in all its intricacies.

The Mindful Movement meditation (see box on page 120) consists of four interlinked stretching exercises that are carried out over a few minutes. These physically realign many of the body's muscles and joints, releasing the stresses that build up in daily *life*. You will find it most helpful to carry out the exercises while listening to the audio online (track 3) as they involve quite precise movements. However, we also give detailed instructions on p. 120, so that you have a solid understanding of what's required. You should aim to do the practice on six out of the next seven days, and move seamlessly from the Mindful Movement meditation on to the Breath and Body meditation (p. 127 and track 4 at http:// bit.ly/rodalemindfulness).

It is natural to feel a bit clunky and uncomfortable when you put time aside to move in this slow way. See if you can explore these sensations, but it is important to be gentle with yourself as you do so. We can't stress enough that the intention here is not to feel pain, or to push beyond the limits of your body. You need to look after yourself during these stretches, letting the wisdom of your body decide what is OK for you: how far to go with any stretch and for how long to hold it.

In particular, if you have a physical problem with your back or any other part of the body, do consult your physician or physical therapist before embarking on even these simple stretches. If you have known physical problems, then as soon as you feel mild discomfort, you should "check in" with yourself. See if you are becoming inclined to push yourself too much. Instead, you could try holding the position for as long as it seems OK to do so, then back off a little. Moment by moment, make wise choices about whether to hold any position for a little longer to explore the sensations or to let go of this posture and move on. You may discover that the sense of solid discomfort comes and goes with the ebb and flow of sensations. Mindful Movement is about cultivating awareness as you do this practice. It is not a competition with yourself or anyone else.

Mindful Movement meditation[5]

Track
3

Preparation

1. Stand in bare feet or socks with your feet about hip-width apart and more or less parallel to each other. The back is straight but not stiff. The head is balanced and the shoulders relaxed, with your hands down by your sides.

2. Remember that it's very important to be gentle with yourself as you do these stretches. Look after yourself during the movement, letting the wisdom of your body decide what is OK for you: how far to go with any stretch and how long to hold it.

3. If you have a physical problem with your back or any other part of the body, then *do* consult your physician or physiotherapist before embarking on even these simple stretches. But whether you have a problem or not, see this practice as a chance to cultivate awareness of the body in even the smallest movement—it's not a competition with yourself or anyone else.

4. As you're standing, notice the contact between your feet and the floor. Perhaps unlock the knees slightly. See how this feels.

Raising arms

5. Then, on an in-breath, slowly and mindfully raise your arms out to the sides until they are parallel to the floor. On another in-breath continue to raise them, slowly and mindfully, until your hands are above your head, with the palms turned toward

each other. Stretch upward, feet firmly grounded on the floor, as you breathe. Stretch up for a few breaths, but stay within your limits.

6. When you are ready, slowly—very slowly—on an out-breath, begin the journey back, allowing the arms to come down. Breath by breath, really tune in to the changing sensations as the arms move, perhaps feeling clothes moving on the surface of the skin. Feel the changing landscape of sensations from the muscles in the arms, until your arms come back to rest, hanging from the shoulders.

7. If your eyes have been open, perhaps close them gently at this point, to help you focus attention on the sensations through-out the body as you stand here. Be aware of the aftereffects of doing this stretch and of the movements of the breath in the body.

Picking fruit

8. Opening your eyes, stretch your right arm up, as if you were picking fruit from a tree that is just out of reach. Looking up, beyond the fingers, bring your full awareness to the sensa-tions throughout the body and to what the breath does as you stretch. Perhaps allow the left heel to come off the floor as you stretch. Feel the stretch right through your body.

9. Now allow the heel to come back to the floor, and begin to lower the hand. Follow the fingers with your eyes if you choose, noticing what colors and shapes your eyes drink in as they follow your hand down.

(continued)

10. Then move your face to the center, letting the eyes close for a few moments as you tune into the aftereffects of this stretch, along with sensations of the breath moving in the body.

11. Now open your eyes again. Stretch up to "pick fruit" with your left hand, allowing the right heel to come off the floor to help the stretch. Once again, see if you can notice what parts of the body are involved in this stretch. Note where the edges are, becoming aware and then letting go of even the slightest tendency to push beyond your limits.

12. Allow the heel to come back to the floor and the arm to return slowly to your side. Follow it all the way with your eyes, noticing what the eyes drink in as they follow the fingers down. Then, when the arm has come to rest, allow the face to come back to center. Let the eyes close. Tune in to the aftereffects of doing this stretch.

Bending sideways

13. Now, on an out-breath, put your hands on your hips, allowing the head and shoulders to bend over to the left very slowly and mindfully, with the hips moving a little to the right. Bending sideways, the body forms a curve that extends from the feet through the hips and torso. Breathe in this position.

14. Remember that it's not important how *much* you bend, it's the quality of attention you bring to even small movements—or even to standing still if you choose to do that instead.

15. On an in-breath, return to standing unpright. Remain here for a moment. Then, on an out-breath, slowly bend over in the opposite direction. On an in-breath, return to standing upright, letting your arms rest by your sides. What aftereffects of this stretch are you aware of as you stand here?

Shoulder rolls

16. Finally, try some shoulder rolls. First, raise the shoulders toward the ears as far as they will go. Then, allow them to move backward, moving the shoulder blades toward each other. Letting the shoulders drop down completely, squeeze them together in front of the body, as if you were trying to touch them together.

17. Now combine these movements in a smooth rolling motion: up, back, down and forward. Letting the breath determine the speed of rotation, breathe in for half the movement and out for the other half. At a certain point, change so the shoulders move in the other direction.

Standing in stillness

18. And now return to stillness, standing straight. Become aware of any and all sensations: the aftereffects of doing these stretches, and the sensations of the breath moving freely in and out of the body.

Mindful Movement can have widely varying effects on different people. Some find it comforting; others find it releases pent-up concerns about their body. Ariel found the stretches were a great comfort to her. "In the previous meditation, my mind was all over the place, but I found it so much easier to concentrate when I was moving," she said.

Marge also found it easier at first, but then found that she was trying too hard. "At one point, I realized that I was gritting my teeth and had a huge frown on my face as I stretched up for that darned fruit!"

This often happens during the stretches. This is why the instructions urge you not only to focus on the physical sensations created by the movements, but also to notice how you are *relating* to these sensations. Marge was trying too hard to stretch beyond her body's capability. Her gritted teeth and frown were a sign of aversion—that she was over-doing it, and something in her didn't like it. It is amazing how the face makes a frown in these situations, as if the furrowed brow would magically help the hand to stretch! "A moment later," Marge said, "I realized what I was doing, and smiled at myself. My body eased up and felt more fluent somehow."

Jac's experience was rather different from Marge's. He found himself afraid to move into any slight discomfort that a stretch might bring, backing off quickly from any sense of intensity. "I injured my back at work a few years ago, and although I got the all-clear from the doctor, I have been afraid of overdoing it since then. So when you said to stretch up, I was looking out for any sign of strain, and when I started to feel a little bit, I came down again quickly."

Jac's experience is important. Meditation and yoga teachers always emphasize being very gentle with the body. But it is possible that Jac's accident has made him overcautious. Here, the instructions are to find and explore the edges near the end of a stretch. There is a "soft edge" where the body begins to feel some intensity. Then there is a "hard edge" where the body has reached the limit of what is possible for it at that moment.[6] The invitation is to stay a little longer near to the "soft edge," finding the middle ground between trying too hard and being afraid to stretch at all, exploring what is happening in the body, maintaining a gentle, warm-hearted awareness that directly senses the muscles and joints being worked as you stretch.

As the stretches unfold, you may feel a range of sensations, from the profoundly soothing to the uncomfortable. These sensations provide an important anchor for the mind. See if you can explore them with full awareness. You might notice that some parts of the body are extremely tight through years of accumulated stresses and worries. Some muscles will feel like solid balls of tension. This may be particularly noticeable in the neck and shoulders. You might be surprised to discover that the body is physically incapable of fully carrying out some stretches that might have been possible some time ago. But this is now, not then. Rather than judging such limits, see if you can explore and accept them. They are, after all, providing the raw material for you to expand your awareness, and teaching you about your limits, and how you can relate to them more skillfully.

Can you stretch without striving?

If you can learn this from the practice, you may find that you can apply it in your daily life as well. Gradually, you may come to see the sensations for what they are—sensations—without ignoring them or driving them away, noticing any judgments that arise. The stretches offer the chance to see how unfamiliar sensations can trigger unsettling thoughts and feelings. You might notice such feelings bubbling up as grumpiness, anger, sadness, fear or just a gentle wistfulness. See if it's possible to note these feelings without becoming enmeshed in them, then escort your attention back to the sensations of stretching or the aftereffects of any stretch.

By intentionally embracing any slight discomfort that arises—both physical and mental—you are offering yourself goodwill and compassion. You are also weakening the tendency to avoid mind and body states that you don't like. So you don't end up overdoing things. Many people say that, in time, initial discomfort ebbs away and is replaced by soothing, almost therapeutic, sensations.

Breath and Body meditation

Week One of the program introduced a short Breath meditation. Here, in Week Three, we return to the Breath and Body, suggesting that you practice it immediately after the Mindful Movement. Many people report that sitting with the mindfulness of Breath and Body after stretching feels very different from sitting without any preparation. Here is a chance to see if this is true for you.

Breath and Body meditation[7]

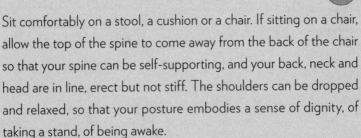

Sit comfortably on a stool, a cushion or a chair. If sitting on a chair, allow the top of the spine to come away from the back of the chair so that your spine can be self-supporting, and your back, neck and head are in line, erect but not stiff. The shoulders can be dropped and relaxed, so that your posture embodies a sense of dignity, of taking a stand, of being awake.

Let your eyes close if that feels comfortable to you, or simply lower your gaze. For a few moments, notice the sensations of your whole body sitting here.

When you are ready, focus your attention on your breathing. Focus on wherever you feel the breath moving most distinctly in and out of your body. This may be the tip of the nose, the chest or down in the abdomen as it rises on the in-breath and falls away on the out-breath. Notice the sensations of each in-breath and each out-breath. Tune in to each breath, noticing its unique qualities. Is it long or short, shallow or deep, rough or smooth?

Remember that there is no right way to feel. Just notice each breath coming in, just as it is, and each breath going out, just as it is. There's no need to control the breath in any way. Allow it to breathe itself.

From time to time, you may notice that the mind wanders to worries, concerns, plans, daydreams, unfinished business. When this happens, simply acknowledge that this is what minds do. It's not a problem, not a mistake. Take this opportunity to notice that you have already woken up. You are aware of the mind-wandering. And this is what the practice is about: seeing the patterns that take us away from the present moment. So when you notice the mind has wandered, take a few moments to notice where it went. Then,

(continued)

gently bring the attention back to the breath. Allow the breath to anchor you in the present moment.

If the mind wanders many times, bring it back just as many times, beginning over and over and over again with the next in-breath or the next out-breath. See each in-breath as a new beginning, and each out-breath as a letting go, a letting be.

Now carry on this work by yourself in silence for a few minutes, checking in from time to time to see where your mind is, and checking in with your posture sometimes, to see if it is as you intended it to be.

When you are ready, deliberately expand the focus of your awareness to the whole body, as if your whole body is breathing now. As well as the sensations of breathing, you also may become aware of all the other sensations that are present in your body as you sit here: from the contact with the chair or stool or cushion, to sensations on the surface of the skin and inside the body.

Hold the whole body in awareness now. Become aware of the space that your body takes up, and the space around the body.

It's not unusual when sitting for a while in this way for intense sensations to arise in your body: sensations of discomfort, stress or tension. If this happens, you have a choice about how to respond. You could intentionally shift your posture, noticing the intention to move, the movement itself and any aftereffects of the movement. Or you could choose not to move, but to stay still and bring your awareness right to the area of intensity, perhaps inviting the breath to "breathe into" that region of the body, exploring what sensations are here in this moment. See if you can notice what is in the bundle of sensations. What is changing from moment to moment, and what is staying the same? There is no need to try to make anything different from how you find it. Simply explore, with openness and curiosity: What is this? And then, if the sensations stop pulling for your attention, return the focus back to the body as a whole, sitting here, breathing, moment by moment.

As you sit in silence, aware of the whole body, check in with your mind and body from time to time. Notice any distractions or restlessness that tends to pull you away from your intention to be fully present in each moment.

And if you become aware of distractions, notice also how you are reacting to them. Notice any frustration or irritation, any physical sensations of contraction or tension. Cradle any and all of these sensations in a larger, more compassionate awareness.

Remind yourself that the deepest stillness and peace does not arise because the world is still or the mind is quiet. Stillness is nourished when we allow the world, the mind and the body to be just as they are for now, moment by moment, and breath by breath.

Dealing patiently with the wandering mind

Thoughts are often more prone to wandering during "sitting practices" like the Breath and Body meditation. It can be deeply frustrating. After two or three weeks of practice, you might feel that you should be seeing some progress, and yet you may feel that you are still incapable of controlling the mind. If it's any consolation, people with many years of experience still feel this way.

And the reason is simple: the aim of meditation is not to control the mind any more than it is to clear it. These are happy by-products of meditation, not the aims. If your aim is to clear the mind, you will end up in a wrestling match with a very skillful opponent. Mindfulness is a far wiser approach than that. It's like a microscope that reveals the deepest patterns of the mind. And when you begin to see the mind in action, you also start to sense when your thoughts are running away with themselves.

When intense sensations arise, you notice how "pain" is created out of discomfort through the thoughts you have about it and especially your thoughts about how long it's going to last. The mere act of observing your thoughts soothes them by holding them gently in a larger space. They tend to diffuse. Your frantic mind becomes still, not because all thought has disappeared, but because you are allowing them to be just as they are. At least for this moment. Your practice, day by day, allows you to remind yourself continuously of this—because it's such an easy thing to forget.

This reminding, re-Mind-ing, is awareness.

The Three-Minute Breathing Space meditation

One of the great ironies of mindful awareness is that it often seems to evaporate just when you need it the most. When you're becoming increasingly burned out, you tend to forget just how useful it can be for dealing with the feelings of being overwhelmed by the world's seemingly relentless demands. When you're becoming angry, it's difficult to remember why you should remain calm. And when you're anxious or stressed, you feel far too rushed to squeeze in a twenty-minute meditation. When you're under pressure, the last thing your mind wishes to be is mindful—tired, old thinking habits are infinitely more seductive.

The Three-Minute Breathing Space[8] was created to deal with such situations. It's a mini meditation that acts as a bridge between the longer, formal meditations and the demands of everyday life. Many people say that it's the most important practice they learn during the whole mindfulness course. And although it's the easiest and quickest to do, remembering to do it is the biggest challenge.

Its impact is twofold: first and foremost, it's a meditation that's used to punctuate the day, so that you can more easily maintain a compassionate and mindful stance, whatever comes your way. In essence, it dissolves negative thought patterns before they gain control over your life—often before you're even aware of them. Secondly, it's an emergency meditation that allows you to see clearly what is arising from moment to moment when you feel under pressure. It allows you to pause when your thoughts threaten to spiral out of control, by helping you to regain a compassionate sense of perspective and to ground yourself in the present moment.

The Breathing Space meditation concentrates the core elements of the Mindfulness program into three steps of roughly one minute each. During Week Three of this course, we suggest that you practice the Breathing Space twice a day. It's up to you when you do it, but it makes sense to find regular times each day to set aside and stick to them, so that this becomes part of your daily routine. You may wish to do the actual practice while listening to the audio files at http://bit.ly/rodalemindfulness (track 8), at least for the first few times that you do it, but then feel free to do it on your own, silently guiding your own practice for about three minutes, keeping the three-step structure. It's also worth reading the printed version of the meditation detailed on the following page, so you can familiarize yourself with its hourglass pattern.

Three-Minute Breathing Space meditation

Step 1: Becoming aware

Deliberately adopt an erect and dignified posture, whether sitting or standing. If possible, close your eyes. Then bring your awareness to your inner experience and acknowledge it, asking: what is my experience right now?

- What *thoughts* are going through the mind? As best you can, acknowledge thoughts as mental events.

- What *feelings* are here? Turn toward any sense of discomfort or unpleasant feelings, acknowledging them without trying to make them different from how you find them.

- What *body sensations* are here right now? Perhaps quickly scan the body to pick up any sensations of tightness or bracing, acknowledging the sensations, but, once again, not trying to change them in any way.

Step 2: Gathering and focusing attention

Now, redirecting the attention to a narrow "spotlight" on the physical sensations of the breath, move in close to the physical sensations of the breath in the abdomen . . . expanding as the breath comes in . . . and falling back as the breath goes out. Follow the breath all the way in and all the way out. Use each breath as an opportunity to anchor yourself into the present. And if the mind wanders, gently escort the attention back to the breath.

Step 3: Expanding attention

Now, expand the field of awareness around the breathing so that it includes a sense of the body as a whole, your posture and facial expression, as if the whole body was breathing. If you become aware of any sensations of discomfort or tension, feel free to bring your focus of attention right in to the intensity by imagining that the breath could move into and around the sensations. In this, you are helping to explore the sensations, befriending them, rather than trying to change them in any way. If they stop pulling for your attention, return to sitting, aware of the whole body, moment by moment.

The hourglass shape of the Breathing Space

It is helpful to view your awareness during the Breathing Space as forming the shape of an hourglass. The wide opening at the top of an hourglass is like the first step of the Breathing Space. In this, you open your attention and gently acknowledge whatever is entering and leaving awareness. This allows you to see if you are entangled in the Doing mode of mind, and if so, to disengage yourself from it and shift into the full awareness of the Being mode. In doing so, you are gently reminding yourself that your current state of mind is not a solid "fact," but is instead governed by interlinked thoughts, feelings, physical sensations and impulses to act. These can, and do, ebb and flow, and you can become aware of them as they do so.

The second step of the Breathing Space is like the narrowing of the hourglass's neck. It's where you focus your attention on the breath in the lower abdomen. You focus on the physical sensations of breathing, gently coaxing the mind back to the breath when it wanders away. This helps to anchor the mind—grounding you back in the present moment.

The third step of the Breathing Space is like the broadening base of an hourglass. In this, you open your awareness. In this opening, you are opening to life as it is, preparing yourself for the next moments of your day. Here you are, gently but firmly, reaffirming a sense that you have a place in the world—your whole mind-body, just as it is, in all its peace, dignity and completeness.

Habit Releaser: valuing the television

Watching TV can be a particularly potent habit, so you can easily take it for granted and stop valuing it. It's all too easy to come home from work, sit down, turn on the TV and watch it. And watch it. And watch it . . . You may feel that there are more interesting things to do, but somehow you just can't bring yourself to do them. You may then start criticizing yourself for watching. You may tell yourself how bad you are for slumping comatose in front of the TV when you could be doing something worthwhile.

Can you make the TV more valuable, and respect it more than you do?

One day this week, see about getting a weekly TV schedule, or looking it up online, to see what program you'd really like to watch: ones that are interesting or enjoyable or both. (Note: if you don't have a TV, then carry out this habit releaser with the radio, or other form of entertainment that you may have come to take for granted.) On your designated day, only watch the program that you have actually chosen to watch and consciously switch off the TV for the times in between. You could read a book or newspaper, phone a friend or relative you haven't spoken to for a while, or perhaps catch up with a few minutes of gardening. You could even do an extra eight-minute session of meditation (or make up for one you've missed out on).

Remember consciously to switch off the television as soon as the chosen program has finished, turning it on again later if there is something else that you particularly want to watch. At the end of the evening, record in a notebook how it went: not only whether it felt good or bad, but what you noticed. What thoughts, feelings, body sensations and impulses were around? Remember that the intention is to help dissolve old habits that have often grown up slowly over many, many years, so don't expect miracles. But if, as a result of any of the practices you undertake this week, you catch a glimpse of another, freer way of living your life, you may be taking the first step to discovering something new: that you don't have to change much of what you do from day to day, but instead learn to do the same things differently; to surround your tasks with the fresh air of awareness and choice.

CHAPTER EIGHT

Mindfulness Week Four: Moving Beyond the Rumor Mill

John was on his way to school.
He was worried about the math lesson.
He was not sure he could control the class again today.
It was not part of a janitor's duty.[1]

What did you notice when you read these sentences? Most people find that they repeatedly update their view of the scene in their mind's eye. First of all, they see a little boy winding his way to school and worrying about his math lesson. Then they're forced to update the scene as the little boy changes into a teacher, before finally morphing into a janitor.

This example illustrates how the mind is continuously working "behind the scenes" to build a picture of the world as best it can. We never see a scene in photographic detail, but instead make inferences based on the "facts" that we are given. The mind elaborates on the details, judging them, fitting them with past experience, anticipating how they'll be in the future and attaching meaning to them. It's a fantastically elaborate mental juggling act. And this whole process is run and rerun every time we read a magazine, recall a memory, engage in conversation or anticipate the future. As a result, events seen in the mind's eye can end up differing wildly from person to person and from any objective "reality": we don't see the world as it is, but as *we are*.

We are constantly making guesses about the world—and we're barely conscious of it. We only notice it when someone comes along and plays a trick on us, as in the John scenario. Then our running commentary on life is laid bare and evaporates—before reformulating itself seamlessly into a new one. Often we're not even aware of the shift. Or, if we are, it gives us a little shiver of vertigo, as if the world imperceptibly shifted beneath our feet. And, if you're lucky, it will make you laugh out loud—this sudden shifting of perspective is how many jokes work.

The way we interpret the world makes a huge difference to how we react. This is sometimes called the ABC model of emotions. The "A" represents the situation itself—what a video camera would record. The "B" is the interpretation given to the scene; the running story we create out of the situation, which often flows just beneath the surface of awareness but is taken as fact. The "C" is our reactions: our emotions, body sensations and our impulses to act in various ways.

Often, we see the "A" and "C" quite clearly, but we are not aware of the "B." We think that the situation itself aroused our feelings and emotions when, in fact, it was our *interpretation* of the scene that did this. It's as if the world were a silent film on which we write our own commentary. But the commentary, with its explanations of what is going on, happens so fast that we take it to be part of the film. It can become progressively more difficult to separate the "real" facts of a situation from its interpretation. And once such a propaganda stream has begun, it can be more and more difficult to argue against it. All future events will be interpreted to support the status quo; competing information is ignored and supporting facts wholeheartedly embraced.

The mind's running commentary on the world is like a rumor. It might be true, it might only be partially true—or it might be completely wrong. Unfortunately, the mind often finds it very difficult to detect the difference between fact and fiction once it has begun to construct a mental model of the world. For these reasons, rumors can be incredibly powerful and derail not just the minds of individuals but of whole societies.

There are few better illustrations of how powerful rumors can be, and how difficult they can be to stop, than the US military's "psychological operations" during the Second World War. During that time, many bizarre and surreal rumors would spread like wildfire across America, often without any foundation or logic at all. For example, claims such as, "The Russians get most of our butter and just use it for greasing their guns," or "The Navy has dumped three carloads of coffee into New York harbor" would appear as if from nowhere and begin to sap morale.

The American government was desperate to scotch such rumors as soon as they appeared and tried all kinds of perfectly reasonable and logical approaches.[2] One of their first tactics was to broadcast special radio programs where they'd take a rumor, discuss it and try to quash it. This soon revealed another problem, in that many listeners would retune their radios partway through a program, so they'd hear only the rumor and not its debunking. This obviously helped to spread the rumors even more.

Next, the government set up special "rumor clinics" in newspapers, where experts would take a rumor and refute it by explaining its psychological underpinnings—how, for example, it represented a form of "self-defense" or a "mental projection." A major problem with this approach soon surfaced too: the experts in the "rumor clinics" often had very little evidence on which to build a case, largely because you can't prove a negative. Quite often, they ended up making things far worse because they would simply dismiss the rumors as nonsense and say that the true facts were "a military secret."

They were up against another major problem too: we often give far more credence to emotionally charged stories than to logic—no matter how rational the arguments.

In many ways, the study of rumors is the study of our minds because: *our thoughts are like rumors in the mind. They might be true, but then again, they might not be.*

In retrospect, we can see how both of the above approaches to debunking wartime rumors were doomed to failure—yet we repeatedly adopt the same techniques when we try to quash the rumors in our own minds. Take self-criticism as an example: when we are feeling stressed or vulnerable, we only hear the inner critic and not the quieter voice of compassion. If we do hear an alternative to the unsettling thoughts, we probably won't believe the answers because the emotional punch behind the thoughts is so powerful that it overwhelms all of our logic. If we dismiss our thoughts as "nonsense" or tell ourselves to "get a grip" or to "pull yourself together" then this further lowers our morale, leaving us wide open to further feelings of weakness and inadequacy. To make matters even worse, every time the tape of self-criticism begins to roll, we immediately start embellishing the story. We begin trawling our minds for supporting evidence and ignore everything to the contrary.

Is it any wonder then, that the rumor mill in our minds can cause us so much unnecessary suffering? Is it so surprising that all of the ways in which we try to quench those rumors only end up making things far, far worse?

Instead of confronting the mind's rumor mill with logic and "positive thinking," it makes far more sense to step outside the endless cycle and just watch the thoughts unfold in all their fevered beauty. But this can be difficult. If you look closely at the "rumors" that start washing around the mind when you feel stressed, you'll see how much a part of you they really appear to be. They carry quite a punch and may be central to what you believe about yourself and the situation in which you find yourself.

Have a look at the following list of common thoughts that pop into people's heads when they feel frantic, stressed, unhappy or exhausted (taken from a questionnaire compiled by one of our colleagues, meditation teacher Hugh Poulton):

- I can't enjoy myself without thinking about what needs to be done.

- I must never fail.

- Why can't I relax?

- I must never let people down.

- It's up to me.

- I must be strong.

- Everyone relies on me.

- I'm the only one who can do this.

- I can't stand this any more.

- I mustn't waste a minute.

- I wish I were somewhere else.

- Why don't they just do it?

- Why am I not enjoying this any more?

- What's the matter with me?

- I can't give up.

- Something has to change.

- There must be something wrong with me.

- Everything will fall apart without me.

- Why can't I switch off?

When we feel stressed and life is frantic, thoughts like these often feel like the absolute *truth* about us and the world. But they are, in fact, *symptoms of stress*, just as a high temperature is a symptom of flu.

As you get more stressed, you believe more strongly in

thoughts such as, *I'm the only one who can do this*. And with loaded thoughts like this, which is in effect saying that you and only you are responsible if things go wrong, then is it any wonder that your mind reacts and wants to find an escape route? You just want to be released from the pressure, so thoughts such as, *I wish I could just disappear,* follow swiftly along behind.

Becoming aware that these thoughts are *symptoms* of stress and exhaustion, rather than facts that must be true, allows you to step back from them. And this grants you the space to decide whether to take them seriously or not. In time, through mindfulness practice, you can learn to notice them, acknowledge their presence and let them go. Week Four of the Mindfulness program will show you how to do this.

Exposing the rumor mill

The first three weeks of the program have been designed to train the mind, while laying the foundations foreveryday mindfulness—the flavor of awareness that allows you to be truly present in the world, rather than simply drifting through it on autopilot. Week Four of the program refines this process by enhancing your ability to sense when your mind and body are signaling that things are turning negative and self-attacking, times when your reactions are pulling you into their vortex. Of course, sensing when your thoughts and feelings are turning against you is one thing; preventing them from gaining unstoppable momentum is quite another. So, Week Four gives you a powerful new tool—the Sounds and Thoughts meditation—to help you.

Practices for Week Four

- An eight-minute Breath and Body meditation (see p. 127, online at http://bit.ly/rodalemindfulness), leading to . . .

- . . . an eight-minute Sounds and Thoughts meditation; we suggest that you practice this sequence *twice a day.* (See page 146 and track 5 online.)

- A Three-Minute Breathing Space meditation (track 8 online) that you do twice a day and also *whenever you need it at any other time.*

Sounds and Thoughts meditation[3]

We are immersed in a soundscape of enormous depth and variety. Just take a moment to listen. What can you hear? At first you might sense a general pulsating, all-encompassing hubbub of noise. You might be able to pick out individual sounds. You might recognize a friendly voice, a radio elsewhere in the building, a door slamming, cars hissing past, a siren in the distance, the hum of air conditioning, an aircraft overhead, tinkling music. The list is endless. Even when you're in a quiet room, you can still pick up muffled sounds. It might be your breath as it moves through your nostrils, or the creaking of the floor or a heating system. Even silence contains sounds.

This constantly fluxing soundscape is just like your thought stream.

It's never still or silent. Our environment fluxes constantly like the waves on the sea and the wind in the trees.

The Sounds and Thoughts meditation gradually reveals the similarities between sound and thought. Both appear as if from nowhere. Both can seem random and we have no control over their arising. Both are enormously potent and carry immense momentum. They trigger powerful emotions that can easily run away with us.

Thoughts come as if from nowhere. Just as the ear is the organ that receives sounds, the mind is the organ that receives thoughts. Just as it is difficult to hear the raw sounds without activating a corresponding concept in the mind, such as "car," "voice" or "central heating," so the flicker of any thought activates a network of associations. Before we know it, the mind has leaped and bound into a past that we had long since forgotten or a future that's been entirely dreamed up and has little basis in reality. We might start to feel angry, sad, anxious, stressed or bitter—just because a thought triggered an avalanche of associations.

The Sounds and Thoughts meditation helps you to discover this for yourself. It also helps you to discover—at the deepest of levels—that you can relate to unsettling thoughts in the same way that you relate to sounds. Your thoughts can be likened to a radio that's been left on in the background. You can listen—or rather observe—but you need not elaborate on what you receive or act on what you feel. You don't usually feel the need to think or behave in a way that a voice on a radio tells you to, so why should you blindly assume that your thoughts portray an unerringly accurate picture of the world? Your thoughts are thoughts. They are your servants. No matter how loud they shout, they are not your master, giving orders that have to be obeyed. This realization gives you immense freedom; it takes you off a hair trigger and gives you the space to make more skillful decisions—decisions that can be made with your mind when it's in full awareness.

There are two key elements to the Sounds and Thoughts meditation—they are receiving and noticing.

Receiving

We receive sounds as they come and go. We see the body as if it were a living microphone that indiscriminately receives sounds as vibrations in the air. We tune in to the raw sensations of each sound with its own volume, tone, pitch, pattern and duration. In the same way, we move from receiving sounds to "receiving" thoughts and any associated emotions they carry—seeing the very moment they appear, seeing how long they hang around and the moment when they dissolve.

Noticing

We notice the layers of meaning that we add to the experience of sounds. We may find that we habitually label them, pursuing those we like or rejecting those we dislike. We see if we can notice this as soon as we become aware that we are doing it and then return to simply receiving the sounds. In the same way, we notice thoughts and feelings and remain fully alive to the way in which they create associations and stories, and how easily we get sucked into their drama.

Sounds and Thoughts meditation[4]

Track 5

Start by sitting for a few moments, grounding yourself by paying attention to your posture, and bring your attention to the breath and body, as described in the Breath and Body meditation on page 127.

When you are settled, bring the focus of your attention to hearing, opening to sounds as they arise from near or far—sounds from in front, the sides, behind, above and below.

Notice any tendency to label sounds as they come or to judge whether you want them to be here, or not. Notice how easily distractions can come, and how easily sounds can create a story. If you notice this, as best you can, bring your attention back to sounds themselves, and allow them to be just as they are.

Imagine hearing these sounds for the very first time, as if each sound you heard were new to you. You may discover a sense of wonder for this ability, which we so often take for granted, to hear so much.

See if it's possible to really hear the raw sensations of sounds—their pitch or loudness or rhythm—and the sounds within sounds.

Some sounds are easily hidden by other more prominent sounds. See if you can be alive to these too, and notice as well if there is a quieter space *between* sounds.

As you focus in this way on your hearing, be aware of the space out of which the sounds arise.

Then, at a certain point, let the sounds fade into the background, and bring your awareness to your thoughts.

These may be thoughts about what you're doing now, or what you're going to be doing, or thoughts about the past. They might be worries or anxieties, or sad, happy or neutral thoughts.

There's no need to try to control your thoughts in any way. Let the thoughts come and go on their own, just as you did with sounds.

Perhaps, when thoughts or images arise in the mind, you might experiment with seeing them like clouds passing across the sky. Your mind is like the sky, and your thoughts are like the clouds—sometimes large, sometimes small, sometimes dark, sometimes light. But the sky remains.

Or you might imagine you are sitting on the bank of a small river or stream, seeing your thoughts as leaves floating past, carried downstream by the water.

Whatever thoughts there are, see if it's possible to see them as mental events that arise in the mind, stay around a while and then move on.

You may be aware of emotions coming up as well. See if it's possible to be open to it all, no matter what it is. Rest in awareness.

If your mind keeps getting drawn into the story created by your thinking, remember that it's always possible to come back to the breath and a sense of the body as a whole, sitting and breathing. This is an anchor to stabilize your awareness in the present moment, before returning again, if you choose, to focus on the coming and going of thoughts and feelings.

For the last few moments of the sitting, focus again on your breathing.

Remember that, wherever you are and whatever your experience, whenever you find your mind scattered and dispersed by the events of your day, the breath is always available to help bring you back into the present moment. It offers you a "place to stand" from which to view thoughts and feelings coming and going in the mind. And as you learn to see your thoughts as mental events, arising and dissolving, you are cultivating, underneath them, a sense of deep stillness and peace.

Observing thoughts and feelings

What do you notice when you do the Sounds and Thoughts meditation? Remember, there is no right or wrong way to feel—no success or failure.

Dana found something strange happened when she turned toward thinking: "When I was focusing on the sounds, then the thoughts were coming thick and fast and interfering with the sounds, but when I started actually to focus on them, the thoughts themselves seemed to go away altogether."

This often happens. In the full daylight of awareness, thoughts seem shy. Why is this? We can think of it like this: thoughts consist of a momentary flicker of activity in a network of the brain, followed by a slower spreading of activation along a much larger network of associations. The flicker may be a very short "pulse" (probably corresponding to a brief image), but what we think of as a "thought" is made up of *both* that momentary pulse *and* a following tail. The tail follows the pulse like a retinue following a king or queen. The retinue is more like inner language with subject and object, verbs, nouns and adjectives, all strung together in a daisy chain of associations that, themselves, provoke further images that evoke further inner speech. Because much of the retinue that follows the pulse comprises mere associations triggered by habit, the act of bringing full awareness to the thinking process dissolves the daisy chain of inner language, leaving you more aware of just the pulses themselves. So, the thoughts soon lose their momentum and run into the sand. Of course, it's often not very long before the thoughts find a gap in awareness just long enough to start another daisy chain, and then, once again, you start to see the retinue that follows the pulse. And so the whole train of thought begins to gather momentum until you are again pulled into the thought stream. It is truly intriguing to witness the activity of your own mind/brain.

During the Sounds and Thoughts meditation, Simon could not focus at all: "I have tinnitus—a high-pitched noise in the background all the time. When I was listening to sounds, the tinnitus became really prominent. I didn't like it at all. Normally, I just try and shut it out, but I get so frustrated. It really spoiled it for me."

Many things can disturb our practice, but tinnitus can be a particularly unwelcome visitor. It is like chronic pain, so unremitting, so intrusive and so intimate. People vary in how they cope with it. During the day when there is a lot of other sound around it can seem OK, but at night, when trying to get to sleep, it can be very troublesome. Meditation on sounds seems just the opposite of coping. So why persist? Simon's experience begins to show why: "I experimented with allowing the ringing in my ears to be there, together with all the other sounds around the place. The noise in the ears did not seem to get any quieter, but my thoughts about it seemed to lessen—I think I was fighting it less, so I was able to relax more. I've tried to relax before, but relaxing always seemed to be about desperately trying to ignore it. I'd never tried allowing it to remain. It felt different somehow. And liberating." Notice Simon's willingness to experiment, to explore. In "turning towards" the very thing that was bothering him, he was noticing that the "tinnitus" consisted not only of the sound, but of the sound plus the whole retinue of "not wanting" and angry thoughts and feelings that were, in the end, attacking him and disturbing his peace of mind.

Sharon's experience shifted dramatically just a few minutes into the meditation. "It felt easy at first because I had no thoughts, I wasn't drifting away. Then—I know this sounds silly—I felt as if my whole body was getting light, floating; it was great, but when it disappeared I felt really disappointed. Then I started to remember other times when I'd felt let down . . . and this made me really sad. What a roller coaster." Sharon had experienced the way in which the weather pattern in the mind can change in an instant. One moment she was enjoying the floating feeling, the next it was gone, and the resulting disappointment left her with a stream of unwanted thoughts and associations.

The thought stream is so powerful that it can pick us up and whisk us away before we're even aware of it. You can imagine yourself sitting on the edge of a stream or small river, watching your thoughts as if they were leaves on the stream floating by. The next moment, you find that you've left your seat and sleepwalked into the middle of the stream. It's only a little later that you wake up and see that, *yet again*, you've become immersed in your thought stream. When this happens—as it surely will—you might congratulate yourself for having woken up, then compassionately acknowledge that your mind is wandering, gently haul yourself back on to the bank of the stream and start over again. The experienced meditator is not someone whose mind does not wander, but one who gets very used to beginning again.

If you're feeling especially wound up or tense, the thought stream isn't a gentle babbling brook, but a tsunami of enormous

Tom's story

Today I learned that failure really doesn't matter that much. I'm still alive. I have all four limbs and my mind seems more or less intact.

While I was meditating, I realized that I was continually losing focus. My mind felt out of control. No matter what I did, my mind would not settle. This was partly because I'd had a particularly bad day at work. I'm a legal clerk. I pride myself on always getting everything ready for a case, come what may. Today I didn't finish on time: I'd mislaid some of the paperwork. I could tell my boss wasn't pleased.

Normally, when I'm stressed, I'll go down to the bar and have a few drinks and then get up the next morning, ready to get going again. But today was different. Instead of drinking, I decided to meditate. It was hard, hard, hard. I hate this feeling of being out of control; I feel as if I'm not good enough—just a failure—and after a while, it felt that I was a loser at meditation too. After twenty minutes of struggling, I opened my eyes and realized that compared to before, and to my normal state of mind, I was actually quite calm. Everything seemed a little bit clearer and more transparent. Far from being a loser at meditation, I'd succeeded in gaining perspective. I learned that when you "fail" at meditation you are actually practicing. If your mind didn't hop around, there would be no chance to spot your furious thoughts in action and to regain awareness of your mind. They kept telling me this during the mindfulness course, but somehow it didn't sink in until I saw it for myself.

After "failing" at meditation I put on a jacket and went and watched a wonderful sunset. I had a glorious night's sleep too. Tomorrow I'll probably learn the same thing again. And the day after that as well . . .

power. It drags you along, kicking and screaming. It might take several minutes before you even realize you've been swept away from the meditation. And, even then, you'll forget where you were. You can struggle to remember if you were focusing on the breath or the body or sounds. This confusion often happens if you're beginning to do the meditation without listening to the audio files. When this happens, you can steady yourself by focusing on the breath as it moves in and out of the body, without giving yourself a hard time. After a few moments, you'll remember the point that you'd reached and will be able to start over, picking up the thread from where you left it.

What is particularly difficult is to notice the thoughts that somehow get under the radar, and are not seen as "thoughts" at all.

You may be sitting quietly, observing thoughts as if they were appearing on a screen or stage in front of you, or as if they were leaves floating past on the stream. Some thoughts are easy to see: perhaps you find yourself thinking, I wonder what's for dinner tonight? And very quickly see, "Ah—there's a thought about dinner." But, sooner or later, you may suddenly remember an email you meant to send, and you find yourself planning when you can get back to the computer. Even then, you may eventually see that this too was a thought. But what if you then say to yourself, "This is not going well—I shouldn't have gone off for so long" or, "I'm just not getting this." It is much more difficult to see *these* intimate self-judgments as "thoughts." They feel more fundamentally true—realistic comments on "me" and how I'm doing.

So if we are imagining watching a movie, we need to be aware, not only of what's on the screen, but the whispers that come as if from the seat behind us. The cinema has "sur-round sound"! And if we are imagining sitting on the bank of a stream, then we need to be aware that there may be a tributary to the same stream that is running behind us as well as in front. Some thoughts just don't feel like thoughts, and these require our special attention, and special reserves of quiet patience. In these times of maximum stress and con-fusion, we learn the most, for it is when we see the most compelling thoughts as mental events—rather than truly reflecting reality—that we glimpse the possibility of freedom most of all.

If some of these practices seem a little repetitive, *it's because they are.* Meditation is a simple practice that gains its power from repetition. It's only through this that we can become aware of the repeating patterns in our own minds. Ironically, medita-tive repetition frees us from endlessly repeating our past mis-takes and the automatic pilot that drives self-defeating and self-attacking thoughts and actions. Through repetition, we gradually tune into the subtle differences that each moment brings.

Think of the meditation as planting seeds. You give young seeds the right conditions, but you don't try to dig them up each day to see if they've grown roots. Meditation is like cultivating a garden: your experience deepens and changes, but this takes place in horticultural time, not clock time.

The Three-Minute Breathing
Space meditation

Now that you have become familiar with practicing the Three-Minute Breathing Space meditation twice a day (see p. 132), you can also use it any time you feel under pressure or when you think it will help you. In time, you will find that you can effortlessly slip in Breathing Spaces whenever you need them. Don't be afraid to use it as many times as you wish. If you feel unsettling or self-attacking thoughts welling up inside you, you can take a Breathing Space to regain perspective.

Used in this way, the Breathing Space is infinitely flexible. You can extend it or shorten it to fit the circumstances you find yourself in. For example, if you feel anxious before a meeting, you may simply close your eyes, and gently run through the practice in the space of a minute or so. Fifteen-year-old Sue-Ellen used the Breathing Space when going into the lessons she found most difficult. As she walked into the classroom, she'd take three breaths to ground herself, gathering her attention on breath and body, ready for whatever would come up in the lesson. In Sue-Ellen's case the Breathing Space took a few seconds at most. But if you feel ready to explode with anger, or feel any other powerful emotion, you

The Intensely Frustrating Line meditation

When you are in line in a supermarket, see if you can become aware of your reactions when something holds up your progress. Perhaps you joined the "wrong" line, and are obsessing about whether to make a dash for another one that seems shorter? At these times, it is helpful to "check in" with what's going on in your mind; seeing what mode of mind you are in. Taking a moment to ask yourself:

- What is going through my mind?

- What sensations are there in my body?

- What emotional reactions and impulses am I aware of?

If you find that you are swept along with needing to "get on," frustrated that things are going more slowly than you had expected, then it is likely that you are in automatic Doing mode. That's fine: it's not a mistake. The mind is doing its best.

Mindfulness accepts that some experiences are unpleasant.

Mindfulness will, however, help by allowing you to tease apart the two major flavors of suffering—primary and secondary. Primary suffering is the initial stressor, such as the frustration of being in a long line. You can acknowledge that it is not pleasant; but it's OK not to like it. Secondary suffering is all of the emotional turbulence that follows in its wake, such as anger and frustration, as well as any ensuing thoughts and feelings that often arise in tandem. See if you can see these clearly as well. See if it's possible to allow the frustration to be here without trying to make it go away.

Stand tall. Breathe. Allow. Be here.

This moment, too, is a moment of your life.

You may still feel pulses of frustration and impatience while you are in line, but these feelings will be less likely to spiral out of control. You may even become, for yourself and for others around you, an oasis of stillness.

could decide to take ten minutes over the Breathing Space. In any case, see if you can retain the hourglass shape we referred to in the previous chapter (see p. 133), with the three distinct "steps," starting by acknowledging the weather pattern of your mind and body. In this first step, you may find it helpful to ask what *thoughts, feelings, body sensations and impulses* are arising from moment to moment. Then, making a graceful shift to the second step, gather and ground yourself by focusing on the breath, before finally opening the focus of attention to your body as a whole in the third step.

The Breathing Space isn't just designed to forestall problems—it's also very useful when your mind has already run away with itself. If you're overwhelmed with sadness, anger, anxiety or stress, then a Breathing Space is the perfect way to ground yourself and regain awareness. In these moments of high emotion and frantic thought, you may learn as much (or more) about your mind than in the formal practices. You may sense the tension in your body, your disturbed breathing and your mind's fevered hopping from thought to thought, each with its own impulse to act. So seize these moments and use them as a powerful laboratory to probe your mind's inner workings.

Once more unto the breach?

It's tempting to use the Breathing Space in precisely the wrong way—as a clever way to fix things or avoid unpleasantness. In its essence, it is not an escape from daily life, not even the equivalent of a cup of tea or a catnap, though these do have their place. Instead, the Breathing Space is a time to regain awareness, to gain a renewed sense of perspective and, thereby, to see clearly any negative thinking patterns that may be gathering momentum in the background. This might seem like a distinction without a difference, so an analogy might help.[5]

Think back to a time you were in a horrible rainstorm. It was relentless. You didn't have a waterproof jacket or umbrella with you. To make matters worse, your shoes leaked like a sieve. After a few moments, you came across a bus shelter and relaxed a little. You felt dry and protected, and a little more in control. After a while, you realized that the rain wasn't going to stop. If anything, it was getting worse. It became obvious that sooner or later you'd have to abandon the shelter and step back into the storm. You had two options at this point.

If you saw the shelter as a break from the rain, then you'll have spent a while cursing your misfortune and becoming more and more unsettled. You might have become annoyed with yourself for not bringing an umbrella. Your mood will have begun to sink lower as your happiness ebbed away. Your thoughts might have gone round and round in circles as you frantically tried to find a way of staying dry. In this case, the shelter will not have been a break from the storm at all, but will instead have ended up enhancing and prolonging your suffering.

If, however, you saw the shelter as a Breathing Space, then your experience had a chance of being completely transformed. Once you realized that the storm was worsening, you might have seen the situation in a different light. You might not have liked it very much, but there was no escaping the fact that you'd soon have to step out into the rain and become soaked to the skin. You'd have seen more clearly that becoming angry and bitter about it would not keep you dry but would, instead, make things worse: wet on the outside *and* bitter on the inside. Once you accepted the inevitable, in the sense not of resignation but of turning toward it, then much of the suffering would have had a chance to melt away. You might even have found some quirky consolations in the experience. You might have paused to notice the unrelenting power of the raindrops and the way they bounced off the pavement to form a thick, watery mist. You might have found it interesting to watch the people scurrying in and out of doorways as they tried to avoid the rain. Or you might have noticed a cat sheltering under a car with a distasteful look on its face. You might even have felt a smile on your face.

In both scenarios, you ended up soaked to the skin—but in the first, your annoyance was compounded by the suffering you inflicted upon yourself, while in the second, your change of perspective might have given you some consolation. Who knows, you might even have been invigorated by the experience.

The Breathing Space is not a break or diversion from reality, but a way of reengaging with it.

After you've completed the Breathing Space, there may be the tendency to immediately (and mindlessly) carry on where you left off. When this happens, it's worth pausing for a few moments to decide how you wish to proceed. Mindfulness gives you the option of acting more skillfully, so it's best to use the quiet moments after meditation to decide—consciously—what you want to do. We will explore four options over the next four weeks. This week's option is simply to reenter the world as you left it before taking the Breathing Space.

Carry on

You can use your rediscovered awareness to carry on with whatever you were doing before you did the Breathing Space, maintaining mindful awareness. Be aware of the thought stream and the tendency to become entangled with it. Approaching the next moment more mindfully may mean prioritizing your time, rather than frantically trying to do everything at once. Or it may mean accepting that your colleagues or family members are behaving in a difficult or unreasonable way and that there's nothing you can do about it. See if you can avoid the temptation to use the Breathing Space as a break or as a way of overtly "fixing" a problem. Breathing Spaces, of themselves, do not solve anything in the short term. But they may give you the perspective to act more skillfully.

Habit Releaser: a visit to the movies

Ask a friend or family member to go with you to the movies—but this time, with a difference. Go at a set time (say 7 p.m.) and *choose whatever movie appeals to you only when you get there.* Often, what makes us happiest in life is the unexpected—the chance encounter or the unpredicted event. Movies are great for all these.

Most of us only go to see a movie when there's something specific we want to watch. If you turn up at a set time and *then* choose what to see, you may discover that the experience will be totally different. You might end up watching (and loving) a film you'd never normally have considered. This act alone opens your eyes and enhances awareness and choice.

Before you go, notice any thoughts that may arise such as, "I haven't got time for pleasure," or, "What if there is nothing showing that I'll enjoy?" You could call these Practice Interfering Thoughts (PITs)—they undermine your enthusiasm for taking action. They are the real "PIT-falls" of daily life, discouraging your intention to do something that might nourish your life in important ways. Once you're inside the theater, just forget about all this and be consumed by the film.

CHAPTER NINE

Mindfulness Week Five: Turning Toward Difficulties

I had my final chemotherapy treatment as the leaves were turning color. Six months passed. I went for my checkup and had another CAT scan. Once again, it was discovered that the cancer was growing. By now, it was spring and the forsythia was just beginning to bud.

Elana Rosenbaum, a meditation teacher at the Center for Mindfulness in Worcester, Massachusetts, was in the middle of teaching an eight-week mindfulness course (about where we are in our program now) when she found that she had a recurrence of her cancer.

My reaction was one of disbelief and shock. My life had just begun to return to normalcy and I was finally finding that I had more energy . . . I was exercising and meditating. I had hoped to prevent a recurrence. I didn't want my life to be interrupted.[1]

Elana knew now that her only hope of survival was a stem-cell transplant and more chemo. She experienced an overwhelming feeling of grief . . . and a fear, as she felt herself girding up to have the strength for more battle. She asked herself whether the risk and hardship she would experience were worth the effort:

I dreaded more treatment, but I also wanted to be alive as long as feasibly possible. I realized it was not only my life I needed to consider, but also my husband's. He didn't want to lose me. This made it very hard to say, "No, I won't have a transplant. I'll take my chances . . ." Being able to finish teaching my class was now impossible and the yoke of responsibility weighed heavy on me. I hoped that I could teach one or two more classes before I'd have to go into the hospital. It was a delicate time in class, and I wanted to be able to guide us through. I didn't like admitting that I was upset and having to exert all my energy to maintain my equilibrium.

I remember sitting down at the next week's teachers' meeting, sighing deeply, and saying, "If I didn't have to, I wouldn't teach tomorrow." All of the teachers looked at me and said, "You don't have to; we'll help you."

I sat there, stunned. It had never occurred to me I could stop teaching . . . I knew I was upset and tired, but until that moment I hadn't realized how tightly I had been holding on to my identity as a teacher, or how forbidden it was for me to admit vulnerability. It felt like shirking responsibility.

Not teaching meant admitting that I was very sick . . . it meant acknowledging that I was tired and scared and that my energy was being zapped by fear and grief and anticipatory worries.

I wanted to be a model for my class, but teaching regardless of circumstances was false. The kindness and compassion of my friends, my colleagues, helped me see the truth of my situation. They didn't say, "You're bad. How could you stop now in the middle of the cycle?"

My "shoulds" and "ought-tos" dissolved, freeing me from the box I hadn't known I had created. As I took in, "You don't have to; we'll help you," struggle ceased. With sadness and relief, it was decided that my colleague, Ferris Urbanowski, would come to my next class with me. I would tell the class what had happened and pass the reins to her. She'd teach this class and the next and then Florence Meyer would teach the final two classes. I would remain as long as I could, but as "patient."

The next day, Ferris and I went to class together. As the class members took their seats along the walls of the room, we placed ourselves in the center. I began with a meditation:

> *Letting go of everything but this moment,*
> *Allow yourself to leave behind work*
> *And the thoughts of the day that has passed,*
> *Or the evening to come.*
> *Simply follow your breath.*
> *As you breathe in, bring your attention fully to the*
> *in-breath,*
> *And as you breathe out, bring it fully to the out-breath,*
> *Allowing it to be as it is*
> *Without trying to change it in any way.*[2]

We sat for a few minutes so that everyone could settle in and then I rang the bells, looked around the room at the people present, took a deep breath, and introduced Ferris.

"Ferris is a good friend and a wonderful teacher. She will

be taking over the class. I've just learned that the lymphoma I've had has returned and I will need more chemotherapy and some hospitalization. I would like to stay in class with you, but now it will be as patient."

In her book, *Here for Now*, Elana describes with simple and painful beauty her journey through these most difficult times. Yet this was not just about surviving cancer. As her colleague, Saki Santorelli, said of her story, "It is about thriving in the face of death; about choosing life in the midst of complete uncertainty; about saying yes (over and over again) to the luminosity that is the core of our human inheritance."

And what about the rest of us? How are we relating to those things, large and small, day in, day out, that remind us of our vulnerabilities? It is to this question that we turn in Week Five of the mindfulness program.

Whenever we're faced with a difficulty—whether it's the stress of a job, illness in ourselves or in a loved one, exhaustion or malignant sadness—it's only natural to try and push it away. We can do this in myriad ways, from endlessly trying to "solve" it or by trying to ignore it or bury it under a pile of distractions. We all use these strategies, even though they may have stopped working many years ago. Why?

First, these methods appeared to work so often in the past that it seems entirely sensible to use the same tactic again and again. Second, there may be an element of denial; we simply do not want to admit that we are helpless and vulnerable because we fear that others will think of us as being not good enough. And deep down, perhaps, we fear that this means that we'll lose some friends and then we'll become lonely and abandoned. So we grind on—and on.

But sooner or later, there comes a point where these strategies no longer work because we either run out of steam or the difficulty we're facing is truly intractable. When we reach this fork in the road we have two options. We can carry on and pretend that nothing is wrong (and lead an increasingly miserable existence), or we can embrace a different way of relating to ourselves and the world. This different approach is one of *acceptance* of ourselves and of *whatever* is troubling us. It means turning toward it, befriending it, even when—indeed, especially when—we don't like it or it scares us.

For many of us, mentioning "acceptance" is heresy of the first order, but this initial reaction stems from the frequent inability of individual words to convey true meaning. Acceptance in the context of mindfulness is not the passive acceptance of the intolerable. It is not "giving up," nor is it resignation or spinelessness. Neither is mindfulness anything to do with detachment—it is not about "not feeling anything" any more. Look at Elana Rosenbaum: she *wanted* with a passion her health, her husband, her life; and to do what she had to do, she had to be attached, very attached—more so than she had ever been in her life.

Mindfulness is not about detachment.

So what do we mean by acceptance? The root of the word (the same root as the words "capture" and "perception") means to receive or take hold of something—and through this, it also means to grasp or understand. Acceptance, in this sense, allows the mind to embrace the true, deep understanding of how things really are. Acceptance is a pause, a period of allowing, of letting be, of clear seeing. Acceptance takes us off the hair trigger, so that we're less likely to make a knee-jerk reaction. It allows us to become fully aware of difficulties, with all of their painful nuances, and to respond to them in the most skillful way possible. It gives us more time and space to respond. And often, we may discover, the wisest way of responding is to do nothing at all.

Paradoxically, taking action in the conventional sense by deploying the mind's Doing mode, is often an automatic reaction. It's not proactive at all. And remaining a slave to our automatic reactions is true resignation to our fate.

In short, mindful acceptance gives us choices.

Perhaps Rumi, the thirteenth-century Sufi poet, summed it up best of all when he wrote "The Guest House":

> This being human is a guest house.
> Every morning a new arrival.
>
> A joy, a depression, a meanness,
> some momentary awareness comes
> as an unexpected visitor.
>
> Welcome and entertain them all!
> Even if they are a crowd of sorrows,
> who violently sweep your house
> empty of its furniture,
>
> still, treat each guest honourably.
> He may be clearing you out
> for some new delight.

The dark thought, the shame, the malice,
meet them at the door laughing and invite
    them in.

Be grateful for whoever comes,
because each has been sent
as a guide from beyond.

Jalaluddin Rumi, in *The Essential Rumi*,
translated by Coleman Barks, 1999

Of course, such acceptance can be very difficult. Some people who have embarked on mindfulness courses stumble at this point. Many people who read this book may stumble too. Some will continue repeating the meditations detailed in the previous chapters and will, no doubt, receive considerable solace from them. Others may abandon mindfulness altogether. We hope that you will continue with Week Five because it's no exaggeration to say that all of the previous chapters have been leading up to this point. The meditations so far have acted as the practices necessary to build the "muscles" of attention. They have enhanced concentration and awareness to such a degree that you are now able to embark on the Exploring Difficulty meditation.

Whatever happens over the coming week or so, always treat yourself with compassion. Repeat the meditations as many times as you choose (but at least see if you can do the recommended minimum). No one is keeping score of your "progress" and you needn't do so either.

The king who found it easier to live with his difficulties[3]

There is a story told of a king who had three sons. The first was handsome and very popular. When he was twenty-one, his father built him a palace in the city in which to live. The second son was intelligent and also very popular. When he became twenty-one, his father built a second palace in the city for him. The third son was neither handsome nor intelligent, and was unfriendly and unpopular. When he was twenty-one, the king's counselors said: "There is no further room in the city. Have a palace built outside the city for your son. You can have it built so it will be strong. You can send some of your guards to prevent it from being attacked by the ruffians who live outside the city walls." So the king built such a palace, and sent some of his soldiers to protect it.

A year later, the son sent a message to his father: "I cannot live here. The ruffians are too strong." So the counselors said: "Build another palace, bigger and stronger and twenty miles away from the city and the ruffians. With more soldiers, it will easily withstand attacks from the nomadic tribes that pass that way." So the king built such a palace, and sent one hundred of his soldiers to protect it.

A year later, a message came from the son: "I cannot live here. The tribes are too strong." So the counselors said: "Build a castle, a large castle, one hundred miles away. It will be big enough to house five hundred soldiers, and strong enough to withstand attacks from the peoples that live over the border." So the king built such a castle, and sent five hundred of his soldiers to protect it.

But a year later, the son sent another message to the king: "Father, the attacks of the neighboring peoples are too strong. They have attacked twice, and if they attack a third time I fear for my life and those of your soldiers."

And the king said to his counselors: "Let him come home and he can live in the palace with me. For it is better that I learn to love my son than that I should spend all the energy and resources of my kingdom keeping him at a distance."

The story of the king holds an important lesson: it's often far easier and more effective in the long run to live with our difficulties than to pour resources into battling and suppressing them.

Tiptoeing toward acceptance

Acceptance comes in two steps. The first involves gently noticing the temptation to drive away or suppress any unsettling thoughts, feelings, emotions and physical sensations. The second step involves actively meeting them "at the door laughing" and greeting them "honourably," as Rumi suggests. This can be a hard and, occasionally, a painful experience, but it's not half as difficult as resigning yourself to a life blighted by unsettling thoughts, feelings and emotions. The secret is to take tiny steps in the direction of acceptance.

The initial sequence for this week of two eight-minute meditations prepares the mind and body for the third Exploring Difficulty meditation: see the first two meditations as ways of

Practices for Week Five

These are carried out on six days out of the next seven. This week, three meditations are practiced in sequence, effectively rolled into one, and practiced once each day in the following order:

- The eight-minute Breath and Body meditation detailed on p. 127 (track 4 at http://bit.ly/rodalemindfulness).

- The eight-minute Sounds and Thoughts meditation detailed on pp. 146–7 (track 5 online).

- The ten-minute Exploring Difficulty meditation detailed on pp. 172–4 (track 6 online).

- Breathing Space meditation on pp. 132–3 (track 8 online); do this as you've done previously with the added instructions at the end of this chapter.

- Habit Releaser—as detailed at the end of this chapter.

grounding yourself, so that you can gain a clearer perspective of yourself and the world.

The Exploring Difficulty meditation very gently invites you to bring unsettling situations to mind and then observe how your body reacts. It's more skillful to work with the body because the mind can become too goal-oriented when directly facing a difficulty. It will want to help by suppressing negativity or by trying desperately to analyze and solve whatever is troubling you. Working with the mind in this context is just too difficult. Focusing on the body, by contrast, puts a tiny sliver of space between you and the problem, so that you don't immediately become entangled within it. In a sense, you are using the body to turn toward negativity rather than using the analyzing mind. You are processing the same raw material, but it is held within a different mode of mind, letting the deepest, wisest part of the mind-body do its own work. This approach has two other benefits as well. First, the body's reactions to negativity often provide a clearer, more coherent "signal," on which it's easier to stay focused. And second, you'll come to realize that physical sensations tend to flux, and this can help to lead toward a deep-seated realization that states of mind also tend to wax and wane from moment to moment.

You will come to learn that everything changes: even the worst-case scenarios imagined in your darkest moments.

And you will see this process unfolding as you use the Exploring Difficulty meditation detailed in the box on page 172 (track 6 online).

Exploring acceptance day by day

When, each day, you are asked to see if you can *deliberately bring to mind a difficulty*, remember that it doesn't have to be a huge issue—just something that you can readily bring to mind that will not overwhelm you. You might consider bringing to the fore a minor disagreement with a friend or colleague, feelings of trepidation over travel plans, or perhaps a decision you've been mulling over without success. You might be surprised by the power of the reaction, but remember to see the tendency to want

Exploring Difficulty meditation

Track 6

Sit for a few minutes. Focus first on the sensations of breathing, then widen your awareness to take in the body as a whole (see Breath and Body, p. 127). Next move your focus to Sounds and Thoughts (see p. 146).

If while you are sitting, you notice that your attention is continually pulled away to painful thoughts or emotions, you can explore something different from what we have been practicing until now.

Up until now, whenever the mind has been distracted by thoughts or feelings, the instruction has been to acknowledge where the mind had been drawn, then gently but firmly to bring the mind back to the breath or the body or whatever you intended to focus on.

Now there's a new possibility. Instead of bringing the mind back from a thought or feeling, now you can allow the thought or feeling to remain in the mind. Then, shifting the attention into the body, become aware of any region of the body where there is tension or contraction, aches or pain—physical sensations that come along with the thought or emotion. These sensations may be very obvious, or they may be quite subtle. But see if you can discern whatever sensations arise when a difficulty is in your mind.

Then when you have identified such sensations, deliberately move the focus of attention to the part of the body where these sensations are strongest. Perhaps imagine you can't "breath into" this region on the in-breath, and "breath out" from it on the out-breath—just as you practiced in the Body Scan. The purpose is not to change the sensations, but to explore them; to see them clearly.

If there are no difficulties or concerns coming up for you now and you want to explore this new approach, then, if you choose, you might deliberately bring to mind a difficulty that is going on in your life at the moment—something you don't mind staying with for a short while. It doesn't have to be very important, but might be something that you are aware of as unpleasant or unresolved. Maybe you had a misunderstanding or an argument. Or perhaps there was a situation where you felt angry, or regretful about something that happened. Or maybe you're worried about something that might happen. If nothing comes to mind, you could choose something from the past, either recent or a long time ago, that once caused unpleasantness for you. So, if you choose to do this, bring such a difficulty to mind now.

Allow it to rest on the workbench of the mind, seeing it vividly, and then let your attention drop into the body, tuning in to any physical sensations that the difficulty is bringing with it.

See if you are able to move close to whatever feelings arise in your body. Tune in to these physical sensations, intentionally directing the focus of your attention to the region of the body where the sensations are strongest, breathing into that part of the body on the in-breath and breathing out from it on the out-breath. Explore the sensations, cradling them in awareness as you watch their intensity change from moment to moment.

Notice how you react to whatever comes up. Hold these reactions in a spacious and compassionate awareness.

Remind yourself that you're not trying to *change* the sensations, but to explore with friendly curiosity the physical sensations coming and going in the body. It may be helpful to say to yourself silently:

(continued)

It's OK to feel this. Whatever it is, it's OK to allow myself to be open to it.

Give the sensations your full attention, breathing with them, letting them be. Remember that you don't have to *like* such feelings in the body—it's OK and natural not to want them around. It may be helpful to repeat phrases such as: *It's OK not to want this. Whatever it is, let's see if I can be open to it, just as it is.* Then, on each out-breath, soften and open to the sensations, wherever they are in the body, letting go of the tendency to tense and brace against them. Say to yourself on each out-breath: *softening, opening.*

See if it is possible to stay with the awareness of these bodily sensations and your relationship to them. Breathe with them, letting them be just as they are.

If you notice that the sensations fade, choose whether to come back to the breath, or to bring the same difficulty, or a new one, to mind. When it has arrived in the mind, allow it to remain, shifting attention to see where it is affecting the body.

If no powerful bodily sensations arise, then you could experiment with "breathing into and out from" any sensations you notice in your body, even if they do not seem to be linked to any particular emotional charge.

And when you are ready, return your focus to the breath, to the sensations of the breath moving in and out of your body, whenever you feel it most vividly—breath by breath.

to engage with the issue, analyzing, problem-solving, brooding. Instead, remind yourself to shift your attention back to the body so you can attend, moment by moment, to its physical reactions to your thoughts. As with previous meditations, see if it is possible to maintain a gentle, compassionate awareness that's imbued with warmth and curiosity.

As you allow this compassionate awareness to enfold the body, see if you can become mindfully aware of the physical location of any discomfort. Tensions will often appear in the shoulders and neck. Fears may start the heart racing. Anticipations may set the stomach churning and make you feel as if you've got butterflies in your stomach. Often, unexpected pains or subtle aches might appear and disappear. Joints may begin to ache or muscles turn to jelly. You might become short of breath or feel light-headed. The body has a million different ways of reacting to unsettling situations, and this meditation gives you the chance to discover where your body might be localizing its suffering on each occasion, making a space for its reactions as they unfold.

Sometimes the body's reactions will be barely noticeable, while on other occasions they might arrive with great swiftness from different places simultaneously. They might behave like a temperamental shower. First, there is nothing, then there's an icy blast, followed by a torrent of scalding hot water. Whatever is the case, allow yourself to focus your awareness on wherever the sensations are strongest. Take a gentle and friendly awareness to this part of the body by "breathing into it" on the in-breath, and "breathing out of it" on the out-breath. After a few moments, when the sensations are in full awareness, silently say to yourself, "It's OK to feel this. It's OK to be open to this."

Stay with these bodily sensations, accepting them, letting them be, exploring them without judgment as best you can. You may find yourself taking the same approach to bodily or mental discomfort as you look towards intense sensations in the yoga practice; as an opportunity to move in close to the edge without forcing anything. Just as you moved up to and explored the "edges" of a stretch in yoga, you could try and do the same with the difficulty you've brought to mind.

If you feel that the mental or physical reaction is becoming too traumatic—if you feel aversion kicking in—remember that you do not have to plunge in all at once. Feel free to take a step back by mentally shifting your attention away from the difficulty, maintaining a flavor of awareness that's infused with warmth, compassion and curiosity. If, after a few moments, you feel sufficiently confident again, take a mental step forward by bringing the difficulty to mind once more, focusing again on your body's accompanying reactions. It's the sensing of your body's reaction that's of importance. You are learning how to dissolve the first step in the chain that drives negative spirals. Your body is processing your troubles in a radically different way. By letting go of the need to "fix" things, a more profound healing has the chance to begin.

As you explore the reactions in your body, see if you can gain—without consciously asking any questions—a detailed sense of how these physical sensations change from moment to moment. What's their character? Are they feelings of "contracting" or "tensing up"? What happens to them when you invite the breath to move into the region of sensations and allow yourself to be open to whatever is here? Is there any sense of expectation, struggle or frustration around this practice, and, if so, are there any sensations associated with this?

Throughout the meditation, hold yourself open in an enquiring way. Be like the explorer: the person who wants to map a new and hitherto undiscovered terrain; someone who is interested in the lie of the land in general, as well as its particular crags and valleys, wanting to know its patterns, the places of barrenness and of fertility, the smooth ground and the jagged rocks. The explorer is mapping the terrain as accurately as possible, for to be inaccurate would be to dishonor what is found there. In the same way, as you approach the last few weeks of the program, your task is to remain curious and interested about whatever comes up in your mind and body from moment to moment, maintaining awareness, so you do not miss seeing the profound beauty that lies at the heart of your life.

Throughout the Exploring Difficulty meditation, as best you can, beware of the temptation to "solve" or "fix" any difficulties that come to mind. Acceptance is linked to positive changes, so it's only natural to use it to fix your difficulties as part of the Doing mode of mind. This may, once again, seem to be a distinction without a difference, but there is a very subtle difference between the two. Remember the mouse in the maze experiment (see pp. 112–13)? This showed that very subtle variations in states of mind lead to vastly different outcomes. It's the same with this week's meditation. If you approach it with the desire to solve a specific problem, then you may simply fire up the mind's autopilot and aversion pathways. You may not even be aware of them kicking into gear, but they may well do so below the level of awareness. Eventually, you may know them by a feeling of sadness or disappointment that "nothing seems to have changed." Of course, it's often extremely difficult—if not impossible—to eliminate such a desire completely, but remember that you are cultivating compassion for yourself. You will not "fail." Every time you realize that you're judging yourself, that realization in itself is an indicator that you've come back to a fuller awareness—central to becoming more mindful day by day. If you find the Exploring Difficulty meditation just too hard, please feel free to leave it for now, simply doing the other meditations each day. You can always return to it at a later date if you wish to explore it further.

Sometimes nothing appears to happen...

The Exploring Difficulty meditation often takes people by surprise. One such situation is when nothing appears to happen. Harry found that when he brought a difficult work situation to mind, he felt nothing at all: "I wondered whether I was doing it right," he said. "Then, suddenly, I felt a contraction right across my chest. It wasn't painful, but it was very definite. It took me by surprise—I'd never really paid attention to what my body does when I'm worried. I didn't try to push it away. I was quite intrigued by it, actually—perhaps because it took time to feel anything. It went up and down, so I decided just to stay with it to see what it did. Eventually, it faded, and when I returned to thinking, the worry that had started it had gone."

Sonya had a similar experience, though she did feel something straightaway: "I knew that the thing that I would focus on was something that someone had said to my husband the other day. I found the phrase 'leaving it on the workbench of the mind' really helpful, as I did not have to do anything with it. I immediately felt a sensation in the lower side of my abdomen, so I focused on it and did what it said to do, imagining the breath was breathing into it, like we'd done in the Body Scan. Some of the sensations stayed the same and others seemed to come and go. Then, without me prompting anything, a quite different thing came into my mind—something to do with my son's school work—and the sensations in the body changed instantly to a feeling of constriction in my upper chest and throat. Then it reversed again. When I held all these in awareness, it really helped to say 'softening, opening' as I breathed out. For the first time, I think I really got the idea of not trying to make anything happen—I was exploring the sensations, not wanting to make them go away."

Like Harry, when Sonya returned to her thoughts, she found that the situations that had been troubling her, although they were still there, did not have the urgency they'd had before. What had happened to them?

Bringing mindful acceptance to our difficulties works for two interconnected reasons. First, it breaks the initial link in the chain that leads to a negative downward spiral. By accepting our negative thoughts, feelings, emotions and bodily sensations—by simply acknowledging their existence—we are preventing the mind's automatic aversion pathways from kicking in. If we do not engage with the downward spiral, we progressively sap its momentum. If we do this during its first all-important twists and turns, as Harry and Sonya did, it never gains enough momentum to perpetuate itself. It just runs into the sand.

Remember the experiment by Richard Davidson and Jon Kabat-Zinn using the sensors on the scalp that measure the electrical activity of the left and right front parts of the brain (see p. 47)? They found that after mindfulness training, the biotech workers were able to maintain an approach-orientated, exploratory mode of mind, even when they were experiencing sad moods. Our own Oxford research published in 2007 has found that even people with a history of depression and suicidal feelings are able to make the same shift toward approaching, rather than avoiding, as indexed by the activity in their brains, after they have participated in a mindfulness course.[4] Harry and Sonya were experiencing the same thing: the release that follows when we are able to approach difficult situations without triggering the body's powerful "aversion" systems.

As we saw earlier, when a difficulty comes to mind, the brain's habitual reaction is to treat it as a real enemy, so it tends to shut down its creative "approach" systems. For some difficulties, it might be necessary to shut down playfulness, but when you are remembering the past or anticipating the future, the difficulty is playing out in our heads and not for real, so this is unnecessary. In fact, it ends up locking things down and blocking creativity: we either feel trapped and the body slumps into submission or the body gears up to fight or flee. Do you remember the brain scanning study we mentioned in Chapter Two (see p. 27)? This found that in people who are low on a scale of mindfulness—those who rush from one thing to another, who find it difficult to stay in the present and who get so focused on their goal that they lose touch with the outside world—the amygdala (at the heart of the fight/flight system) is chronically overactive.[5] You may think that rushing through life gets more done, but you are instead activating the brain's aversion system and undermining the very creativity you're seeking.

The second reason why bringing mindful acceptance to our difficulties works is because it allows you to become aware of the *accuracy* of your thoughts. Take the thought: *I can't cope. I'm going to scream.* If you observe how you react to the thought, and actively feel the clenching muscles in the shoulders and stomach, before the sensations eventually fade away, you'll see more clearly that it was a fear and not a fact. You did cope with the situation; you didn't scream. It was a powerful and compelling fear, but it was never a fact. Cross-checking thoughts with reality is a powerful antidote to negativity in all its forms.

Breathing Spaces: applying your learning to everyday life

Over the past few weeks, you've been practicing the Breathing Space twice a day and whenever you felt that you needed it. Now we suggest that *whenever* you feel troubled in your body or mind, you should see the Breathing Space meditation as your first port of call.

After completing a Breathing Space, you have four options open to you. As we said last week, the first option is to simply carry on as before, but with enhanced awareness. This week we suggest that after a Breathing Space you should gently and seamlessly "drop into" the body to explore any physical sensations that arise as difficulties appear in the mind. This week's Breathing Space is very similar to the one you've used over the previous weeks, but it has been refined to help you explore difficulties with a greater degree of compassion. It is this week, perhaps more than any other, that the Breathing Space acts as a bridge between the longer, more formal meditation sessions and daily life. You should carry out the three steps of the meditation as usual, but incorporate the extra refinements detailed below. Your awareness should follow the usual hourglass shape. In addition to this, you are asked to pay special attention to the extra instructions in Step Three, as these will help you explore difficulties with greater warmth and compassion.

Step 1. Awareness

You have already practiced observing—bringing the focus of awareness to your inner experience and noticing what is happening in your thoughts, feelings and bodily sensations. Now you may like to experiment with *describing, acknowledging* and *identifying* them by putting the experiences into words. For example, you might say in your mind: *I can feel anger growing* or, *Self-critical thoughts are here.*

Step 2. Redirecting attention

You have already practiced gently *redirecting* your full attention to the breath by following it all the way in and all the way out. This week you could also try saying at the back of your mind, *Breathing in . . . breathing out.*

You could also try counting each breath in and each one out. For example, you can say to yourself on the first in-breath, "breathing in—one," and when you exhale, you can say to yourself, "breathing out—one." On the next in-breath you can say "breathing in—two" . . . and so on all the way up to five, before starting again at one.

Step 3. Expanding attention

You have already practiced allowing your attention to expand to the whole body. This week, rather than resting in full awareness for a while, as you've done previously, gently allow your consciousness to include any sense of discomfort, tension or resistance, just as you did with the Exploring Difficulty meditation. If you notice any of these sensations, bring your attention right up to and into them by "breathing into" them. Then breathe out from them, softening and opening as you do so. At the same time, say to yourself, "It's OK to feel this. Whatever it is, it's OK to be open to it." If the discomfort dissolves, return to focusing on the spaciousness of the body.

If you feel able, allow this step to take more than the customary minute or so, staying with the awareness of your bodily sensations and your relationship to them, breathing with them, accepting them, letting them be, allowing them to be just as they are. See it as an extra step, if that helps, or perhaps as a bridge back to daily life. So rather than immediately carrying on with your life where you left off, rest awhile in awareness and explore the messages your body is sending you within the space of awareness.

As best you can, bring this expanded awareness
to the next moments of your day.

Habit Releaser: sow some seeds (or look after a plant)

Nurturing a plant, or sowing some seeds, are among those very simple things in life that can have a surprisingly big benefit. It might even save your life. In the late 1970s, Harvard University psychologist Ellen Langer and her team conducted a now classic series of experiments in which they asked a group of elderly people in a care home to look after a plant in their room.[6] They were told it was their responsibility to water it and make sure it received enough food and light. At the same time, another group of elderly people had a plant placed in their room, but were told "not to worry about it." The nurses would look after it for them. The researchers then measured the levels of happiness in the two groups of people and found, to their surprise, that those asked actively to look after a plant were noticeably happier and healthier. They lived longer too. Just the act of caring for another living thing had markedly improved their life.

So this week, why not sow some seeds or buy or borrow a plant from a friend? If you plant seeds, why not sow those that bees can feed off? There's something mesmerizing about bees at work. Alternatively, why not sow the seeds of a plant you can later eat, such as tomatoes, lettuce or spring onions? As you sow the seeds, feel their texture and that of the soil. Is there any tension in your body, perhaps localized in your neck and shoulders? As you sprinkle the soil over the seeds, watch how it falls through your fingers. Now do it at half speed. Does it feel any different? What does the soil smell like? Does it have a deep, earthy aroma or the slightly acidic smell of sandy soil? When you water the seeds or the young plants, pay close attention to the way the light glints off the droplets. Why not spend a little time finding out more about the plants you'll be nurturing?

And what about Elana?

In the preface to the second edition of her book, *Here for Now*, Elana Rosenbaum wrote:[7] "Sometimes people ask me: 'Are you cured?' 'Cured of what?' I ask them."

She concludes: "I am alive. I am well. I continue to challenge myself to be fully here for now. What about you?"

CHAPTER TEN

Mindfulness Week Six: Trapped in the Past or Living in the Present?

K ate sat silently. The psychologist sat with her, allowing the silence to be there for a while, as the noise of the busy hospital corridor outside the interview room continued. She'd been admitted twenty-four hours earlier, after taking an overdose of her antidepressants. Physically, she was well, the effect of the pills having worn off—but she still felt exhausted. She also felt ashamed, angry with herself, and wished she had not done it; she felt very sad and alone.

When asked by the nurse why she had taken the pills, Kate said she didn't really know—that she'd felt desperate, that she'd had to do something and couldn't think of anything else to do. She did not really think that she would die—she did not actually *want* to die. It was more a feeling of wanting to escape for a while—to pull the bedclothes over her head to make the world go away. Life had gotten too complicated. So many people depended on her and she felt she'd let them all down. "Perhaps," she felt, "if I take myself out of the way, everyone else's life would be so much better."

As she began to talk to the psychologist, more of her story came out. Things in life had been pretty straightforward at one time: school, college, her job as a secretary, a mother and father that lived a few hours away, steady boyfriends—no one special right now, but not too lonely—a good circle of friends ("What will they think?" she suddenly asked, and began to cry).

Kate's life had been thrown into turmoil eighteen months before when she'd had a car accident that she felt was her fault, although the insurance companies had decided that no one was at fault. No one in either vehicle had been injured, but for Kate, the scars were in her mind, not on her body. She had been taking her six-year-old niece, Amy (her sister's daughter), to the mall. Amy was also OK after the crash, and even seemed to be able to talk about what had happened without being scared or traumatized at all. And Kate's sister had just been relieved that nothing too serious had happened to her daughter and to her beloved sister.

But Kate could not forgive herself. She replayed the accident in her mind's eye over and over again. What if Amy had not been strapped in (she had been); what if the other car had been going faster (it wasn't)? what if Amy had been injured or even killed (she wasn't). Kate's mind was doing what minds often do: creating imaginary scenarios that then become adhesive. Try as she might, she could not dismiss them from her mind. More and more, she found herself focusing on these as often or more than on the actual events themselves. She had developed what is sometimes called posttraumatic stress disorder (PTSD),[1] and she was also depressed: tired all the time, feeling low. The joy had gone out of her life, and she'd lost interest in things she used to take pleasure in. Eventually, all these feelings had accumulated into a state of mind that could only be described as prolonged mental pain: Kate alternated between feelings of emptiness and hopelessness on the one hand, and of turmoil and confusion on the other. Now she thought less of the event, but more about the mental pain itself. Her thoughts went round and round on themes that anyone in such pain can experience (see box, below).[2]

Mental pain: the thoughts that just keep going round and round . . .

- There is nothing I can do.

- I am falling apart.

- I have no future.

- I am completely defeated.

- I have lost something I'll never find again.

- I am not my old self any more.

- I am worthless.

- I am a burden to others.

- Something in my life has been damaged forever.

- I can't find meaning in my life.

- I am completely helpless.

- The pain will never go away.

Kate's story illustrates in a very direct way some of the states of mind that can entrap us. In many subtle ways, we find that we cannot forgive ourselves for things we have done or failed to do in the past. We carry around the dead weight of past failures, unfinished business, relationship difficulties, unresolved arguments, unfulfilled ambitions for ourselves and others. It may not be as traumatic an event as Kate's, but her experience reveals aspects of her mind that she shares with all of us: the difficulty in letting go of the past, the brooding about things that did or didn't happen or worrying about things that haven't yet happened. When the mind gets into such ruts and will not let go, you can find yourself overthinking. Try as you might, you cannot disengage the mind from its own goals and imaginings: a state that has been called "painful engagement."[3] In fact, at times like these, it can seem that if you ever allowed yourself to feel happy again, you'd be betraying some person or principle. How could Kate feel happy after what she'd done? She felt she didn't deserve it.

It is not hard to see why any and all of us might feel guilty for much of the time. It's all around us. Western society has been built from the ground up on guilt and shame. We can feel guilty for not being able to cope; guilty for being a bad person or a poor husband, wife, mother, father, brother, sister, daughter or son; guilty for not achieving our potential. We can feel shame for not living up to our own expectations, or for feeling anger, bitterness, jealousy, sadness, meanness and despair. Guilty for enjoying life. Guilty for feeling happy . . .

And the foundation for much of this guilt and shame is fear—the inner bully that we all carry around in our heads: fear that we're not good enough; fear that if we relax we'll begin to fail; fear that if we let ourselves off the leash, all hell will break loose; fear that if we don't maintain our defenses we'll be over-whelmed . . . And if we fear that others will criticize us, why not play safe and attack ourselves with a few homemade criticisms first?[4] One fear leads to another, which feeds into another, in an endless debilitating cycle that saps our energy, leaving us like a hollow shell drifting through life.

But there's also something else in Kate's experience that may easily go unnoticed: the theme of *irreversibility* in all her thoughts. After the accident she felt different in some unchange-able way. And struggling in the midst of her trauma and depres-sion, with the antidepressants not really helping, she'd felt that her life was irreversibly damaged; that she'd lost something that she'd never find again. Any of us can fall into the same mental trap. We can carry with us a hidden assumption that, because of what has happened to us, nothing at all can ever be the same again.

But why does this happen? The answer lies in the way we remember events from the past. Scientific research has made great progress in understanding how memory for events in our life works and how it can go wrong. In experiments conducted over many years by Mark Williams and colleagues, volunteers recall an event in the past when they felt happy. It does not nec-essarily have to have been an important one, but one that lasted less than a day from any time in the past. Most of us find it easy to recall something. Perhaps we'd remember some good news or walking in the hills and seeing a dramatic view, a first kiss or a day out with a good friend. Notice that the memory has worked smoothly, retrieving a specific event—something that happened on a particular day and time and place (even if you cannot recall exactly when it took place). You could try more examples for yourself using the questions in the box on page 190.

Memories of real events

Look at the words below. Think of a real event that has happened to you, and that comes into your mind when you see each of these words. Keep in mind or write down what happened. (It doesn't matter whether the real event happened a long time ago or only recently, but it should be something that lasted for less than one day.)

For example, if "fun" was one of the words, it would be OK to say, "I had fun when I went to Jane's party," but it would not be OK to say, "I always have fun at parties," because that doesn't mention a particular event. Do your best to write something for each word.

In each case, remember to come up with something that lasted for less than one day.

Think of a time when you felt:

- Happy

- Bored

- Relieved

- Hopeless

- Excited

- Failure

- Lonely

- Sad

- Lucky

- Relaxed

But it is not always easy to be specific. Research has found that if we've experienced traumatic events in the past, or if we are depressed or exhausted or locked into a brooding preoccupation about our feelings, then our memory shows a different pattern. Instead of doing the work of retrieving one specific event, the retrieval process stops short when it has only completed the first step of recollection: retrieving a summary of events. Very often, the result is what psychologists call an "overgeneral memory."

So when Kate was asked if could she think of something— any particular event in the past—that made her feel happy, she said, "Me and my roommate used to go out on the weekends." Her memory had stopped short of producing a particular episode. And when asked to recall any specific event that had made her feel sorry, she said, "Arguments with my mom." When asked if she remembered any *particular* time, she simply said, "We always argued."

Kate's response is not unique. Research conducted by our team at Oxford, and in other labs throughout the world, has discovered that this pattern is very common for some people, particularly those who are too tired or frantic to think straight, those who are prone to depression or those with traumatic life histories. At first, the impact that this memory difficulty might have was unclear. Then it was found that the more people tended to retrieve memories in this nonspecific way, the more difficulty they had in letting go of the past and the more affected they were by things going wrong in their lives right *now* and rebuilding their lives again after an upset.[5] For example, in 2007 Professor Richard Bryant, working in Sydney, Australia, found that firefighters who showed this pattern of memory when they joined the fire service were later found to have been more traumatized by what they had to witness as part of their stressful jobs.[6] Another colleague, Professor Anke Ehlers, found that those with this overgeneral memory pattern were more likely to suffer PTSD after an assault. When they investigated further, they found that this memory difficulty went along with a tendency to brood, and also, importantly, with the feeling that the assault had in some way changed things permanently and irreversibly.[7]

The dance of ideas

Imagine you're in a crowded bar and see a friend talking to one of your work colleagues. You smile and wave at them. They are looking in your direction, but don't seem to notice you.

What thoughts go through your mind? How do you feel?

You might think that such a scene is clear-cut, but it's actually highly ambiguous. Show it to half a dozen people and you will get a range of answers that depend more on the state of mind of the person being asked than on any concrete "reality." If something has recently happened to make you happy, you will probably assume that your friends didn't see you waving at them. The scene will soon be forgotten. But if you are unhappy or distressed for some reason (any reason), the dance of ideas will be choreographed differently and the scene will take on an entirely different meaning: you may conclude that your friends are trying to avoid you or that maybe you had lost more friends. You might think:

They are avoiding me. Here we go again. Maybe she never liked me and spent ages trying to lose me. Why is friendship so transient? The world is becoming increasingly shallow.

Such "self-talk" can quickly turn a period of fragile sadness into a longer and deeper bout of unhappiness that leaves you questioning many of your most cherished beliefs. Why?

Our minds are always desperately trying to make sense of the world—and they do this in the context of baggage accumulated over many years together with the mood of the moment. They are constantly gathering up scraps of information and trying to fit them together into a meaningful picture. They do this by constantly referring back to the past and seeing if the present is beginning to pan out in the same way. They then extrapolate these models into the future and see, once again, if a new pattern or theme emerges. Juggling such patterns is one of the defining characteristics of being human. It's how we impose meaning on the world.

When the dance freezes

This dance of ideas is amazing to behold, until it starts to "freeze." Overgeneral memory tends to freeze the past as a by-product of its tendency to summarize—the summary is then taken as true forever. So once you have interpreted your friends' behavior in the bar as "rejection," you rarely go back to the actual details of the situation and consider other interpretations. You overgeneralize, especially if you are tired or preoccupied with your own problems. And when the dance of ideas freezes, all you remember later is yet another example of people rejecting you. Your world loses its texture and color and becomes black or white—win or lose.

What we now understand from this research is something hugely important: that the feeling that "things are irreversible" or that "I have been damaged forever" is a very toxic aspect of a pattern of mind. But it is a pattern of mind in which we can easily get stuck, because the very thought itself seems to say: *I am permanent: there is nothing you can do about me: I am with you forever.* This sense of permanence arises from a tendency to be *trapped in the past*, recalling events in an overgeneral way. And this overgenerality is fed by a tendency to suppress memories of events we don't like or by simply brooding about them. Suppression and brooding are exhausting, and this also feeds overgeneralized recall. And once our memories are overgeneral, we don't return to the specifics of what has actually happened in the past; instead, we get caught and trapped inside our sense of guilt for what has happened and hopelessness about anything ever changing in the future. It *feels* permanent, but the good news is that it is temporary. Despite the propaganda it represents, it *can* change. Our research has found that eight weeks of mindfulness training makes memory more specific and less overgeneral.[8] Mindfulness releases us from the trap of overgenerality.

If you have been following along with the meditations up to this point, you may have experienced this for yourself. Acceptance of the "guilts" and "fears" from the past—seeing them as mere straws in the wind—may have begun to allow you some respite. You may be finding oases of peace in your life. Perhaps you have found yourself recalling with a greater sense of ease events from the past—events that you had previously found difficult to bring to mind without huge emotional

Treating yourself with kindness

How harsh and judgmental are you toward yourself? Treating yourself with kindness and ceasing to judge yourself harshly are cornerstones of finding peace in a frantic world. Ask yourself the following questions:[9]

- Do I criticize myself for having irrational or inappropriate emotions?

- Do I tell myself I shouldn't be feeling the way I'm feeling?

- Do I believe some of my thoughts are abnormal or bad and I shouldn't think that way?

- Do I make judgments about whether my thoughts are good or bad?

- Do I tell myself that I shouldn't be thinking the way I do?

- Do I think some of my emotions are bad or inappropriate and I shouldn't feel them?

- When I have distressing thoughts or images, do I judge myself as good or bad, depending what the thought/image is about?

- Do I disapprove of myself when I have irrational ideas?

If you endorsed strongly more than one or two of these questions, you may be being too hard on yourself. Could you begin treating yourself with more compassion? The trick with this questionnaire is to understand that you're being too harsh on yourself without seeing this fact as a criticism. See your responses as an aid to awareness, rather than as a sign of success or failure.

turbulence. You may still feel the pain of them, perhaps even acutely, but begin to sense that these events actually belong to the past, and could be let go of, placed back in the past where they rightly belong.

This is because, day by day, you have been exploring an alternative to the automatic brooding "avoidant" mode of mind that induces overgenerality, getting you stuck in the past, putting a fog over the future. The Raisin meditation, the Breath and Body meditation, the Body Scan, the Mindful Movement, the learning to relate to thoughts as you relate to sounds, the exploration of the difficult by working through the body—each of these has contributed to learning that there is, for you, a new possibility. There is a possibility of dwelling, moment by moment, in a state of mind that cradles you in a nonjudgmental and compassionate wisdom.

In teaching mindfulness classes, we see many examples of people discovering the freedom that comes when they realize that something they thought was permanent was, in fact, changeable. But sometimes, all of the meditations you've prac-ticed up to now can leave a corner of the mind untouched. Somehow, many people seem to be able to meditate for weeks, months or years, and never really hear the message of kind-ness for themselves. They think of meditation as another thing *to do*.

So, you need to go one step further if you want not only to bring about the bone-deep peace that comes from cultivating mindfulness, but also to help sustain it in the light of the stresses that life throws at you. You need to relate to the world with kindness and compassion, and you can only do this if you come home to who *you* are, accepting yourself with deepest

Practices for Week Six

- There is one new meditation this week. It is the ten-minute Befriending meditation detailed on page 198 (track 7 online at http://bit.ly/rodalemindfulness)—to be done on six days out of the next seven. Each time you come to do it, prepare yourself by sitting quietly, using track 1 or 4 online to guide you (Weeks One and Three), or, if you feel able, without the help of any tracks at all.

In addition:
- Continue with the Three-Minute Breathing Space meditation (see p. 132), aiming to do this twice a day and whenever you feel you need it.

- You should also try to carry out one of the Habit Releasers detailed at the end of this chapter.

respect, honor and, yes, love. The last meditation we are going to invite you to share is a befriending meditation. In this meditation you acknowledge that however hard you find it to be compassionate to *others*, it can feel even harder to bring kindness to *yourself*.

Week Six helps you bring kindness back into your life—kindness not just for others but for yourself too.

The Befriending meditation[10]

Track
7

Take a few minutes now to become settled in a warm and comfortable place where you can be by yourself for a while, relaxed and alert.

Find a posture that, for you, embodies a sense of dignity and wakefulness. If you are sitting, allow the spine to be strong, the shoulders relaxed, the chest open and the head balanced.

Focus on the breath, and then expand attention to the whole body for a few minutes, until you feel settled.

When the mind wanders, acknowledge where it went, remembering that you have a choice now: either to escort it back to whatever you had intended to focus on or, instead, to allow your attention to drop into the body to explore where you are experiencing the trouble or concern. Feel free to use any previous meditations as part of your preparation for this one.

When you are ready, allow some—or all—of these phrases to come to mind, changing the words if you choose, so that they connect to you and become, for you, your own gateway into a deep sense of friendliness toward yourself:

May I be free from suffering.
May I be as happy and healthy as it is possible for me to be.
May I have ease of being.

Taking your time, imagine that each phrase is a pebble dropped down into a deep well. You are dropping each one in turn, then listening to any reaction in thoughts, feelings, bodily sensations or impulse to act. There is no need to judge what arises. This is for you.

If you find it difficult to bring forth any sense of friendship toward yourself, bring to mind a person (or even a pet) who, either in the past or present, has loved you unconditionally. Once you have a clear sense of their love for you, see if you can return to offering this love to yourself: *May I be free from suffering. May I be happy and healthy. May I have ease of being.*

Remain with this step for as long as you wish before moving to the next.

At a certain point, bring to mind a loved one, and wish them well in the same way (using he, she, or they, as you prefer): *May he (she/they) be free from suffering. May he (she/they) be as happy and healthy as it is possible for them to be. May he (she/they) have ease of being.*

Once again, see what arises in mind and body as you hold the person in mind and heart, wishing them well. Once again, allow responses to come. Take your time. Pause between phrases— listening attentively. Breathing.

When you are ready to move on, choose a stranger. This may be someone you see regularly, perhaps in the street or on the bus or train—someone you recognize, but may not know the name of; someone you feel neutral about. Recognize that, although you do not know them, they probably also have a life full of hopes and fears as you have. They too wish to be happy, as you do. So, keeping them in heart and mind, repeat the phrases and wish them well.

Now, if you choose to extend this meditation further, you might wish to bring to mind someone whom you find difficult (past or present). This does not have to be the most difficult person in your life, but whomever you choose, now intentionally allow

(continued)

them to be in your heart and mind, acknowledging that they, too, may wish (or have wished) to be happy, and to be free from suffering. Repeat the phrases: *May he (she) be free from suffering. May he (she) be happy and healthy. May he (she) have ease of being.* Pausing. Listening. Noticing sensations in the body. Seeing if it is possible to explore these feelings without censoring them or judging yourself.

Remember that if at any time you feel overwhelmed and drawn away by intense feelings or thoughts, you can come back to the breath in the body to anchor yourself back in the present moment, treating yourself with kindness.

Finally, extend loving-kindness to all beings, including your loved ones and strangers and those whom you find difficult. The intention here is to extend love and friendship to all living beings on the planet—and remembering that all living beings includes you! *May all beings be free from suffering. May all beings be happy and healthy. May all of us have ease of being.*

At the end of this time of practice, take time to sit with the breath and the body, resting in clear awareness of the present moment. Whatever your experience of this practice, acknowledge your own courage in taking the time to nourish yourself in this way.

And it can be hard...

It is hard to bring genuine loving-kindness and friendship to yourself, so taking the time to explore this practice takes some commitment. But it can be done anywhere, at any time, as well as during the formal daily practice. Gradually, you may become aware that it is impossible to nourish others without also nourishing yourself; impossible to be truly loving to others while you are attacking yourself for not being good enough. This is what Cara found when she took one of our courses:

"I started by steadying myself," said Cara. "After a moment, I started bringing the phrases to mind: 'May I be free from suffering . . .' After a while, I started noticing something coming to mind—a sense of being overwhelmed with the sheer busyness of my life. I returned to the meditation, but it kept coming up. So I stayed with this, seeing if I could bring friendliness to my sense of busyness."

What was Cara sensing? Afterwards, she reflected further on her experience. "Although I *knew* I was very busy in my life, I never thought of it as something that was actually doing me harm—that I was actually *suffering* because of it. It reminded me of another phrase that I had once heard—'May I be safe from inner and outer harm'—and I thought, yes, that's it. I have always thought that it was the *world out there* that makes me busy: my job, my family—the whole thing. But what I was hearing now was: Ah, yes, but this is me too—I'm harming myself. I think that I *need* to be busy; this is a really old pattern for me. And here it was, coming up, in reaction to the 'wishing myself well' in this practice. I thought, hmm . . . I wonder what I'm going to discover?"

Cara certainly felt that she was running to keep up with her life, but in the midst of her loving-kindness meditation, she had a deep sense of not only the suffering that this brought about, but the way in which she was contributing to it. Interestingly, in the context of her mindfulness, there was no self-blame, just a quiet knowing of how things were. Later, she was able to say that, as part of her ongoing practice, she had written five questions to ponder:

- How can I nourish myself?

- How can I slow down in the midst of my rushing?

- How can I stand back?

- How can I make choices?

- How can I be kind to myself?

Gradually, Cara learned that friendship is the quiet voice inside. It all too easily gets drowned out by the louder voices of fear and guilt. Fear of failure had, for her, tried to "protect" her from love. It told her she'd lose out by being kind-hearted. It warned her that if she was not constantly vigilant, she'd be ripped off, double-crossed and resoundingly used and abused by those around her. It had persuaded her, instead, to be angry with the world. It reminded her constantly that "you are indispensable, so you need to keep going whatever the cost" and that "nobody understands the situation like you do" and "nobody cares."

By the time Cara came to a mindfulness course, she had begun to feel ashamed about all of the powerful reactions that fear had dredged up. It was in the Befriending meditation— coming after all the other practices that had gradually allowed her to see her mind and body with greater kindness—that she was so forcibly struck by what she had been doing to herself.

Further, Cara realized that she was also compounding her suffering, not only by saying, "I must be busy," but also by repeating to herself, "Things used to be different. This is so relentless. Nothing will ever be the same again." She saw how much these and other thoughts were driving wedges between her and the world. They had progressively separated her from her family, friends and colleagues. Her life really had begun to resemble the one in her darkest fears—one that was founded on cynicism and bitterness. She had become very lonely inside, separate from everyone who did not conform to her standards— even herself. Cara realized that she was saying these things to herself even when she was lying in bed at night or walking the dog. Now, at last, something new happened: she saw that at the moment when she was lying in her bed, she *was* actually in bed, not at work—and that "this is relentless" was actually a (very adhesive) thought she could let go of, regardless of whatever else it might pretend to be!

Jesse agreed: "Yes—you chide yourself for being angry, selfish and cynical. On top of all this, another layer of guilt is imposed on you by society. It's all-pervading and supremely powerful."

Jesse's experience had been a feeling of being "put upon" by everyone since his school days. "It comes down from the Church, the state, our schools and our bosses. They always told me that I was no good—'flawed goods,' one teacher told me—and they make us all strive ever harder, even though we all know perfection is impossible. They teach us to feel guilty for not working hard enough."

Cara recognized these pressures too. She said, "Later, if we have children, we are blamed for not looking after the kids *and* juggling a career."

By doing the Befriending meditation, both Cara and Jesse recognized that no one had ever taught them to treat themselves kindly. Virtually every facet of their lives was hemmed in by rules and regulations to such a degree that even breathing seemed like a subversive act.

The antidote to all this fear and guilt was, for them, to take a step back and listen to the quiet voice of the heart. They were discovering what countless numbers of people have discovered over the centuries: that if we are to find true peace, we have to listen to the quiet voice of compassion and ignore the bellowing ones of fear and guilt and shame. Meditation can help us to do this, but we have to imbue it with kindness, otherwise we run the risk of finding temporary respite, but not the true peace that lies beyond the ups and downs of daily life. We end up dampening down the noise, but remain deaf to a better, more wholesome way of living. Many studies have now shown this to be true. Kindness transforms things: the "aversion" pathways in the mind are switched off and the "approach" ones switched on instead. This change in attitude enhances openness, creativity and happiness, while at the same time dissolving the fears, guilts, anxieties and stresses that lead to exhaustion and chronic discontent.

Rebecca's experience was similar: "I'm training to be a counselor. I started a few months ago. Actually I did a bit of counseling a few years ago before the children were born. When I did the meditation, I remembered one of my clients who had not done very well—he'd needed to be hospitalized, and I blamed myself, even though no one else thought it was my fault. It brought up all the old fears I used to have about things being my responsibility if anything went wrong at all.

"As I sat, I felt very vulnerable—but also a sense of empathy and kindness for myself that I'd never had before. I think that I had reacted to my vulnerability by trying to be strong, as if retraining now would make me less likely to get hurt. The meditation reminded me that if I ever stopped being vulnerable to being hurt, I'd stop being the sort of counselor that I believe is most helpful to those who seek help."

Kindness in practice

Kindness arises through empathy—a deep, shared understanding of another person's predicament. Brain research shows that the part of the brain that is activated when we are feeling genuine empathy for another is the same part that we saw being activated by mindfulness meditation: a part called the insula[11] (see p. 49).

Although we often talk about having empathy for others, it's equally important to be open to receiving it ourselves. We often have very little empathy for our own thoughts and feelings and frequently try to suppress them by dismissing them as weaknesses. Or we might try indulging our emotions with treats (mostly accompanied by a slightly bitter feeling of entitlement), such as overeating (because we feel we deserve it). But it may be helpful to imagine that our deepest thoughts and feelings don't want indulging (or dismissing). They just want to be heard and understood. They just want us to empathize with the feelings that are giving rise to them. We could try seeing them as we might relate to a baby that is crying inconsolably. Sometimes, once we have done everything we can, the only thing left to do is cradle the baby in our arms, with warmth and compassion—just to be there. We don't have to *do* anything more than just be there.

Some people think that it's a little selfish to start by focusing on themselves during the meditation rather than trying to cultivate kindness for others, but this is to misunderstand the long-term intentions of the practice. By spending a little time cultivating friendship toward yourself, you are gradually dissolving the negative forces of fear and guilt within. This reduces your adhesive preoccupation with your own mental landscape, which, in turn, releases a wellspring of happiness, compassion and creativity that benefits everyone. A good way of looking at this is to see kindness as a crystal-clear pool fed by a small spring. You can try and conserve the pool by rationing the water, giving each person you meet a small thimbleful as they pass by. Alternatively, you can unblock the spring that feeds the pool, ensuring that it's continuously replenished and provides ample sustenance for all. Meditation unblocks the spring.

The Befriending meditation may become part of daily life as much as any other practice you've learned so far. See if you can, as much as you are able to, infuse your life with empathy for others. This may not be easy. Many people can genuinely appear selfish, unkind and ice cold, but this may often be a reflection of their own busyness and lack of awareness of the effect they have on others. If you bring kindness to bear toward such people, you'll soon realize that they are, to a greater or lesser extent, just like us all: stumbling through life trying to find happiness and meaning. See if it is possible to feel their predicament.

Although in the early stages, the Befriending meditation might seem a little difficult, remember that it has already begun its work. Brain-imaging research has shown that within a few minutes of beginning the meditation, the parts of the brain governing the "approach" qualities of kindness and empathy begin to fire.[12]

Extending the Breathing Space to negative thoughts

In Chapter Eight we said that there were four options open to you after completing the Breathing Space. The first is to carry on with what you were doing before you began the meditation, but with enhanced awareness. The second option is to consciously "drop into" your body to help you deal more skillfully with difficulties. This week we'll explore a third possibility; relating differently to your thoughts. Earlier in this chapter we explained how your thoughts can trap you by shouting their bad advice, often based on memories that are overgeneral, so that you often only get a biased summary of events that have happened to you. Now, when you have finished taking a Breathing Space, spend a few moments noting your thoughts and feelings. *See if you can relate differently to your thoughts.*[13] You might:

- write down your thoughts

- watch the thoughts come and go

- view your thoughts as thoughts, not as objective reality

- name your thought patterns, such as "morbid thoughts," "worrying thoughts" or "anxious thoughts," or simply just "thinking, thinking"

- ask yourself whether you're overtired, jumping to conclusions, overgeneralizing, exaggerating the significance of the situation or unreasonably expecting perfection

Habit Releaser

Choose one of the Habit Releasers shown below and try to carry it out at least once this week. If you prefer, you can do both.

1. Reclaiming your life[14]

Think back to a time in your life when things seemed less frantic, before the time when some tragedy or increase in workload took over your daily existence. Recall in as much detail as you can some of the activities that you used to do at that time. These may be things you did by yourself (reading your favorite magazines or taking time to listen to a track from a favorite piece of music, going out for walks or bike rides) or together with friends or family (from playing board games to going to the theater).

Choose one of these activities and plan to do it this week. It may take five minutes or five hours, it might be important or trivial, it might involve others or it could be by yourself. It is only important that it should be something that puts you back in touch with a part of your life that you had forgotten—a part of you that you may have been telling yourself was lost somehow, that you could not get back to. Don't wait until you *feel* like doing it; do it anyway and see what happens. It's time to reclaim your life.

2. Do a good-natured deed for someone else

Why not carry out a random act of kindness? It needn't be something big. You could help a colleague tidy their desk, assist a neighbor in carrying their shopping or do something for your partner that you know they hate doing themselves. If you've finished a good book or a newspaper, why not leave it on a bus seat?[15] Why not get rid of a few possessions that you no longer need and that have been cluttering up your home? Instead of throwing them away or recycling them, try Freecycling them. (Freecycling is an international movement that allows you to get rid of your old stuff by giving it away to people who need it and are willing to collect it. This includes small items like old computer cables, half-used bags of plaster or even fully functioning TVs or DVD players. Have a look at: www.freecycle.org.)

There are numerous other ways of helping others too. Think

about your friends, family and colleagues. How can you make their lives a little bit better? Perhaps a colleague is hard pressed on a particular job and you could cheer them up by leaving a little treat on their desk first thing in the morning. A bunch of flowers could transform their entire day. You don't always have to tell them you're the one who did it—just do it for the sake of it, with warmth and understanding. If an elderly person near you lives alone, why not give them your phone number in case of emergency? There's no need to tell anyone else about it. Give for the sake of giving and imbue it with warmth and empathy. If you see someone needing help today, why not give them a hand? Once again, you don't need to wait until you feel like doing it—see the action as a meditation in itself, an opportunity for learning and exploring your reactions and responses. See how it affects your body. Make a mental note of how you feel.

The genius and wisdom of Einstein

This chapter has been about cultivating friendliness and kindness toward yourself and others. Even as you are reading, you may notice some resistance to these ideas. You may become aware of a rumor at the back of the mind. The rumor says that if you ever let go of striving, or became more compassionate and accepting, you'd lose your "edge" and become too soft for your own good.

Albert Einstein, along with countless scientists and philosophers throughout the ages, always emphasized the importance of kindness, compassion and curiosity in daily life. Although Einstein viewed such qualities as good in themselves, he also knew that they led to clearer thinking and a better, more productive way of living and working. He did not fall into the trap of thinking that being harsh on yourself and others leads to success. Einstein knew that this view arose because we all tend to misattribute success to the harsh, driving voices in our heads, rather than to the quieter, more reasonable ones. He wrote:

> A human being is a part of the whole called by us the universe, a part limited in time and space. He experiences himself, his thoughts and feeling as something separated from the rest, a kind of optical delusion of his consciousness. This delusion is a kind of prison for us, restricting us to our personal desires and to affection for a few persons nearest to us. Our task must be to free ourselves from this prison by widening our circle of compassion to embrace all living creatures and the whole of nature in its beauty. Nobody is able to achieve this completely, but the striving for such achievement is itself a part of the liberation, and a foundation for inner security.[16]

CHAPTER ELEVEN

Mindfulness Week Seven: When Did You Stop Dancing?

It was eleven-thirty at night and Marissa was struggling with her Breathing Space meditation. And today, of all days, she really needed a breathing space. She was desperate to calm down so she could get a good night's sleep, but almost as soon as she'd begun her meditation, she was interrupted by the irritating buzz of a message arriving on her phone in the next room. She knew who it would be from: her boss at the unit where she worked; and she could guess what it would say: "Marissa—have you double-checked the end-of-year figures for the department's budget?—Leanne."

Marissa's manager never rested and saw no reason why anyone else should do so either. Marissa was at her wits' end dealing with Leanne. She was someone who genuinely couldn't see a distinction between her job and the rest of her life. The manager worked twelve-hour days and routinely bombarded people with texts and emails late at night. Some people had a

211

life; Marissa's boss had a smartphone. She was a walking management textbook who spoke all of the right jargon about "empowerment," "cross-cutting strategies" and "thinking outside the box," but somehow she never managed to put any of it into practice, particularly when it came to dealing with her subordinates. To her colleagues she seemed bad-tempered, aggressive and impulsive. To cap it all, she was becoming inefficient, forgetful and devoid of creativity. Her private life—such as it was—was equally chaotic. Her second husband had recently left her, and her seventeen-year-old daughter was a "disappointment" because of her devotion to art and drama, rather than to economics and business studies. Leanne was genuinely stunned that her daughter didn't want a lucrative career on Wall Street and a life focused around designer clothes and expensive wines.

It was easy to blame Leanne, but she was, of course, also a victim, unable to step outside of a punishing work schedule and a disintegrating private life.

Ironically, Marissa had many of the same problems as Leanne until she'd discovered mindfulness two years previously. It was an epiphany. After years of unhappiness, stress and exhaustion, she'd learned to relax and had begun to live again. Mindfulness had improved her life no end, but she still had moments of high stress—usually when it came to dealing with Leanne's demands. But at least she now knew how to handle them a little more skillfully.

Marissa returned to her Breathing Space meditation. She sensed the tightness in her neck and shoulders, the pulse in her temples and her fast and shallow breathing. They were all signs that she was under intense pressure and, if she wasn't careful, she'd soon become exhausted and quite possibly depressed too.

The previous few weeks had been hellishly difficult, but she was determined not to be pulled back into the dark pit of the Exhaustion Funnel.

As Marissa learned during her mindfulness classes, many of life's problems, such as unhappiness, anxiety and stress, can be likened to drifting down a funnel of exhaustion that progressively drains away your life and energy.

Exhaustion Funnel

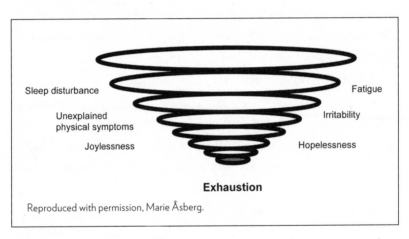

Sleep disturbance

Fatigue

Unexplained physical symptoms

Irritability

Joylessness

Hopelessness

Exhaustion

Reproduced with permission, Marie Åsberg.

The Exhaustion Funnel

Our colleague, Professor Marie Åsberg, from the Karolinska Institute in Stockholm, is an expert on burnout. She uses the Exhaustion Funnel to describe how this can happen to any of us.

The circle at the top represents how things are when we are living a full and balanced life. As things get busier, however, many of us tend to give things up to focus on what seems "important." The circle narrows, illustrating the narrowing of our lives. But if the stress is still there, we give up more—and more. The circles narrow further.

Notice that very often, the very first things we give up are those that nourish us the most but seem "optional." The result is that we are increasingly left with only work or other stressors that often deplete our resources, and nothing to replenish or nourish us—and exhaustion is the result.

Professor Åsberg suggests that those of us who continue downward furthest are likely to be those who are the most conscientious, those whose level of self-confidence is closely dependent on their performance at work, i.e., those who are often seen as the best workers, not the lazy ones. The diagram also shows the sequence of accumulating "symptoms" experienced by Marissa as she lived out her assumption that a social life was superfluous—the funnel narrowed and she became more and more exhausted.

The funnel is created as you narrow the circle of your life to focus on solving your immediate problems. As you spiral down the funnel, you progressively give up more and more of the enjoyable things in life (which you come to see as optional) to make way for the more "important" things such as work. As you slide ever further down, you give up even more of the things that nourish you, leaving yourself increasingly exhausted, indecisive and unhappy. You are eventually spat out at the bottom, a shadow of your former self.

It's all too easy to get sucked into the Exhaustion Funnel. If you are overworked, or otherwise have too much on your plate, it's entirely natural to make space by temporarily streamlining your life. This generally means giving up a hobby or part of your social life so that you can focus on your work; in Marissa's case, this meant abandoning her weekly choir practice. But what she didn't take into account was how nourishing the choir practice was for her soul. The weekly practice had become central to her life, but she'd bought into the idea that a social life was somehow optional, or even superfluous. In Marissa's mind, her social life could be suspended when something more "important" came along. Although it seemed like a temporary fix to free up more time for work, it soon backfired. Without the weekly respite of choir practice, she gradually became less energized, creative and efficient. She ended up accomplishing less and taking more time to do so.

To free up even more space for work, she abandoned her monthly book club, largely because she never had any spare time to read the novels she'd normally devour. This, too, soon backfired as she became still less efficient at work. So after a further few months, pressures of work once again forced her to put a little more of her life on hold. This time Marissa extended her working day by a couple of hours by enrolling her nine-year-old daughter in an after-school club. But this also had an unexpected downside. She soon started feeling guilty about seeing less and less of her daughter. The guilt often ate into her sleep and she became increasingly inefficient at work.

Leanne came up with a solution: a laptop. This allowed Marissa to work when her daughter was watching her favorite TV programs. As you'd expect, this also meant that Marissa began working later into the night, analyzing spreadsheets and banging off emails so that her bosses could see her commitment. Needless to say, after a while something had to give, and this time it was her diet.

Both Marissa and her daughter Ella loved the occasional takeout, but soon they were eating them night after night and

becoming bored with the fatty, salty, low-nutrient food. But
Marissa and her daughter hadn't just given up wholesome food
to save time cooking; they'd also lost something that often goes
unnoticed: conversation. Long chats in the kitchen with her
growing daughter gave way to the occasional exchange of gossip
about TV soap characters in the commercial breaks. Inch by
inch, Marissa was giving up all of the things she loved and that
nourished her, for the thing she'd come to dislike: work. Not
only had Marissa used to love her work; now it had become a
trap for her, and it was draining away her life, leaving her
exhausted and increasingly unhappy.

Yet again her boss had a solution: a smartphone. Now she
could even work in bed if she chose. At first, it was thrilling
to be able to exchange high-powered emails and texts twenty-
four hours a day. (Never mind that Leanne had once confided
in Marissa that her second marriage had started to go down-
hill when she used her smartphone to complete and send off a
report for work—on her honeymoon.) Marissa felt reinvigor-
ated and empowered—that lasted for a few weeks. Then, it
quickly became apparent that her bosses were all vying with
each other by working later and later. It was clear that
exchanging emails late at night made her colleagues and
bosses feel important. Marissa was wiser than that, but was
still unsure as to how she could escape the trap she'd been
seduced into.

In the end, it was an occupational therapist at the hospital
where Marissa worked who sprung her free. The therapist was
running a mindfulness course as part of a clinical trial to see
whether meditation could help normally mentally healthy people to reduce their levels of job stress and become happier and
more relaxed. It was only when Marissa began the course that

it became obvious to her—and the therapist—that she was in pretty poor mental shape. During the pre-class interview, she was handed a sheet listing the most common symptoms of stress, depression and mental exhaustion. Marissa ended up checking most of the boxes. For Marissa, they included such things as:

- becoming increasingly bad-tempered or irritable

- a narrowing of her social life, or simply "not wanting to see people"

- not wanting to deal with such normal business as opening the mail, paying the bills, or returning phone calls

- becoming easily exhausted

- giving up on exercise

- postponing or overshooting deadlines

- changes in sleeping patterns (either sleeping too much or too little)

- changes in eating habits[1]

Do any of these seem familiar to you?

On the outside, Marissa had successfully maintained the façade of the busy, efficient worker, but deep inside she was crumbling under the strain. At first, she refused to believe she had a problem. She felt that all she needed was a few good nights' sleep. The meditations she learned certainly allowed her to sleep, but as all of the other benefits of mindfulness began to accrue, Marissa realized just how close she'd come to a breakdown. Her life had almost completely trickled away down the Exhaustion Funnel.

All work and no play?

As Marissa's experiences with the Funnel show, some activities are more than just relaxing or enjoyable—they actually nourish us at a far deeper level too. They help us to build up our resilience to life's stresses and strains, but also to become more sensitive to life's more beautiful nuances. Other activities deplete us. They drain away our energy, making us weaker and more vulnerable to the dips in life's roller coaster ride. They also eat away at our capacity to enjoy life fully. Very quickly, these depleting activities can begin monopolizing our lives. And if we're under pressure, the things that nourish us are gradually abandoned, almost without notice, driving us into the heart of the Exhaustion Funnel.

Take this little test for yourself to see how much of your life is devoted to activities that nourish you and how much to those that deplete you. First, mentally run through the different activities that you do in a typical day. Feel free to close your eyes for a few moments to help bring these to mind. If you spend much of your day apparently doing the same thing, try breaking the activities down into smaller pieces, such as talking to colleagues, making coffee, filing, word processing and eating lunch. And what sort of things do you find yourself doing in a typical evening or weekend?[2]

Now, write it all down, listing maybe between ten and fifteen activities of a typical day in a column on the left-hand side of your page.

Activities you do in a typical day	N/D

When you have your list in front of you, ask yourself these questions:

1. Of the things that you have written, which nourish you? What lifts your mood, energizes you, makes you feel calm and centered? What increases your sense of actually being alive and present, rather than merely existing? These are nourishing activities.

2. Of the things that you have written, which deplete you? What pulls you down, drains away your energy, makes you feel

tense and fragmented? What decreases your sense of actually being alive and present, what makes you feel that you are merely existing, or worse? These are depleting activities.

Now, complete the exercise by putting an "N" for "nourishing" or a "D" for "depleting" on the right-hand side, corresponding to each activity. If an activity is both, put down your first reaction, or if you simply cannot choose, put N/D or D/N. You may find that you want to say, "It depends," and, if so, it may be useful to notice what it depends on.

The aim of this exercise is not to shock or unsettle you, but to give you an idea of the balance in your life between the things that nourish you and those that deplete you. The balance does not have to be perfect, as one nourishing activity that you love might easily outweigh any number of depleting ones. Nevertheless, it is wise to have at least a handful of nourishing activities (and preferably do at least one each day) to balance the depleting ones. This may be as simple as taking a long bath, reading a book, going for a brisk walk or indulging in your favorite hobby. The old saying, "All work and no play makes Jack a dull boy" contains more than a grain of truth. Many other societies have similar homilies. And in some cultures, doctors don't ask, "When did you start to feel depressed?" but, "When did you stop dancing?'

Learning to dance again

Understanding how much of your life is devoted to depleting activities is one thing, but it's also important to take action to either spend less time doing them or to devote more effort to nourishing pastimes. A central focus of Week Seven of the mindfulness course is devoted to taking action to redress the balance between the things that nourish you and those that deplete you.

Step One: Rebalancing your daily life

Spend a few minutes reflecting on how you can begin to redress the balance between the nourishing and depleting activities that you listed in the table earlier. Perhaps you can do this together with someone with whom you share your life—a family member or trusted work colleague, for example?

There will be some aspects of your life that you simply cannot change for now. If, say, your job is the source of your difficulties, you might not have the luxury of being able to quit (even if you feel that this is the most appropriate solution). If you cannot fundamentally change a situation then you have two options. First, you can try, as best you can, to increase the time and gentle effort you devote to nourishing activities and to decrease the time and effort you give to depleting ones. Or second, you could try to approach the depleting ones in a different way, to practice being fully present with them, even if you find them boring or unpleasant. You could try to become fully mindful of them instead of judging them or wishing them away. By being present in more of your moments, and making mindful decisions about what you really want and need during those times, you can become progressively more accepting of the good and bad points of your day. You will also discover unexpected routes to happiness and fulfillment.

Take the case of Beth. She was a clerk in the back office of a major bank—always, as she said, run off her feet with one thing after another. There was no obvious time for her to relax, let alone meditate. After a few weeks of mindfulness practice at home, she started to pay more attention to the busyness of her day. She noticed that tiny gaps opened up even at the most hectic times. For example, she realized she spent a lot of time trying to contact other parts of the company by phone or email to track down missing files. She'd often phone or email several times but get nowhere. This was one of the most annoying parts of her job—waiting for someone else to reply. She'd often find herself muttering angrily: "Why aren't they at their desks—getting on with their jobs, like me!"

Then, she had a light bulb moment: here was time that she could reclaim for herself; a moment of silence that she could use to ground and reconnect with herself. She started to use these gaps to take mini breathing spaces, in which she could mentally step back from the hubbub. After a while, she started to notice many other times when she could step back from the melee—for example, when waiting for her computer to start up each morning, waiting for the drinks machine to deliver her drink, walking to meetings or standing in line for sandwiches at lunchtime. Before this, she'd thought that mindfulness practice was best done when taking a lunch break or nipping outside for a coffee. Now, she found she could look for gaps throughout the day, times that could be used to transform her thoughts, feelings and behavior. It wasn't necessary for her to increase dramatically the time she devoted to nourishing activities, or to reduce the amount she spent on depleting ones—she simply altered her relationship to those unavoidable depleting ones. She had begun to discover that even in the busiest days, there were "cracks" in what seemed an impenetrable wall of work.

In her own way, Beth had found a way of "turning toward," rather than escaping or avoiding her experiences. This is the mindfulness you have been learning too; to hold the difficult aspects of your daily life, as well as your beliefs or expectations about them, and to move in closer to them. This is what you've been learning during the previous six weeks of practice by focusing on your bodily sensations, feelings and thoughts.

Now it's time to draw up your own map that you can use to alter the balance between the depleting and nourishing things in your life. In the space on the following page, if you can, write down five ways in which you plan to alter the balance. Don't worry if you can't immediately think of five—just write in the extra ones when they occur to you later. Focus on the small things in life; this is a crucial part of the practice. Don't write down "Give up work" or "Take up mountain climbing," for example. Choose things that are easily achievable for you, such as "Take a coffee break every two hours," "Walk the kids to school, rather than drive" or "Eat one less takeout meal each week and cook dinner instead." You could try breaking down depleting things into smaller chunks as well. For example, clean a cupboard or tidy a corner of your desk for five minutes, rather than carrying on until it's perfect. Or you might decide to finish work in a different way, turning off your computer a quarter of an hour earlier to give you time to consider what is on the agenda for tomorrow, rather than answering emails up to the last minute, then suddenly realizing you are late for whatever it is you planned to do after work. Note how sometimes it is possible to deal more skillfully with a depleting activity simply by leaving enough time to do it. See if it is possible to take a small pause before and after it, so it has its own space in your life. It also pays to bear in mind that what you find depleting is unique to you, so it is fine to focus on the things in your own life without comparing them to what others find nourishing or depleting.

I will alter the balance between nourishing and depleting
activities by:

_____

_____

_____

_____

_____

_____

And most important of all: see if it's possible to remain mindful when you're carrying out both the nourishing and depleting
activities—and especially when you are consciously shifting
the balance between them. See if you can sense how even the
tiniest—seemingly inconsequential—changes can alter how
you think and feel, and how this affects your body.

You could refer back to the list often, perhaps weekly, and
certainly if you feel your mood worsening. And remember, you
don't have to make major changes in direction: tiptoes are perfectly fine.

Many of us find numerous ways to avoid or put off altering
the balance between nourishing and depleting activities in our
lives; usually for very solid-sounding and altruistic reasons.
Some may say, for example: "I'm balancing being a mom, a
career woman, a wife and a homemaker. Where do I find the
time for myself?" Others will point to the large projects at work
or home, and say, "Not now, not yet; maybe some day—when
this project is finished."

On the surface, this approach seems reasonable; but try to

see if it is possible to take the long view. In time, if we don't rebalance our lives, we will become less effective at everything we do. We will become joyless, sleepless and witless. Here are other common reasons people have given for not rebalancing their lives:[3]

- There are things in life that I don't have a choice over, like going to work.

- If I don't keep up, I fall behind.

- It's shameful to show weakness at work.

- I wasn't raised to take time for myself.

- I can only do something that I enjoy once all my obligations to others, or to my work, have been completely satisfied.

- I have so many caring responsibilities. It would be wrong to put myself first.

If any of these reasons, and countless others like them, sound familiar to you, then perhaps you are now in a position to see how many of them depend on old habits of black-and-white thinking in which there seems no middle way. Mindfulness helps you to get beyond the extremes, to see how you can find creative ways of helping to nourish yourself in many subtle and not-so-subtle ways. Like Beth, you might start finding gaps in your day. And, in the long run, it's best foreveryone, including yourself, to find a balance between nourishing and depleting activities.

Seeing clearly the balance between the things that nourish

you and those that deplete you is important. But they also have a deeper underlying message too. First, they help you to explore the connections between your actions and your mood. Deep down, we all feel that when we're unhappy, stressed or exhausted there's nothing we can do about it. It feels like a set point. If you feel at your wits' end through stress, then you feel helpless—you *are* stressed. Period. Likewise, if you feel exhausted, devoid of energy or lacking in vigor, you feel that "this is just the way things are" and "there's nothing I can do to change it."

Taking time to see how you can rebalance your daily life encourages you to see these thoughts as just thoughts—as "propaganda" that prevents you from even testing whether it is true or not.

Furthermore, if you can more easily sense a shift in the balance between the nourishing and the depleting, this can act as an early warning signal for worsening mood. It also acts as a route map back to a balanced and happy life. If you know which activities nourish you, you can do more of them should you start to feel unhappy or unduly stressed or tired. They also give you a menu of activities from which to choose should you feel your mood worsening. This map may prove to be of huge significance because chronic low-level unhappiness, stress and exhaustion sap your capacity to make decisions. If you have preplanned for such an eventuality, a minor dip in mood can become a springboard to greater happiness rather than a stepping-stone to misery. Depleting and negative thoughts are part of the territory of living in a frantic world, but that does not mean you have to buy into them.

Practices for Week Seven

Over the coming week, we suggest you carry out three meditations on six days out of the next seven. This week is not as
prescriptive as the previous six. We suggest that you tailor your
own formal meditation practice by choosing two of the meditations at http://bit.ly/rodalemindfulness that you've carried out
before.

Choose one of the meditations because you felt it gave you some
appreciable nourishing benefits, such as helping you to relax or simply making you feel good about the world. Choose the other because
you felt that you didn't fully get to grips with it first time around,
because it was difficult in some way or because you feel that you'd
benefit from repeating it. Devote about twenty to thirty minutes to
the two combined meditations.

As with the previous ones, you could carry them out in
sequence while listening to the appropriate tracks online, or do
them at different times of the day. The order in which you do
the two meditations isn't important. It might be worth setting up
a playlist for the two meditations on your MP3 player. And try to
remember that it's the spirit of the meditations that's important
rather than the detail.

Write the two meditations you plan to do here (you can mull this
decision over for a while if you wish):

1. _____

2. _____

3. The Three-Minute Breathing Space meditation (twice a day at
   set times and when needed—see p. 132).

Step Two: Breathing Space plus taking further action

The first theme of this chapter has been to bring you to greater awareness of the balance between depleting and nourishing activities, and to help you optimize this balance. The second theme develops the first, by coupling the Three-Minute Breathing Space with concrete action to make an immediate and meaningful difference to how you feel. The Breathing Space can be more than a means of reconnecting with your expanded awareness. It can also act as a powerful springboard to help you take skillful action.

You may have already experienced through your practice of mindfulness that the tint in the lenses through which you routinely see the world has, progressively, become more obvious, allowing you to survey reality with a bit more clarity. With this in mind, after "grounding" yourself through meditation you are in a better position to take skillful action. So this week, when you feel stressed, as always, take a breathing space first, then afterward consider what action you might take. This need not be productive in a business sense, or even in a personal sense, but should be something that just feels right and appropriate. It should not be impulsive or habitual but, rather, an activity that will actively enhance your life.

As we have already seen, often the most skillful course of action will be to remain mindful and let the situation resolve itself. However, during this week in particular, we'd like you to focus on taking a specific action that you can do almost as a behavioral experiment. We use the word "behavioral" to remind you that you do not have to *feel like* doing it—you just have to do it! This is because research has found that when our mood is low, our usual motivation process is reversed. Usually, in daily life, we are motivated to do something, then we do it. But when mood is low, we have to do something *before* the motivation comes. Motivation follows action, rather than the other way around. You may have noticed this, for instance, if there has been a time when you almost decided not to go out with friends, saying, "I'm too tired; I won't enjoy it," and then discovered to your surprise that you had a great time. Curiously, although this may have happened many times, we find it difficult to learn from it because when our mood is low next time, its propaganda—blocking our memory from accessing positive times in the past, and telling us there is no point in doing anything now—is so strong that we are, once again, caught in its trap.

In summary, when you feel tired, unhappy, stressed or anxious, waiting until you feel motivated may not be the wisest course of action. You have to put the action first.

When mood is low, motivation follows action,
rather than the other way around. When you put
the action first, motivation follows.

So, after you have used the Breathing Space at times of stress this week, pause momentarily and ask yourself:

- What do I need for myself right now?

- How can I best take care of myself right now?

You have three options for skillful action:

- You can do something pleasurable.

- You can do something that will give you a sense of satisfaction or mastery over your life.

- Or you can continue acting mindfully.

Why these three options? Because the sort of exhaustion and stress that can be most undermining for your quality of life particularly affects these three: your capacity for enjoyment, your ability to keep on top of business and your motivation to be mindful. We'll explore each in turn.

Doing something pleasurable Exhaustion, stress and low mood ensure that instead of genuinely enjoying life, you experience "anhedonia"—that is, you can't find *pleasure* in life. The things you used to enjoy now leave you cold—you feel as if a thick fog has put a barrier between you and simple pleasures, and few things seem rewarding any more. Research suggests that much of this is because the "reward centers" of the brain have become insensitive to the things that used to activate them. So gradually, by taking mindful action, you start, in small ways, to wake up these neglected pathways, selecting activities you used to enjoy or think you might now enjoy, and trying, as an experiment, to discover if they give you pleasure.

Enhancing feelings of mastery or control Anxiety, stress, exhaustion and unhappiness reduce your sense of *control* over your life. Research over many years has found that when we feel out of control in one area of our life, this can spread like a virus affecting other areas too. We end up feeling inexplicably helpless, saying to ourselves, "There's nothing I can do" or "I just don't have the energy."

When this "helplessness virus" kicks in it is extremely powerful, affecting even little things. So you can end up feeling like you don't want to walk down the road to mail a letter or pay that bill, even though it might only take five minutes. It just lies there, accusing you each day, reminding you that you are not coping. Gradually, there is an accumulation of little things, and you seem to have lost control over the most intimate aspect of your life. So, in gradual steps, you select tiny actions that *can* be done and, once done, they communicate with the deepest aspects of yourself that you are not as helpless as you thought.

Enhancing mindfulness As you have seen throughout each week of this course, stress and exhaustion arise from (and contribute to) the Doing mode of mind that volunteers to help when you are stressed, but has the side effect of narrowing your life, paving it over with overthinking, striving, suppression of "weakness," automatic pilot, mindless eating, mindless walking and, well, mindless everything really. So following the Breathing Space this week, you have another option—act mindfully and return to your senses: what do your eyes see, your ears hear, your nose smell? What can you touch? What is your posture, your facial expression? What is right here, if you take a moment of mindful awareness?

Choosing actions—being specific Choose what feels most appropriate. Some ideas are shown below, but don't feel limited to them. Do what feels the best. Don't feel guilty about doing something for the hell of it. And don't expect miracles. See if you can carry out what you have planned as best you can. Putting extra pressure on yourself by expecting this to alter things dramatically may be unrealistic. Rather, activities are helpful experiments—done whether you feel like doing them or not—to rebuild your overall sense of pleasure, control and mindful awareness in the face of shifts in your mood.

1. Do something pleasurable[4]

- *Be kind to your body.* Have a nice hot bath; have a nap for thirty minutes or less;[5] treat yourself to your favorite food without feeling guilty; have your favorite hot drink.

- *Engage in an enjoyable activity.* Go for a walk (maybe walk the dog for a friend); visit a friend; get together what you need so you can do your favorite hobby; do some gardening; get some exercise; phone a friend you have been out of contact with for a while; spend time with someone you like; bake a cake; go shopping; watch something funny or uplifting on TV; go to the movies; read something that gives you pleasure (not "serious" reading); listen to some music that you have not listened to in a long while; do one of the Habit Releasers from a previous chapter.

What things can you add to this list?

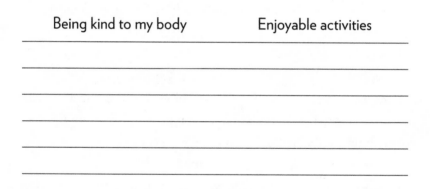

Being kind to my body   Enjoyable activities

2. Do something that gives you a sense of mastery,
   satisfaction, achievement or control[6]

These are sometimes difficult to do because they can seem to add to exhaustion, rather than relieve it. We suggest doing *small* amounts of an activity, and doing it as an *experiment*, specifically when you feel helpless or out of control. Try not to prejudge how you will feel after it is completed. Keep an open mind about whether doing the activity will be helpful in any way. It may be something like cleaning a room in your house; clearing out a cupboard or drawer; writing a thank-you letter or other "catching-up" letters; paying a bill; doing something that you have been putting off; getting some exercise. If you like, break them down into smaller steps and only tackle one step at a time. It's especially important to congratulate yourself whenever you complete a chosen task or even *part* of one. For example, if you resolve to clean a room, only do it for, say, five minutes rather than ten or twenty. Savor the feelings of satisfaction, achievement and control it gives you.

What things could you add to this list?

What gives me a sense of mastery, satisfaction, achievement or control?

_____

_____

_____

_____

_____

_____

_____

_____

_____

3. Act mindfully[7]

Whatever you are doing, mindfulness is only one breath away. It is as easy as focusing your entire attention solely on what you are already doing *right now*. In this way, see if it is possible to bring your mind to each present moment, for example: ("Now I am standing in a line . . . Now I can feel the basket in my hand . . . Now I'm walking forward . . . Now I'm reaching for my bag . . ." Be aware of your breathing as you do other things; be aware of the contact of your feet with the floor as you stand and as you walk. No one else need know that you are doing a mindfulness practice, and it could change your whole day.

The truth is that often, tiny changes in what you do—whether you feel like doing them or not—can fundamentally alter the way you feel. You can become reenergized, destressed or have your spirits lifted by taking a few baby steps forward. For example, a short walk may dissolve exhaustion, a cup of tea may lift your spirits, or ten minutes reading your favorite magazine may reduce stress. Taking mindful action helps you to discover which activities most soothe your frantic nerves in moments of crisis. They may be unique to you and they will quite often seem like tiny steps—almost inconsequential tiptoes forward. However, when you couple these small actions with the Breathing Space meditation, you produce something of profound power and importance. This is something that each of us has to feel for ourselves; you may be told this a thousand times and shown all of the scientific evidence, but none of this will be anywhere near as powerful as actually sensing it for yourself (see box, opposite). And this is the core message of Week Seven:

Tiny actions can fundamentally alter your relationship
to the world for the better.

Mindfulness bells

Pick a few ordinary activities from your daily life that you can turn into "mindfulness bells," that is, reminders to stop and attend. There's a list below of things you might like to turn into bells. Why not photocopy this page and the next and stick them on your fridge as a gentle reminder?

• **Preparing food** Any food preparation is a great opportunity for mindfulness—vision, hearing, taste, smell, touch. Focus on the feel of the knife as it slices through vegetables of different texture, or the smell released as each vegetable is chopped.

• **Eating** Try having part of a meal in silence or without the distraction of TV or the radio. Really focus on the food—colors, shapes, perhaps thinking about how this food came to you, the sensations of eating. See how easily you taste the first mouthful and no other. What does the fourth mouthful taste like?

• **Washing the dishes** A great opportunity for exploring sensations, constantly coming back to the present moment, rinsing this dish, water flowing, sensation of temperature, etc.

• **Driving** Be aware of deciding where to focus your mind while you are driving. If you decide to focus on the upcoming meeting, etc., know that this is the decision you have made. If you decide to make your primary focus something other than the actual driving, notice how quickly you can shift driving into the foreground of your attention when the situation demands. Notice if you are leaving the actual act of driving too much in the background of your attention! Take some of your driving time to make your primary focus the driving—all the sensations, the movement of your

(continued)

hands, feet and so on, the visual scanning you are doing, the shifting of your vision from close up to far away and so on.

- **Walking** Pay attention to the actual sensations of walking; notice when the mind goes elsewhere and come back to "just walking."

- **Become a model citizen!** When crossing the street, use the pedestrian signals as an opportunity to stand quietly and focus on your breath, rather than an opportunity to try to beat the lights.

- **Red lights** An opportunity to sit quietly, peacefully and be aware of your breath.

- **Listening** When you are listening, notice when you are not listening—when you start to think of something else, what you are going to say in response, etc. Come back to actually listening.

When stress and exhaustion are overwhelming—what Marissa realized

Sometimes, Marissa found that, despite her mindfulness practice, feelings of being overwhelmed by life came out of the blue. Everything seemed to be going smoothly when, suddenly, she might wake up feeling very tired and listless, or with angry or sad thoughts going through her mind.

When things came out of the blue like this, they always set off patterns of thinking that drew on her own unique history. So because she had been down in the past, her tiredness *now* triggered old habits of thought that were particularly damaging: full of overgeneralized memories, predictions that this would go on forever and repeated thoughts claiming, "I'm no good."

She found that all of these patterns were very adhesive; she found them very difficult to dismiss but, after a while, she began recognizing them through one salient feature that all of them shared: *they all undermined her motivation for taking any action to nourish herself.* When this happened, she found it useful to tell herself: "Just because I am feeling like this now does not mean that things have to stay like this."

Marissa would ask herself: "What can I do to look after myself to get me through this low period?" She would take a breathing space to help gather herself. She found it particularly useful to start by using the Week Five practice of dropping her attention into the body to see how her mood was reflected in her physical sensations, and allow her attention to dwell in the body for a while. This helped her to see her situation from a wider perspective. This wider perspective, in turn, allowed her to become aware of both the pull of the old habits of thinking, as well as the skillful action that she could take, either immediately or later so that she could better take care of herself during this vulnerable period.

Everyday life offers endless opportunities for you
to stop, to focus, to remind yourself to be fully awake
and present to what is happening right now.

CHAPTER TWELVE

Mindfulness Week Eight: Your Wild and Precious Life

It matters that you care.
It matters that you feel.
It matters that you notice.

FROM "HOKUSAI SAYS," ROGER KEYES[1]

There is an old story told about a king who wished to move his palace.[2] But because he feared that his enemies might take advantage of this to attack him and steal his treasures, he summoned his trusted general. "My friend," he said, "I have to move my palace, and must do so within twenty-four hours. You have been my trusted servant and soldier for so long. I do not trust anyone but you to help me with this task. Only you know the network of underground passages between this palace and the other. If you are able to do this for me, and move all my most precious treasures by yourself, I will give you and your family your freedom: you may retire from my service, and as a reward for your faithfulness over so many years, I will give to you such a portion of both my wealth and my lands that you will be able to settle, and you, your wife and children and their children and grandchildren will be financially secure."

The day came when the treasures were to be moved. The general worked hard. He was not a young man, but he persisted in his efforts. He knew that the task needed to be completed within the twenty-four-hour window. After this, it would become unsafe to continue. With minutes to spare, he completed the job. He went to see his king, who was delighted. The king was a man of his word and gave him the portion of the treasure he had promised, and the deeds to some of the most beautiful and fertile lands in the kingdom.

The general returned to his home and took a bath, and as he lay there, he looked back on all that he had achieved, and he relaxed: he felt a great satisfaction that he could now retire, that things were dealt with, and that his major tasks were finished. For that moment, he had a sense of completeness. The story ends here.

Do you know what that moment is like? Perhaps you have experienced a similar moment when things have gone well for you in the past? You have felt a sense of completeness. A sense that tasks have been done.

One of the most difficult aspects of the frantic rush through a busy life is that we often do not allow even the smallest notion of "completion" to enter the picture of our daily lives. We often rush from task to task, so much so that the end of one task is just the invitation to start another. There are no gaps in between in which we could take even a few *seconds* to sit, to take stock, to realize that we have just completed something. Just the reverse: how many times do we hear ourselves say, "I haven't achieved anything at all today"? And we say this most often when things have been at their busiest. Is there an alternative approach?

If you can practice cultivating a sense of completeness—even a glimmer, right now, in this moment, with the little things of life—there is a chance that you would be better able to cope with those aspects of mind that keep telling you that you are not there yet; not yet happy, not yet fulfilled. You might learn that you are complete, whole, just as you are.

As you became immersed in the detail of each week's practice, you may have found that you lost sight from time to time of the overall aim and structure of the program, so here is a brief reminder of what you have been practicing.

The aim of the early sessions was to give you, through formal and informal mindfulness practice, many opportunities to recognize the Doing mode in its many forms, and to begin the cultivation of the alternative Being mode. Since attention is so often hijacked by current concerns, the first meditations helped you to learn how to pay sustained attention to one single thing, using as the focus of attention things that any of us tend to take for granted, such as the taste of food, sensations in the body, the breath or the colors and shapes of an ordinary visual scene. You learned to see the patterns of mind that distract you, and how the constant chatter of the mind can dull your senses, draining the color and texture from each present moment. You learned to come back again and again to whatever you had been intending to focus on, without judgment or self-criticism. The core theme at this stage was how to pay attention, intentionally, with kindness. Practice in the simple act of giving the mind just one thing to do provided, and still provides, many opportunities to wake up and recognize that the Doing mode of mind is asserting itself.

You learned that the Doing mode of mind is not a mistake, nor is it an enemy to get rid of. It only becomes problematic when it volunteers for a job it can't do, then refuses to let go, so that you go on working at a problem or a project long after you are too tired to make any sensible progress. Your projects and preoccupations then become adhesive and all-consuming, and you cannot see how to let go.

So, the training in later sessions focused on widening awareness so that you could recognize when, in everyday life, the stress of frantic daily living is starting to trigger overuse of the Doing mode. You learned to disengage from Doing mode and then to enter Being mode. You learned strategies that could provide you with a range of options for responding more skillfully when you feel overwhelmed by the overbusyness, stress and exhaustion of life. Central to these was the ability to step away from using your Doing mind to *overcome* your mind—and to cultivate kindness toward yourself and others.

Mindfulness practice does not *compel* us to let go of Doing, but it does give us the choice, and the skills to do so if we so choose. And with an insight into how to let go, practiced many times in the small moments of daily living, there are many opportunities to learn ways in which, even when difficult and uncomfortable emotions arise, you can *make space* even for *them*, exploring them with compassion and courage when you feel it is right to do so.

Finding peace in a frantic world

Finding peace in a frantic world is not easy. In our darkest hours it can seem as if the entire world has been designed from the ground up to maximize our distress and drive us to exhaustion. Stress and anxiety can seem overwhelming, and full-blown depression can appear to be only a hair's breadth away. While the attitude that "the world is against me" is understandable, it also limits us. It means that we do not see how many of our troubles arise from the way *we* live our lives. Simply put, we get in our own way. Anxiety, stress, unhappiness and exhaustion are often symptoms of a wider and deeper malaise. They are not free-floating afflictions, but symptoms arising from the way we relate to each other, ourselves and to the world itself. They are signals that there is something wrong in our lives. They are signs to which we need to pay attention.

If you accept all this, then the door is opened to a radically different approach to living—one that encourages you, from moment to moment, to actually live your life to the full *right now*, rather than putting it off until tomorrow. We all have the tendency to postpone our lives. How many times have you told yourself, *I'll catch up with my sleep on the weekend, When things let up a bit I'll see more of the kids* or *Next summer I'll relax and take a proper holiday*? Well, here it is: *now* is the future that you promised yourself last year, last month, last week. *Now* is the only moment you'll ever really have. Mindfulness is about waking up to this. It's about becoming fully aware of the life you've already got, rather than the life you wish you had.

Mindfulness is not an alternative version of psychotherapy or another "self-help" approach to improving your life. It's not a technique for understanding the past or for correcting "aberrant" or "incorrect" ways of thinking in the present. It doesn't paper over the cracks, but looks for patterns in them, seeing them as our teachers. Mindfulness doesn't directly "treat" our difficulties, but instead reveals and brings a penetrating yet kindly awareness to their underlying driving forces. It deals with the subliminal themes of all our lives. And when these are held up to the light of awareness, something remarkable happens: the negative themes gradually start dissolving of their own accord. Our endless striving, tunnel vision and brooding, our tendency to get lost in our own thoughts, to be driven by the autopilot, to become consumed by negativity and abandon the things that nourish our souls—these all represent the Doing mind working as hard as it can. When we let go of seeing this as an enemy to be overcome, all of these tendencies are able to melt away in the light of openhearted awareness.

We can tell you this—we can even prove it to you with the most powerful tools that science has to offer—but you must experience it for yourself to truly *understand* it.

We constantly weave false dreams for ourselves, but what we really need to weave is a parachute to use when life starts to become difficult or begins to fall apart. Mindfulness has been compared to weaving such a parachute.[3] But there's no point in doing this when we're falling headlong towards destruction. We have to weave our parachute every day, so that it's always there to hold us in an emergency. The first seven weeks of the Mindfulness program helped you begin to taste this process, but Week Eight is as important as them all.

Week Eight is the rest of your life.

The task now is to weave the practices into a routine that is sustainable in the long term.

Weaving your own parachute: using mindfulness to maintain your peace in a frantic world[4]

Mindfulness can serve as an emergency parachute. It needs weaving every day, so that it's ready and waiting should you encounter an emergency. Here are some tips:

- **Start the day with mindfulness** When you open your eyes, gently pause before taking five deliberate breaths. This is your chance to reconnect with your body. If you feel tired, anxious, unhappy or in any way distressed, see these feelings and thoughts as mental events condensing and dissolving in the space of awareness. If your body aches, recognize these sensations as sensations. See if you can accept all of your thoughts, feelings and sensations in a gentle and compassionate way. There is no need to try and change them. Accept them—since they are already here. Having stepped out of automatic pilot in this way, you might choose to scan the body for a minute or two, or focus on the breath, or do some gentle stretches before getting out of bed.

- **Use Breathing Spaces to punctuate your day** Using Breathing Spaces at preset times helps you to reestablish your focus in the here and now, so that you can respond with wisdom and compassion to thoughts, feelings and bodily sensations as you move through the day.

- **Maintain your Mindfulness practice** As best you can, continue with your formal meditation practice. They are the practices that support your Breathing Spaces and help you to maintain mindfulness throughout as much of your daily life as possible.

- **Befriend your feelings** Whatever you feel, as best you can, see if you can bring an open and kindhearted awareness to *all* of your feelings. Remember Rumi's "Guest House" poem (see p. 166)?. Remember to roll out the welcome mat to even your most painful thoughts, such as fatigue, fear, frustration, loss, guilt or sadness. This will diffuse your automatic reactions and transform a cascade of reactions into a series of choices.

- **When you feel tired, frustrated, anxious, angry or any other powerful emotion, take a Breathing Space** This will "ground" your thoughts, diffuse your negative emotions and reconnect you with your bodily sensations. You will then be in a better position to make skillful decisions. For example, if you feel tired you may choose to do some stretches to reawaken and reenergize your body.

- **Mindful activities** Whatever you do, see if you can remain mindful throughout as much of the day as possible. For example, when you are washing dishes, try to feel the water, the plates and the fluctuating sensations in your hands. When you are outside, look around and observe the sights, sounds and smells of the world around you. Can you feel the pavement through your shoes? Can you taste or smell the air? Can you feel it moving through your hair and caressing your skin?

- **Increase your level of exercise** Walking, cycling, gardening, going to the gym—anything physical can be used to help weave your parachute. See if you can bring a mindful and curious attitude to your body as you exercise. Notice the thoughts and feelings as they arise. Pay close attention if you feel the need to "grit your teeth" or you start to feel the first stirrings of aversion or other negative thoughts or sensations. See if you can gently observe the sensations as they unfold. Breathe with, and into, their intensity. Gently increase the length and intensity of your exercises, but always try and remain mindful.

- **Remember the breath** The breath is always there for you. It anchors you in the present. It is like a good friend. It reminds you that you are OK just as you are.

It's important to be realistic. Each of us needs a positive reason to carry on meditating. But the word "positive" does not capture the full potential of what is available to us. If you've got this far into the program, then you probably already know why you wish to continue, but it is, nonetheless, important to ask, *really ask*, why it might be important, based on your experience of mindfulness, to continue cultivating it.

A good way of doing this is to close your eyes and imagine dropping a stone down a deep well. The stone represents the question: *What is it that is most important to me in my life that this practice could help with?*

Sense the stone dropping down into and beneath the surface of the water. There's no rush to find answers. If one answer comes, let the stone fall further—see if other answers come. When you hear some answers—even if they're only tentative—take some time to reflect, then write them on a postcard or piece of paper and keep it somewhere safe, ready to be looked at should you ever become despondent about the practice. You may find several answers to the question. Perhaps:

- for my parents

- for my children

- to safeguard my happiness

- to remain calm and energized

- to remain freer from anger, bitterness and cynicism

The aim of allowing the question to be asked is to show you how sustaining your practice will help you to reclaim your life in a profound way, day by day, and moment my moment, rather than seeing it as yet another thing to "do" or "get done" for some negative or prescriptive reason. Most of us do not need another "should" or "ought" to add to the already long list of things we have to do each day. So, writing your own answers on a card and keeping it safe ensures that you have something that reminds you of the *positive discoveries* that you have made in the practice of mindfulness that encourage you to explore further. There will be many times in the future when your commitment to practice falls away or wears thin. At such times, you can easily become despondent or angry with yourself. When this happens, it is good to have your original motivations readily at hand.

Making the choice

It is time for you to decide which practice or combination of practices you think is sustainable for *you* in the long term. You should be realistic and remember that your choice is not set in stone. You can change it from day to day, from week to week or from year to year, to match the demands being made upon you and what it is you want to explore through your practice. Sometimes, you may feel the need for reconnecting with the body in the Body Scan (see p. 97), while at other times, you might choose deliberately to bring a worry or problem right into the center of your practice, using the Exploring Difficulty meditation from Week Five (see p. 172). The choice is yours. You now have the skills to decide for yourself.

How long should you meditate for? The practice itself will teach you. Recall that meditation was first developed when humans lived in and off the fields. Indeed, one of the words that we translate into English as "meditation" actually means "cultivation" in the original Pali language. It originally referred to cultivation of crops in the fields and flowers in the garden. So how long should the cultivation of the mindfulness garden take each day? It is best to go into the garden and see for yourself. Sometimes ten minutes in the garden of meditation practice will be needful, but you may find, once there, that your cultivation will slip effortlessly into twenty or thirty minutes. There is no minimum or maximum time. Clock time is different from meditation time. You could simply experiment with what feels right and with whatever gives you the best chance to renew and nourish yourself. Every minute counts.

Most people find that it is most helpful to combine some regular (every day) formal practice with mindfulness in the world. There is something about the "everyday-ness" of the practice that is important. By every day we mean that a majority of days each week will find you taking yourself away to be by yourself for a period, no matter how short.

Remember the advice of yoga teachers: the most difficult move in yoga is the move on to your mat. Similarly, the most difficult aspect of formal mindfulness practice is getting on to your chair or stool or cushion. So, if you find you have missed it for a while, why not come and sit for one minute?

Just one minute.

Listen to your mind's reaction. *What? Just one minute! That'd be no good. There's absolutely no point in doing anything unless I can do it properly.* Listen to the tone of voice that has appeared in your mind. Is it helpful or is it hindering your best intentions with its hectoring perfectionism?

Come. Just come—for one minute. There's no need to try and stop the hindering voice. Carry it with you as you come and give yourself the rich blessing of one precious minute of sitting—one moment in which to remind your mind and body that there is a different, wiser, quieter voice to be heard.

And that is enough for today.

Whichever practices you decide upon, many find that making space in the day for the Breathing Space is a great blessing. It's always there for you in moments of stress or unhappiness. It's the perfect way of checking in with yourself during the day. In many ways, the main meditation practice that you eventually decide upon is there to support your Breathing Spaces. It's your parachute. Many people on our courses say that it's the most important thing they've ever learned.

Practice as if your life depended on it,
as in many ways, it surely does. For then you
will be able to live the life you have—and
live it as if it truly mattered.

Sometimes poetry captures the soul of an idea more than anything else. This poem, by Roger Keyes, was inspired by the paintings of Japanese artist Katsushika Hokusai (1760–1849). Hokusai's message in his paintings—captured in this poem— sums up the message of this book and its invitation. We offer it to you as food for the journey.

Hokusai Says[5]

Hokusai says   Look carefully.
He says pay attention, notice.
He says keep looking,   stay curious.
He says there is no end to seeing.

He says Look Forward to getting old.
He says keep changing,
You just get more who you really are.
He says get stuck, accept it, repeat
yourself as long as it's interesting.

He says keep doing what you love.

He says keep praying.

He says every one of us is a child,
Every one of us is ancient,
Every one of us has a body.
He says every one of us is frightened.
He says every one of us has to find
A way to live with fear.

He says everything is alive—
Shells, buildings, people, fish,
Mountains, trees. Wood is alive.
Water is alive.

Everything has its own life.

Everything lives inside us.

He says live with the world inside you.

He says it doesn't matter if you draw,
Or write books. It doesn't matter
if you saw wood, or catch fish.
It doesn't matter if you sit at home
And stare at the ants on your verandah
Or the shadows of the trees
And grasses in your garden.
It matters that you care.

It matters that you feel.

It matters that you notice.

It matters that life lives
through you.

Contentment is life living through you.
Joy is life living through you.
Satisfaction and strength
Is life living through you.
Peace is life living through you.

He says don't be afraid.
Don't be afraid.

Look, feel, let life take you by the hand.
Let life live through you.

—Roger Keyes

Notes

CHAPTER ONE

1. Ivanowski, B. & Malhi, G. S. (2007), "The psychological and neurophysiological concomitants of mindfulness forms of meditation," *Acta Neuropsychiatrica*, 19, pp. 76–91; Shapiro, S. L., Oman, D., Thoresen, C. E., Plante, T. G. & Flinders, T. (2008), "Cultivating mindfulness: effects on well-being," *Journal of Clinical Psychology*, 64(7), pp. 840–62; Shapiro, S. L., Schwartz, G. E. & Bonner, G. (1998), "Effects of mindfulness-based stress reduction on medical and premedical students," *Journal of Behavioral Medicine*, 21, pp. 581–99; Siegel, D. *Mindsight: The New Science of Transformation* (New York; Random House, 2010).
2. Fredrickson, B. L. & Joiner, T. (2002), "Positive emotions trigger upward spirals toward emotional well-being," *Psychological Science*, 13, pp. 172–5; Fredrickson, B. L. and Levenson, R. W. (1998), "Positive emotions speed recovery from the cardiovascular sequelae of negative emotions," *Cognition and Emotion*, 12, pp. 191–220; Tugade, M. M. & Fredrickson, B. L. (2004), "Resilient individuals use positive emotions to bounce back from negative emotional experiences," *Journal of Personality and Social Psychology*, 86, pp. 320–33.
3. Baer, R. A., Smith, G. T., Hopkins, J., Kreitemeyer, J. & Toney, L. (2006), "Using self-report assessment methods to explore facets of mindfulness," *Assessment*, 13, pp. 27–45.
4. Jha, A., et al. (2007), "Mindfulness training modifies subsystems of attention," *Cognitive Affective and Behavioral Neuroscience*, 7,

pp. 109–19; Tang, Y. Y., Ma, Y., Wang, J., Fan, Y., Feng, S., Lu, Q., et al. (2007), "Short-term meditation training improves attention and self-regulation," *Proceedings of the National Academy of Sciences (US)*, 104(43), pp. 17152–6; McCracken, L. M. & Yang, S. Y. (2008), "A contextual cognitive-behavioral analysis of reha-bilitation workers' health and well-being: Influences of acceptance, mindfulness and values-based action," *Rehabilitation Psychology*, 53, pp. 479–85; Ortner, C. N. M., Kilner, S. J. & Zelazo, P. D. (2007), "Mindfulness meditation and reduced emotional interfer-ence on a cognitive task," *Motivation and Emotion*, 31, pp. 271–83; Brefczynski-Lewis, J. A., Lutz, A., Schaefer, H. S., Levinson, D. B. & Davidson, R. J. (2007), "Neural correlates of attentional expertise in long-term meditation practitioners," *Proceedings of the National Academy of Sciences (US)*, 104(27), pp. 11483–8.

5. Hick, S. F., Segal, Z. V. & Bien, T., *Mindfulness and the Therapeutic Relationship* (Guilford Press, 2008).

6. Low, C. A., Stanton, A. L. & Bower, J. E. (2008), "Effects of acceptance-oriented versus evaluative emotional processing on heart rate recovery and habituation," *Emotion*, 8, pp. 419–24.

7. Kabat-Zinn, J., Lipworth, L., Burncy, R. & Sellers, W. (1986), "Four-year follow-up of a meditation-based program for the self-regulation of chronic pain: Treatment outcomes and compliance," *The Clinical Journal of Pain*, 2(3), p. 159; Morone, N. E., Greco, C. M. & Weiner, D. K. (2008), "Mindfulness meditation for the treatment of chronic low back pain in older adults: A randomized controlled pilot study," *Pain*, 134(3), pp. 310–19; Grant, J. A. & Rainville, P. (2009), "Pain sensitivity and analgesic effects of mindful states in zen meditators: A cross-sectional study," *Psychosomatic Medicine*, 71(1), pp. 106–14.

8. Speca, M., Carlson, L. E., Goodey, E. & Angen, M. (2000), "A randomized, wait-list controlled trail: the effect of a mindfulness meditation-based stress reduction program on mood and symp-toms of stress in cancer outpatients," *Psychosomatic Medicine*, 62, pp. 613–22.

9. Bowen, S., et al. (2006), "Mindfulness Meditation and Substance

Use in an Incarcerated Population," *Psychology of Addictive Behaviors*, 20, pp. 343–7.

10. Davidson, R. J., Kabat-Zinn, J., Schumacher, J., Rosenkranz, M., Muller, D., Santorelli, S. F., Urbanowski, F., Harrington, A., Bonus, K. & Sheridan, J. F. (2003), "Alterations in brain and immune function produced by mindfulness meditation," *Psychosomatic Medicine*, 65, pp. 567–70.

11. Godden, D., & Baddeley, A. D. (1980), "When does context influence recognition memory?" *British Journal of Psychology*, 71, pp. 99–104.

CHAPTER TWO

1. www.who.int/healthinfo/global_burden_disease/projections/en/index.html.

2. Zisook, S., et al. (2007), "Effect of Age at Onset on the Course of Major Depressive Disorder," *American Journal of Psychiatry*, 164, pp. 1539–46, doi: 10.1176/appi.ajp.2007.06101757.

3. Klein, D. N. (2010), "Chronic Depression: diagnosis and classification," *Current Directions in Psychological* Science, 19, pp. 96–100.

4. Twenge, J. M. (2000), "Age of anxiety? Birth cohort changes in anxiety and neuroticism, 1952–1993," *Journal of Personality and Social Psychology*, 79, pp. 1007–21.

5. Michalak, J. (2010), "Embodied effects of Mindfulness-based Cognitive Therapy," *Journal of Psychosomatic Research*, 68, pp. 311–14.

6. Strack, F., Martin, L. & Stepper, S. (1988), "Inhibiting and facilitating conditions of the human smile: A nonobtrusive test of the facial feedback hypothesis," *Journal of Personality and Social Psychology*, 54, pp. 768–77.

7. Way, B. M., Creswell, J. D., Eisenberger, N. I. & Lieberman, M. D. (2010), "Dispositional Mindfulness and Depressive Symptomatology: Correlations with Limbic and Self-Referential Neural Activity During Rest," *Emotion*, 10, pp. 12–24.

8. Watkins, E. & Baracaia, S. (2002), "Rumination and social problem-solving in depression," *Behavior Research and Therapy*, 40, pp. 1179–89.

CHAPTER THREE

1. The distinction between Doing and Being modes of mind was first made in Kabat-Zinn, J., *Full Catastrophe Living: Using the Wisdom of Your Body and Mind to Face Stress, Pain and Illness* (Piatkus, 1990), pp. 60–1 and 96–7.

2. See Jon Kabat-Zinn's *Coming to Our Senses: Healing Ourselves and the World Through Mindfulness* (Piatkus, 2005) for more detailed discussion of these issues.

3. Adapted with permission from Brown, K. W. & Ryan, R. M. (2003), "The benefits of being present: Mindfulness and its role in psychological well-being," *Journal of Personality and Social Psychology*, 84, pp. 822–48.

4. In this book, we provide an eight-week course for you to taste the benefits of mindfulness directly. In our clinic, participants are invited to do longer meditations over eight weeks, and if you wish to sample these, you could look at www.mindfulnessCDs.com and the book that describes MBCT, which this book is based on: *The Mindful Way Through Depression: Freeing Yourself from Chronic Unhappiness* by Mark Williams, John Teasdale, Zindel Segal & Jon Kabat-Zinn (Guilford Press, 2007).

5. Davidson, R. J. (2004), "What does the prefrontal cortex 'do' in affect: Perspectives on frontal EEG asymmetry research," *Biological Psychology*, 67, pp. 219–33.

6. Davidson, R. J., Kabat-Zinn, J., Schumacher, J., Rosenkranz, M., Muller, D., Santorelli, S. F., et al. (2003), "Alterations in brain and immune function produced by mindfulness meditation," *Psychosomatic Medicine*, 65, pp. 564–70.

7. Lazar, S. W., Kerr, C., Wasserman, R. H., Gray, J. R., Greve, D., Treadway, M. T., McGarvey, M., Quinn, B. T., Dusek, J. A., Benson, H., Rauch, S. L., Moore, C. I. & Fischl, B. (2005), "Meditation experience is associated with increased cortical thickness," *NeuroReport*, 16, pp. 1893–7.

8. Craig, A. D. (2004), "Human feelings: why are some more aware than others?" *Trends in Cognitive Sciences*, vol. 8, no.6, pp. 239–41.

9. Farb, N., Segal, Z. V., Mayberg, H., Bean, J., McKeon, D., Fatima, Z. & Anderson, A. (2007), "Attending to the present: Mindfulness

meditation reveals distinct neural modes of self-reference," *Social Cognitive and Affective Neuroscience,* 2, pp. 313–22.

10. Singer, T., et al. (2004), "Empathy for Pain Involves the Affective but not Sensory Components of Pain," *Science,* 303, p. 1157.

11. Farb, N. A. S., Anderson, A. K., Mayberg, H., Bean, J., McKeon, D. & Segal, Z. V. (2010), "Minding one's emotions: Mindfulness training alters the neural expression of sadness," *Emotion,* 10, pp. 225–33.

12. Fredrickson, B. L., Cohn, M. A., Coffey, K. A., Pek, J. & Finkel, S. M. (2008), "Open hearts build lives: Positive emotions, induced through loving-kindness meditation, build consequential personal resources," *Journal of Personality and Social Psychology,* 95, pp. 1045–62. See Barbara Fredrickson's Web site at www.unc.edu/peplab/home.html.

13. Shroevers, M. J. & Brandsma, R. (2010), "Is learning mindfulness associated with improved affect after mindfulness-based cognitive therapy?" *British Journal of Psychology,* 101, pp. 95–107.

14. See http://www.doctorsontm.com/national-institutes-of-health.

15. Schneider, R. H., et al. (2005), "Long-Term Effects of Stress Reduction on Mortality in Persons ≥ 55 Years of Age With Systemic Hypertension," *American Journal of Cardiology,* 95 (9), pp. 1060–64 (www.ncbi.nlm.nih.gov/pmc/articles/PMC1482831/pdf/nihms2905.pdf).

16. Ma, J. & Teasdale, J. D. (2004), "Mindfulness-based cognitive therapy for depression: Replication and exploration of differential relapse prevention effects," *Journal of Consulting and Clinical Psychology,* 72, pp. 31–40; Segal, Z. V., Williams, J. M. G. & Teasdale, J. D., *Mindfulness-based Cognitive Therapy for Depression: A New Approach to Preventing Relapse* (Guilford Press, 2002).

17. Kenny, M. A. & Williams, J. M. G. (2007), "Treatment-resistant depressed patients show a good response to Mindfulness-Based Cognitive Therapy," *Behavior Research & Therapy,* 45, pp. 617–25; Eisendraeth, S. J., Delucchi, K., Bitner, R., Fenimore, P., Smit, M. & McLane, M. (2008), "Mindfulness-Based Cognitive Therapy for Treatment-Resistant Depression: A Pilot Study," *Psychotherapy and Psychosomatics,* 77, pp. 319–20; Kingston, T., et al. (2007), "Mindfulness-based cognitive therapy for residual depressive

symptoms," *Psychology and Psychotherapy*, 80, pp. 193–203.

18. Godfrin, K. & van Heeringen, C. (2010), "The effects of mindfulness-based cognitive therapy on recurrence of depressive episodes, mental health and quality of life: a randomized controlled study," *Behavior Research & Therapy*, doi: 10.1016/j.brat.2010.04.006.

19. Kuyken, W., et al. (2008), "Mindfulness-Based Cognitive Therapy to Prevent Relapse in Recurrent Depression," *Journal of Consulting and Clinical Psychology*, 76, pp. 966–78; Segal, Z. et al. (2010), "Antidepressant Monotherapy versus Sequential Pharmacotherapy and Mindfulness-Based Cognitive Therapy, or Placebo, for Relapse Prophylaxis in Recurrent Depression," *Archives of General Psychiatry*, 67, pp.1256–64.

20. Weissbecker, I., Salmon, P., Studts, J. L., Floyd, A. R., Dedert, E. A. & Sephton, S. E. (2002), "Mindfulness-Based Stress Reduction and Sense of Coherence Among Women with Fibromyalgia," *Journal of Clinical Psychology in Medical Settings*, 9, pp. 297–307; Dobkin, P. L. (2008), "Mindfulness-based stress reduction: What processes are at work?" *Complementary Therapies in Clinical Practice*, 14, pp. 8–16.

CHAPTER FIVE

1. You can check out this experiment in the video at http://viscog.beckman.illinois.edu/flashmovie/12.php, or a similar one on YouTube here: www.youtube.com/watch?v=yqwmnzhgB80.

2. Kabat-Zinn, J., *Full Catastrophe Living: Using the Wisdom of Your Body and Mind to Face Stress, Pain and Illness* (Piatkus, 1990); Santorelli, S., *Heal Thy Self: Lessons on Mindfulness in Medicine* (Three Rivers Press, 2000); Williams, J. M. G., Teasdale, J. D., Segal, Z. V. & Kabat-Zinn, J., *The Mindful Way Through Depression: Freeing Yourself from Chronic Unhappiness* (Guilford Press, 2007).

CHAPTER SIX

1. Wells, G. L. & Petty, R. E. (1980), "The effects of head movements on persuasion," *Basic and Applied Social Psychology*, vol.1, pp. 219–30.

2. T. S. Eliot, *Burnt Norton* in *Four Quartets* (Faber and Faber, 2001).

3. In our clinical programs, we use a Body Scan lasting between thirty and forty-five minutes once each day. See Kabat-Zinn, J., *Full Catastrophe Living: Using the Wisdom of Your Body and Mind to Face Stress, Pain and Illness* (Piatkus, 1990), pp. 92–3; Williams, J. M. G., Teasdale, J. D., Segal, Z. V. & Kabat-Zinn, J., *The Mindful Way Through Depression: Freeing Yourself from Chronic Unhappiness* (Guilford Press, 2007), pp. 104–6. In this book, we offer a fifteen-minute Body Scan for you to do twice a day. If you wish to try a longer practice, see Resources on page 265.

4. From David Dewulf, *Mindfulness Workbook: Powerfully and Mildly Living in the Present*, by permission. See www.mbsr.be/Resources.html.

CHAPTER SEVEN

1. Douglas Adams, *The Hitchhiker's Guide to the Galaxy* (Pan Macmillan, 1979).

2. Friedman, R. S. & Forster, J. (2001), "The effects of promotion and prevention cues on creativity," *Journal of Personality and Social Psychology*, 81, pp. 1001–13.

3. Steve Jobs speaking at Stanford University in June 2005. See www.ted.com/talks/steve_jobs_how_to_live_before_you_die.html.

4. If you choose, you can continue with the Body Scan once a day in addition to these Week Three practices. The Mindful Movement meditation and the Breath and Body meditation are based on: Kabat-Zinn, J., *Full Catastrophe Living: Using the Wisdom of Your Body and Mind to Face Stress, Pain and Illness* (Piatkus, 1990)—see also www.mind fulnessCDs.com—and Williams, J. M. G., Teasdale, J. D., Segal, Z. V. & Kabat-Zinn, J., *The Mindful Way Through Depression: Freeing Yourself from Chronic Unhappiness* (Guilford Press, 2007). The Three-Minute Breathing Space meditation is from Segal, Z. V., Williams, J. M. G. & Teasdale, J. D., *Mindfulness-based Cognitive Therapy for Depression: A New Approach to Preventing Relapse* (Guilford Press, 2002), p. 174 and Williams, J. M. G., Teasdale, J. D., Segal,

Z. V. & Kabat-Zinn, J., *The Mindful Way Through Depression: Freeing Yourself from Chronic Unhappiness* (Guilford Press, 2007), pp. 183–4.

5. See previous note.

6. See Vidyamala Burch, *Living Well with Pain and Illness,* Chapter 8 (Piatkus, 2008).

7. See note 4.

8. See note 4.

CHAPTER EIGHT

1. Segal, Z. V., Williams, J. M. G. & Teasdale, J. D., *Mindfulness-Based Cognitive Therapy for Depression: A New Approach to Preventing Relapse* (Guilford Press, 2002).

2. Allport, G. W. & Postman, L., *The Psychology of Rumor* (Holt & Co., 1948).

3. For "soundscape" see Kabat-Zinn, J., *Coming to Our Senses: Healing Ourselves and the World Through Mindfulness* (Piatkus, 2005), pp. 205–210. The Sounds and Thoughts meditation is based on Kabat-Zinn, J., *Full Catastrophe Living: Using the Wisdom of Your Body and Mind to Face Stress, Pain and Illness* (Piatkus, 1990) and Williams, J. M. G, Teasdale, J. D, Segal, Z. V. & Kabat-Zinn, J., *The Mindful Way Through Depression: Freeing Yourself from Chronic Unhappiness* (Guilford Press, 2007).

4. See previous note.

5. Adapted from Segal, Z. V., Williams, J. M. G. & Teasdale, J. D., *Mindfulness-Based Cognitive Therapy for Depression: A New Approach to Preventing Relapse* (Guilford Press, 2002).

CHAPTER NINE

1. Rosenbaum, Elana, *Here for Now: Living Well with Cancer through Mindfulness*, pp. 95ff (Hardwick, Satya House Publications, 2007).

2. Rosenbaum, p. 99.

3. Segal, Z. V., Williams, J. M. G. & Teasdale, J. D., *Mindfulness-based Cognitive Therapy for Depression: A New Approach to Preventing Relapse* (Guilford Press, 2002).

4. Barnhofer, T., Duggan, D., Crane, C., Hepburn, S., Fennell, M. & Williams, J. M. G. (2007), "Effects of meditation on frontal alpha asymmetry in previously suicidal patients," *Neuroreport*, 18, pp. 707–12.

5. Way, B. M., Creswell, J. D., Eisenberger, N. I. & Lieberman, M. D. (2010), "Dispositional Mindfulness and Depressive Symptomatology: Correlations with Limbic and Self-Referential Neural Activity during Rest," *Emotion*, 10, pp. 12–24.

6. Rodin, J. & Langer, E. (1977), "Long-term effects of a control-relevant intervention among the institutionalised aged," *Journal of Personality and Social Psychology*, 35, pp. 275–82.

7. Rosenbaum, p. 12.

CHAPTER TEN

1. For more information about PTSD, see www.rcpsych.ac.uk/mentalhealthinfo/problems/ptsd/posttraumaticstressdisorder.aspx.

2. Based on Israel Orbach's research on mental pain: Orbach, I., Mikulincer, M., Gilboa-Schechtman, E. & Sirota, P. (2003), "Mental pain and its relationship to suicidality and life meaning," *Suicide and Life-Threatening Behavior*, 33, pp. 231–41.

3. "Painful engagement" refers to the feeling that your goals are unattainable, yet at the same time you are not able to let them go, for your happiness feels like it depends on them. See MacLeod, A. K. & Conway, C. (2007), "Well-being and positive future thinking for the self versus others," *Cognition & Emotion*, 21(5), pp. 1114–24; and Danchin, D. L., MacLeod, A. K. & Tata, P. (submitted), "Painful engagement in parasuicide: The role of conditional goal setting."

4. For an extended discussion of these ideas, see Paul Gilbert, *The Compassionate Mind* (Constable, 2010).

5. See Williams, J. M. G., Barnhofer, T., Crane, C., Hermans, D., Raes, F., Watkins, E. & Dalgleish, T. (2007), "Autobiographical memory specificity and emotional disorder," *Psychological Bulletin*, 133, pp. 122–48.

6. Bryant, R. A., Sutherland, K. & Guthrie, R. M. (2007), "Impaired specific autobiographical memory as a risk factor for posttraumatic

stress after trauma," *Journal of Abnormal Psychology,* 116, pp. 837–41.

7. Kleim, B. & Ehlers, A. (2008), "Reduced Autobiographical Memory Specificity Predicts Depression and Posttraumatic Stress Disorder After Recent Trauma," *Journal of Consulting and Clinical Psychology,* 76(2), pp. 231–42.

8. Williams, J. M. G., Teasdale, J. D., Segal, Z. V. & Soulsby, J. (2000), "Mindfulness-Based Cognitive Therapy reduces overgeneral autobiographical memory in formerly depressed patients," *Journal of Abnormal Psychology,* 109, pp. 150–55.

9. Adapted from Baer, R. A., et al. (2006), "Using self-report assessment methods to explore facets of mindfulness," *Assessment,* 13, pp. 27–45. Used with permission of Dr. Baer and Sage Publications.

10. This is sometimes called Loving Kindness meditation—but "befriending" is a better translation of the original Pali word (Metta) on which it is based.

11. Singer, T., et al. (2004), "Empathy for Pain Involves the Affective but Not Sensory Components of Pain," *Science,* 303, p. 1157, doi: 10.1126/science.1093535.

12. Barnhofer, T., Chittka, T., Nightingale, H., Visser, C. & Crane, C. (2010), "State Effects of Two Forms of Meditation on Prefrontal EEG Asymmetry in Previously Depressed Individuals," *Mindfulness,* 1 (1), pp. 21–7.

13. Williams, J. M. G., Teasdale, J. D., Segal, Z. V. & Kabat-Zinn, J. (2007), *The Mindful Way Through Depression: Freeing Yourself from Chronic Unhappiness* (Guilford Press), p. 202.

14. The idea of reclaiming your life arises directly from the research findings of Anke Ehlers and her colleagues showing how much we tend to assume that everything is irreversibly changed by trauma: Kleim, B. & Ehlers, A. (2008), "Reduced Autobiographical Memory Specificity Predicts Depression and Posttraumatic Stress Disorder After Recent Trauma," *Journal of Consulting and Clinical Psychology,* 76(2), pp. 231–42.

15. See www.bookcrossing.com.

16. Einstein writing to Norman Salit on March 4, 1950.

CHAPTER ELEVEN

1. Segal, Z. V., Williams, J. M. G. & Teasdale, J. D., *Mindfulness-based Cognitive Therapy for Depression: A New Approach to Preventing Relapse* (Guilford Press, 2002), pp. 269–87.
2. See previous note.
3. See note 1.
4. See note 1.
5. Note that sleep researchers advise that any nap during the day should not exceed thirty minutes or we run the risk of entering so deep a sleep that we feel groggy on waking.
6. This section comes from Segal, Z. V., Williams, J. M. G. & Teasdale, J. D., *Mindfulness-based Cognitive Therapy for Depression: A New Approach to Preventing Relapse* (Guilford Press, 2002), pp. 286–7.
7. See previous note.

CHAPTER TWELVE

1. From Keyes, R., "Hokusai Says." See page 250 for the entire poem.
2. Retold from a story told by Youngey Mingpur Rinpoche, *Joyful Wisdom: Embracing Change and Finding Freedom* (Harmony, 2009).
3. Jon Kabat-Zinn, "Meditation" in Bill Moyers (ed.), *Healing and the Mind*, pp. 115–44 (Broadway Books, 1995).
4. Adapted from *Mindfulness for Chronic Fatigue* (unpublished) by Christina Surawy, Oxford Mindfulness Centre.
5. Sometimes poetry captures the soul of an idea more than any number of explanations. This poem, by Roger Keyes, was inspired by his many years spent studying the paintings of Japanese artist Katsushika Hokusai (1760–1849), famous for *The Great Wave off Kanagawa* and for painting to a very great age. We are grateful for Roger Keyes' permission to reproduce it here.

Resources

WEB SITES

www.franticworld.com Our Web site to accompany this book. It contains a forum to discuss your experiences and to learn from others. There are links to further meditations and books that you might find useful, plus a section listing upcoming talks, events and retreats.

www.oxfordmindfulness.org Our Oxford-based Web site: general introduction to MBCT; includes information on training and how you can support our future work in mindfulness.

www.gaiahouse.co.uk Gaia House, West Ogwell, Newton Abbot, Devon TQ12 6EW. A retreat center in the insight meditation tradition.

www.dharma.org Information about centers offering experience of the insight meditation tradition.

www.bangor.ac.uk/mindfulness Training in mindfulness-based approaches to healthcare, up to Master's level, is offered at the University of Bangor, where Mark Williams was based before coming to Oxford.

www.stressreductiontapes.com For tapes/CDs of meditation practices recorded by Jon Kabat-Zinn.

www.amazon.com For copies of a videotape about the work of Jon Kabat-Zinn: *Mindfulness and Meditation: Stress Reduction.*

www.octc.co.uk For CDs of meditation practices recorded by Mark Williams.

www.umassmed.edu/cfm Web site of the Center for Mindfulness, UMass Medical School.

www.investigatingthemind.org Web site of the Mind and Life Institute.

USA AND CANADIAN RESOURCES

If you wish to deepen your meditation practice, the best way is to have on-going personal contact with an experienced meditation teacher and support from others who are also practicing. There are many different forms of meditation. Therefore, it is best to find an approach that is compatible with the Mindfulness program on which this book is based: the westernized insight meditation tradition. Information about these centers can be obtained from the following: Insight Meditation Society in Barre, Massachusetts (www.dharma.org) or Spirit Rock in Woodacre, California (www. spiritrock.org).

The Center for Mindfulness at UMass Medical Center, founded by Jon Kabat Zinn (the director is Saki Santorelli) was where the application of mindfulness in the modern healthcare started. It can be found at www.umassmed.edu/content.aspx?id=41252

For Jon Kabat-Zinn's own Web site, see www.mindfulnesstapes.com/

The Center for Mindfulness at University of California San Diego (Steven Hickman) can be found at http://health.ucsd.edu/specialties/psych/mindfulness/index.htm.

The North American site for MBCT, hosted by Professor Zindel Segal and his team in Toronto, is http://mbct.com.

The Ann Arbor Centre for Mindfulness (Libby Robinson) is at www. aacfm.com/Libby_Robinson.html.

The Mindful Awareness and Research Centre (MARC) at UCLA is at http://marc.ucla.edu/.

Longer meditations narrated by Mark Williams and used by the Oxford Mindfulness Center, UK, can be found at http://itunes. apple.com/gb/album/mindfulness-meditations-mark/id429733506.

AUSTRALIAN AND NEW ZEALAND RESOURCES

Interest Groups

MBSR-MBCT ANZ@yahoogroups.com is an online group established by a Sydney-based MBCT teacher, Chrissie Burke, who updates members regularly with news of relevant conferences, research articles and mindfulness events. Members can ask questions, network and collaborate. To join the list of members, email Chrissie (chrissie.burke@gmail.com).

Meditation Centers

www.dharma.org.au Information about the centers that follow the Insight
  Meditation traditions (which are closest to the mindfulness practices
  taught in MBCT and MBSR) can often be found on this Web site.

Other Online Resources of Interest

www.openground.com.au For information on MBSR courses and
  training around Australia.
www.canberramindfulnesscenter.com.au MBSR courses and training
  in Canberra.
www.mindful-well-being.com/index.php For information on MBCT
  courses in Sydney.
www.mindfulness.org.au The Melbourne Mindfulness information site.
www.mindfulness.net.au A Tasmanian site offering mindfulness integrated with CBT.
www.mindfulexperience.org The home of the Mindfulness Research
  Guide, a comprehensive resource that:
  • Provides information to researchers and practitioners on the sci-
    entific study of mindfulness including research publications,
    measurement tools and mindfulness research centers.
  • Hosts the *Mindfulness Research Monthly*, a bulletin for the pur-
    pose of keeping researchers and practitioners informed of
    current advances in research.
Centre for the Treatment of Anxiety and Depression (CTAD) For fur-
  ther information on MBCT training and courses in Australia,
  email ctad@health.sa.gov.au.

MBCT MANUAL FOR THERAPISTS

Segal, Z. V., Williams, J. M. G. & Teasdale, J. D., *Mindfulness-Based
  Cognitive Therapy for Depression: A New Approach to Preventing
  Relapse* (Guilford Press, 2002).

SELF-HELP GUIDE

Williams, J. M. G., Teasdale, J. D., Segal, Z. V. & Kabat-Zinn, J.,
  *The Mindful Way Through Depression: Freeing Yourself from
  Chronic Unhappiness* (Guilford Press, 2007).

SUMMARY TEXT

Crane, R., *Mindfulness-based Cognitive Therapy* (Routledge, 2008).

268   Resources

MEDITATION

The selection below is meant as an introduction to insight meditation and as an invitation to explore. Many of these teachers and authors have written more books than are listed here and have meditation tapes/CDs you can buy. (Dates/publishers of recent paperback editions cited when possible.)

Beck, C. J., *Everyday Zen: Love and Work* (Thorsons, 1997).

Boorstein, S., *It's Easier Than You Think: The Buddhist Way to Happiness* (HarperSanFrancisco, 1996).

Chödrön, P., *The Wisdom of No Escape: How to Love Yourself and Your World* (Element, 2004).

Dalai Lama, *Advice on Dying: And Living a Better Life*, translated and edited by Jeffrey Hopkins (Rider & Co., 2004).

Goldstein, J., *Insight Meditation: The Practice of Freedom* (Newleaf, 1994).

Goldstein, J., *One Dharma: The Emerging Western Buddhism* (HarperSanFrancisco, 2002).

Goldstein, J. & Salzberg, S., *Insight Meditation: A Step-by-Step Course on How to Meditate* (Sounds True Inc., 2002).

Gunaratana, B. H., *Mindfulness in Plain English* (Wisdom Publications, 2002).

Hanh, T. N., *The Miracle of Mindfulness: Manual on Meditation* (Rider & Co., 1991).

Hanh, T. N., *Peace Is Every Step: The Path of Mindfulness in Everyday Life* (Rider & Co., 1995).

Kabat-Zinn, J., *Full Catastrophe Living: Using the Wisdom of Your Body and Mind to Face Stress, Pain and Illness* (Piatkus, 1990).

Kabat-Zinn, J., *Wherever You Go, There You Are: Mindfulness Meditation foreveryday Life* (Piatkus, 1994).

Kabat-Zinn, J., *Coming to Our Senses: Healing Ourselves and the World Through Mindfulness* (Hyperion/Piatkus, 2005).

Kornfield, J., *A Path with Heart* (Rider & Co., 2002).

Kornfield, J., *After the Ecstasy, the Laundry: How the Heart Grows Wise on the Spiritual Path* (Bantam Books, 2001).

McLeod, K., *Wake Up to Your Life* (HarperSanFrancisco, 2002).

Orsilo, S. M. and Roemer, L., *The Mindful Way through Anxiety* (Foreword by Segal, Z. V.) (The Guilford Press, 2011).

Rabinowitz, I. (ed.), *Mountains Are Mountains and Rivers Are Rivers:*

Applying Eastern Teachings to Everyday Life (Hyperion, 2000).

Rinpoche, S., *The Tibetan Book of Living and Dying* (Rider & Co., 1998).

Rosenberg, L. with Guy, D., *Breath by Breath: The Liberating Practice of Insight Meditation* (Shambhala Publications, 2004).

Rosenberg, L. with Guy, D., *Living in the Light of Death: On the Art of Being Truly Alive* (Shambhala Publications, Boston, Mass., 2001).

Salzberg, S., *Loving-kindness. The Revolutionary Art of Happiness* (Shambhala Publications, 2004).

Santorelli, S., *Heal Thy Self: Lessons on Mindfulness in Medicine* (Three Rivers Press, 2000).

Shafir, R. Z., *The Zen of Listening: Mindful Communication in the Age of Distraction* (Quest Books, 2003).

Sheng-Yen (Master) with Stevenson, D., *Hoofprint of the Ox: Principles of the Chan Buddhist Path as Taught by a Modern Chinese Master* (Oxford University Press, 2002).

Smith, J. (ed.), *Breath Sweeps Mind: A First Guide to Meditation Practice* (Riverhead Trade, 1998).

Tolle, E., *The Power of Now: A Guide to Spiritual Enlightenment* (Hodder, 2001).

Wallace, B. A., *Tibetan Buddhism From the Ground Up: A Practical Approach for Modern Life* (Wisdom Publications, 1993).

MEDITATION AND PSYCHOLOGY

Bennett-Goleman, T., *Emotional Alchemy: How the Mind Can Heal the Heart* (Harmony Books, 2001).

Brazier, C., *A Buddhist Psychology: Liberate Your Mind, Embrace Life* (Robinson Publishing, 2003).

Epstein, M., *Thoughts without a Thinker: Psychotherapy from a Buddhist Perspective* (Basic Books, 2005).

Epstein, M., *Going to Pieces Without Falling Apart: A Buddhist Perspective on Wholeness* (Thorsons, 1999).

Epstein, M., *Going on Being: Buddhism and the Way of Change, a Positive Psychology for the West* (Broadway Books, 2001).

Goleman, D., *Emotional Intelligence* (Bantam Books, 1995).

Goleman, D., *Working with Emotional Intelligence* (Bantam Books, 1998).

Goleman, D., *Destructive Emotions: How Can We Overcome Them? A Scientific Dialogue with the Dalai Lama* (Bantam Books, 2004).

Index

Underscored page references indicate sidebars. **Boldface** references indicate illustrations.

ABC model of emotions, 137–38
Acceptance
  of difficulties, 171, 179, 180
  meaning of, 165–66
  poem about, 166–67
  in Exploring Difficulty meditation, 177
  mindful, 40, 45, 166, 180
  of past, 194, 196
  of self, 60, 104, 165, 197
  steps toward, 169
Amygdala, overactive, 27, 180
Analysis, in Doing mode, 38–39
Anger, 4, 8, 19, 25, 47, 48, 58, 71, 90, 102, 116, 126, 130, 144, 149, 154, 155, 156, 157, 173, 182, 185, 188, 202, 203, 236, 245, 246, 247
Anhedonia, 230
Animals, responses to danger by, 26
Antidepressants, 3, 52, 189
Anxiety, 2, 3, 8, 10, 12, 16, 18, 23, 26, 28, 40, 60, 66, 72, 95, 115, 242
  chronic, increase in, 17
  Exhaustion Funnel and, 213
  mindfulness meditation reducing, 5, 6, 37, 46, 56, 156
  moods creating, 8
  motivation and, 229
  reduced sense of control from, 230
  self-feeding nature of, 19

Anxious feelings or thoughts, 2, 8, 11, 16, 37, 47, 72, 114, 130, 144, 154, 207, 229, 244, 245
Appreciative attention exercise, 108–9
Approaching
  vs. avoiding, 41–42, 47, 48, 180
  difficulties, 39, 44, 206
Approach-orientated puzzles, 113–14
Arm raising, in Mindful Movement meditation, 120–21
Attention
  appreciative, exercise on, 108–9
  in Breathing Space meditation, 132–33, 181, 182–83
  focusing, 117, 240
  in Body Scan meditation, 58, 97, 98, 99, 100
  on breath, 4, 4, 81, 163
  likened to resistance training, 101–2
  on present, 35
  full
    benefits of, 77, 78
    in Habit Releasers, 57
    paying, 79
    steps toward, 79
  intermittent, 69
  paying
    in Mindfulness of the Body and Breath meditation, 83, 84, 85
    to routine activities, 76–77

in Raisin meditation, 72, 73, 76
Audio tracks, on meditation, 14, 56, 82, 103, 106, 119, 131, 152
Autonomy, mindfulness meditation increasing, 50–51
Autopilot, 58, 88, 142, 153, 177, 231, 243, 244
  advantages of, 69, 70
  disadvantages of, 71–72
  in Doing mode, 37–38, 43, 105, 106
  example of, 67–68
  experiments on, 68
  mindfulness and, 70
Aversion, 113, 114, 115, 124, 176, 177, 179, 180, 204, 245
Avoidance, 41, 44, 47, 114
Avoidance-orientated puzzles, 113
Awareness
  anchoring, in moving body, 118
  in Being mode, 38
  in Body Scan meditation, 95
  in Breathing Space meditation, 181, 182
  in controlling automatic pilot, 71
  cultivating, 87–88
  in Exploring Difficulty meditation, 175, 176, 178
  focusing, 72
    on everyday activities, 78
  of mind, 11, 31, 112
  power of, 31

thinking process and, 148
in Three-Minute Breathing
   Space meditation, 132

Balanced life
   achieving, 220, 221–26
   represented in Exhaustion
      Funnel, 213, **213**
Befriending meditation,
   59, 197, 198–200,
   200–206
Befriending your feelings,
   244–45
Being mode, 34–35, 36,
   37–43, 60, 133, 240,
   241
Bending sideways, in Mindful
   Movement meditation,
   122–23
Body. See also Body Scan
   meditation
   connecting with, 94
   as emotional radar, 95
   in Exploring Difficulty
      meditation, 170, 171,
      172, 175, 178, 179
   ignoring and mistreating
      of, 92–93
   mind connected with,
      20–22, 23, 91–92
   in Mindfulness of the Body
      and Breath meditation,
      83–85
   as sensitive to feelings, 58
Body Scan meditation, 58,
   118, 178, 196, 247
   beginning, 106
   handling difficulty with,
      101–4
   instructions for, 97–100
   as pleasant experience,
      104–5
   preparing for, 95–96
   revealing Doing mode,
      105–6
Brain
   amygdala of, 27, 180
   changes in, from
      mindfulness
      meditation, 46–49,
      179–80
   imaging of, 27, 36, 46, 47,
      49, 206
   insula of, 48, 205
   prefrontal cortex of, 47
   reward centers of, 230

Breath
   in Befriending meditation,
      198
   in Body Scan Meditation,
      97–100, 178
   in Exploring Difficulty
      meditation, 172, 173,
      174, 178
   in mindfulness meditation,
      4–5, 80–81, 163, 244
   in Mindfulness of the Body
      and Breath meditation,
      81–82, 83–85
   in Sounds and Thoughts
      meditation, 146, 147
   for starting day with
      mindfulness, 244
   for weaving your
      parachute, 245
Breath and Body meditation,
   126, 127–29, 143, 146,
   172, 196
Breathing Space. See also
   Three-Minute
   Breathing Space
   meditation
   case history about, 211, 212
   hourglass shape of, 133–34,
      156, 181
   for maintaining peace in
      frantic world, 244, 245
   making time for, 249
   rainstorm analogy and,
      157–58
   uses for, 153–54, 156–58,
      159
   in Week Five, 181–83
   in Week Six, 206–7
Brooding, 30, 41, 45, 93, 175,
   188, 191, 194, 195,
   196, 243
Brushing your teeth, paying
   full attention to, 77
Bullying script, 114
Burnout, 41, 115, 130, 213
Busyness, 8, 24, 36, 43, 59,
   68, 85, 96, 105, 201,
   206, 222, 241

Cancer
   mindfulness meditation
      and, 6
   story about, 161–64
Cartoon experiment, on
   mind-body connection,
   21–22

Chair changing, as Week One
   Habit Releaser, 88–89
Chocolate meditation, 14, 54,
   55, 72
Chronic pain, 6
Compassion, 5, 8, 12, 19, 40,
   42, 45, 46, 49, 54, 59,
   60, 85, 117, 126, 129,
   131, 139, 163, 167,
   173, 175, 176, 177,
   181, 182, 195, 196,
   197, 204, 205, 209,
   210, 241, 244
Completeness, achieving
   sense of, 239–40
Context, effect on memory, 10
Control, enhancing feelings
   of, 230–31, 232–33
Creativity, influences on, 5, 60,
   113, 180, 204, 206, 212

Daily life
   rebalancing, 221–26
   weaving mindfulness into,
      117–19, 120–23,
      124–26, 127–29
Dance of ideas, 192–93
Death, 46, 117, 164
Demobilization, 115
Denial of difficulties, 164
Depleting activities, 43, 218–
   20, 221, 223–24, 226
Depression, 2, 16, 115, 180,
   189, 242
   clinical, 18
   effect on memory, 191
   effect on movement, 21
   increase in, 17
   mindfulness meditation
      preventing or reducing,
      3, 5, 6, 51–52
   moods creating, 8
   recurrence of, 17, 52
   symptoms of, 217
Difficulties. See also
   Exploring Difficulty
   meditation
   acceptance of, 165–67,
      179–81
   facing, stories about,
      161–64, 168–69
   ineffective methods of
      dealing with, 164–65
   mind vs. body for dealing
      with, 171, 175–78
   turning toward, 222–23

Doing mode, 28–29, 31, 34, 35, 36, 37–43, 105–6, 115, 133, <u>155</u>, 166, 177, 231, 240, 241
Driving, as mindfulness bell, <u>235–36</u>

Eating, as mindfulness bell, <u>235</u>
Eight-Week Mindfulness Program. *See also individual entries for Weeks One through Eight*
　caution about, 63–66
　equipment for, 63
　overview of, 56–61
　setting up time and space for, 61–63, 96
Einstein, Albert, 209–10
Emotions
　ABC model of, 137–38
　acknowledging vs. solving, 28
　components of, 19, **20**
　connected to thoughts and body, 20, 23, 29–30, 91
　constellations of, 25–26
　empathic sharing of, 116–17
　habits and, 71–72
　negative, 9, 10, 11, 25, 28
　past influencing, 25–26, 27
　positive, <u>6</u>, 19, 46, <u>50</u>
　as secondary suffering, <u>155</u>
　set-point of, 46–47, 48
Empathy, 19, 44, 46, <u>49</u>, 54, 60, 94, 116–17, 204, 205–6, 209
Equipment, for Eight-Week Mindfulness Program, 63
Exercise(s), <u>245</u>
　stretching, in Mindful Movement meditation, 118–19, <u>120–23</u>, 124–26
Exhaustion, 1–2, 3, 8, 18, 19, 28, 41, 56, <u>59</u>, 69, 71, 72, 114, 115, 118, 140–41, 142, 164, 191, 212, 217, 226, 230, 231, 232, 234, 236–37, 242. *See also* Tiredness

Exhaustion Funnel, 213–18, **213**
Exploring Difficulty meditation, <u>59</u>, 167, 196, 247
　instructions for, 171, <u>172–74</u>, 175–78
　overview of, 170–71
　preparing for, 169–70
　results from, 178–81
　role of mind vs. body in, 170–71, 175–78
External circumstances, happiness linked to, 34, 35

Failure, 24, <u>59</u>, 64, 102, 104, 117, 139, 148, <u>151</u>, 188, <u>195</u>, 202
Fatigue. *See* Exhaustion; Tiredness
Fear, 10, 19, 24, 25, 40, 41, 42, 81, 91, 94, 113, 117, 126, 162, 164, 175, 181, 188–89, 194, 202, 203, 204, 205, <u>245</u>
Fight-or-flight response, 22, 27
Food preparation, as mindfulness bell, <u>235</u>
Forgetfulness, 68, 69
Franticness, common negative thoughts with, 140–41
Frantic world, 2, 8, 13, <u>59</u>, <u>195</u>, 239
　finding peace in, 241–43, <u>244–45</u>
Freecycling, 208
Freedom, 35, 40, 63, 79, 115, 145, 153, 196
Friendship. *See* Befriending meditation; Befriending your feelings
Frustration, <u>245</u>
　dealing with, <u>154–55</u>
Future, living in, 78, 105

Gardening analogy, describing meditation, 153
Gardening Habit Releaser, 183–84
Gratitude exercise, ten-finger, <u>109</u>

"Guest House, The" (Rumi), 166–67, <u>244</u>
Guilt, 188, 194, 203, 204, 205, 215

Habit breaking, 12–13
Habit Releasers, 232
　purpose of, 56–57, 61
　Week One, changing chairs, 88–89
　Week Two, going for a walk, 106–7, 109
　Week Three, valuing the TV, 134–35
　Week Four, going to the movies, 159–60
　Week Five, sowing some seeds or looking after a plant, 183–84
　Week Six
　　random act of kindness, 208–9
　　reclaiming your life, 207–8
Habits
　automatic pilot and, 69–71
　driving routine behavior, dissolution of, 79
　power of, 68
Happiness, 2, 8, 19, 34, 35, 45, 46, 47–48, 66, <u>108</u>, 159, 184, 204, 205, 206, 221, 226, 246
Hardiness, 53, 54
Headphone experiment, on body's influence on thoughts, 91–92
Health, mindfulness meditation improving, <u>50–51</u>
Helplessness, 114, 230–31
"Hokusai Says" (Keyes), 238, 249, <u>250–51</u>
Holocaust survivors, hardiness traits of, 53
Hourglass shape, of Breathing Space, 133–34, 156, 181
Hypertension, meditation reducing, <u>6</u>

Ideas, dance of, <u>192–93</u>
Immune system, meditation strengthening, <u>6</u>, 48

Inattention, 68, 77
Inner critic, 9, 25, 139. *See also* Self-criticism
Insula, of brain, 48
    empathy and, 49, 205
Interpretation of world, ABC model and, 137–38
Interruptions, during meditation, 63
Irreversibility of thoughts, 189, 194
Irritability, 5, 6, 8, 10, 11, 25, 26, 71, 217

Job dissatisfaction, case histories about, 16, 23–25, 90–91, 94, 211–13, 214–18, 221–22
Judgmentalism, 9, 11, 13, 30, 39, 44, 45, 105, 195

Keyes, Roger, poem by, 238, 249, 250–51
Kindness, 60, 64, 163, 195, 196, 197, 200, 202, 204, 205–6, 209, 240, 241. *See also* Loving-kindness
Kindness Habit Releaser, 208–9
Kings' stories
    on facing difficulties, 168–69
    on finding completeness, 238–39

Lake analogy, describing wandering mind, 86
Life expectancy, mindfulness increasing, 36–37
Listening, as mindfulness bell, 236
Love, self-feeding nature of, 19
Loving-kindness, 50, 59, 200, 200, 201

Mastery, enhancing feelings of, 230–31, 232–33
Maze experiment, 112–14, 177
MBCT. *See* Mindfulness-based cognitive therapy

Meditation, mindfulness. *See* Meditations, specific; Mindfulness and Mindfulness meditation
Meditations, specific
Befriending meditation, 59, 197, 198–200, 200–206
Body Scan meditation, 58, 95–96, 97–100, 101–6, 118, 178, 196, 247
Breath and Body meditation, 126, 127–29, 143, 146, 172, 196
Chocolate meditation, 14, 54, 55, 72
Exploring Difficulty meditation, 59, 167, 169–81, 196, 247
Mindful Movement meditation, 58, 118–19, 120–23, 124–26
Mindfulness of the Body and Breath meditation, 58, 81–82, 83–85, 86–87
One-Minute meditation, 4
Raisin meditation, 72, 73–75, 76–79, 196
Sounds and Thoughts meditation, 59, 142, 143–45, 146–47, 148–53, 172, 196
Three-Minute Breathing Space meditation, 57, 130–31, 132–33, 133–34, 197, 227, 228–34 (*see also* Breathing Space)
Memory(ies)
    bad, triggers of, 10, 11, 30
    in Doing vs. Being modes, 42, 43
    echoing emotional state, 9
    effect of context on, 10
    impact of, on mind and body, 23, 25
    mindfulness meditation improving, 5, 6
    overgeneral, 191–92, 193, 194, 207
    of past, 9, 11, 27, 42, 43, 48, 144, 146, 189, 191, 193, 229
    of real events, 189, 190

suppression of, 194
    of threats, 27
    working, limitations of, 69
Mental pain, 187, 187
Mental time travel, 42
Mind
    analytic side of, 11
    approach vs. avoidance system of, 114
    aversion pathways of, 113, 177, 179
    awareness of, 11, 31
    busyness of, as problem, 78–79
    connected with memory, 9
    conscious, 42, 70, 72
    in Exploring Difficulty meditation, 170, 171, 172
    on full alert, 26
    inferences made by, 136–38
    problem-solving mode of, 28–30
    restless, turning toward, 79
    threat perception by, 26–27
    training, to focus, 79
    wandering, 64–65, 82, 85, 86–87, 94–95, 101, 102, 103, 127–28, 129–30, 151, 198
Mind-body connection, 20–22, 23, 91–92
Mindful eating
    in Chocolate meditation, 14, 54, 55, 72
    in Raisin meditation, 72, 73–75
Mindful Movement meditation, 58
    guidelines for, 118–19, 196
    reactions to, 124–26
    stretches in, 120–23
Mindfulness and mindfulness meditation
    audio tracks on, 14, 56, 82, 103, 106, 119, 131, 152
    autopilot and, 70
    Being mode awakened by, 35, 38, 39, 40, 41–42, 43
    benefits of, 5, 6, 11–12, 35–36, 44–45, 50–52, 212, 216, 217
    for boosting resilience, 53–54

Mindfulness and mindfulness
    meditation (*cont.*)
  brain changes from, 46–49
  choosing practices for, 247
  compared to parachute
    weaving, 243
  core program of, 12
    time frame for, 13
  effectiveness of, 3
  enhancing, in Week Seven,
    231, 233–34
  feelings of failure about, 151
  finding gaps for practicing,
    222–23
  focusing on breath in, 4–5
  gardening analogy and, 153
  habit breaking in, 12–13
  for increasing life
    expectancy, 36–37
  for maintaining peace in a
    frantic world, 244–45
  for managing negative
    thoughts, 11
  myths about, 6–7
  overview of, 240–41
  positive reason for
    continuing, 246–47
  purpose of, 242–43
  repetition in, 153
  struggles with, 167
  subtle changes from, 116
  time spent on, 56, 57,
    247–49
Mindfulness-based cognitive
    therapy (MBCT), 3,
    51–52
Mindfulness bells, 235–36
Mindfulness of the Body and
    Breath meditation, 58,
    81–82, 83–85, 86–87
Mindfulness Program.
    See Eight-Week
    Mindfulness Program
Mood
  as driver of thoughts, 19, 20
  influences on, 10–11, 20, 26
  low
    persistence of, 26
    preventing pleasure, 230
    mindfulness meditation
    improving, 50
  motivation and, 229
  subtle changes in, 16, 18
  thinking producing, 8, 9
  warning signals about, 226
Mortality, meditation
    reducing, 51

Motivation, 228–29
Mouse in the maze
    experiment, 112–14,
    177
Movement. *See also* Mindful
    Movement meditation
    depression and, 21
Movie going Habit Releaser,
    159–60

Negativity, 5, 9, 13, 25–26,
    28, 30–31, 34, 42, 50,
    57, 59, 61, 71, 109,
    116, 138, 181, 205,
    226, 243
  Breathing Space and, 157,
    206–7, 245
  downward spirals of,
    10–11, 40, 71–72, 115,
    131, 176, 179
  Exploring Difficulty
    meditation and,
    170–71
  mouse and movement
    experiment and,
    113–14
Nourishing activities
  in Being mode, 43
  exercise for assessing,
    218–20
  giving up, 59–60, 214–16
  importance of, 218
  for rebalancing life, 221,
    223–24, 226

One-Minute meditation, 4
Overthinking, 30, 34, 35, 44,
    59, 114, 188, 231

Pain, chronic, 6
Painful engagement, 188
Parachute, weaving, 243,
    244–45
Passivity, 112
Past
  acceptance of, 194, 196
  difficulty letting go of,
    188, 191
  entrapment in, 188, 194,
    207
  influence of, 24–25, 26,
    114, 137
  living in, 77, 105
  memories of, 9, 11, 27, 42,
    43, 48, 144, 146, 189,
    191, 193, 229
  re-living, 42, 43

Peace, 2, 8–12, 13, 24, 34,
    59, 62, 63, 85, 93, 100,
    129, 134, 147, 194,
    195, 196, 204, 241–47
Perfectionism, 114, 249
Perspective, changes in, 33,
    34, 156, 158
Physical health, mindfulness
    meditation improving,
    50–51
Picking fruit, in Mindful
    Movement meditation,
    121–22
PITs (Practice Interfering
    Thoughts), 160
Planning, in Doing vs. Being
    modes, 42, 43
Plant care Habit Releaser,
    183–84
Playfulness, 113, 115, 180
Pleasure, reclaiming, 230,
    231–32
Poems
  "Hokusai Says," 238, 249,
    250–51
  "The Guest House,"
    166–67, 244
Positivity, 6, 19, 46, 47, 50,
    140
Postponement of life, 242
Posttraumatic stress disorder
    (PTSD), 186–87, 192
Practice Interfering Thoughts
    (PITs), 160
"Practices of the week" box,
    57
Prefrontal cortex, showing
    mood shifts, 47
Present moment
  living in, 42–43
  paying attention to, 78
Problem-solving, 12, 28–30,
    34, 175
PTSD, 186–87, 192
Pushing too hard
  donkey story about, 112–13
  pitfalls of, 112
Puzzles, approach- vs.
    avoidance orientated,
    112–14

Rainstorm analogy,
    Breathing Space and,
    157–58
Raising arms, in Mindful
    Movement meditation,
    120–21

Raisin meditation, 72, _73–75_, 76–79, 196
Rational critical thinking, 28
Reaction times, mindfulness meditation increasing, 5, _6_
Real events, memories of, 189, _190_
Rebalancing daily life, 221–26
Reclaiming your life Habit Releaser, 207–8
Relationships, meditation improving, _6_
Repetition, in meditation, 153
Resignation, vs. mindful acceptance, 40, 45
Resilience, mindfulness boosting, 53–54
Reward centers of brain, 230
Risk taking, 115
Routine activities
  focusing on, _76–77_, 78
  normally missed, _76_
  waking up to, 117
Rumi, Jalaluddin, 166–67, _244_
Rumors, 138–40, 209

Sadness, 3, 8, 10, 12, 19, 25, 29, 42, 48, 71, 116, 126, 156, 164, 177, 188, _193_, _245_
Seed sowing Habit Releaser, 183–84
Self-criticism, 9, 13, 15, 25, 86, 117, 139–40, 240. _See also_ Inner critic
Senses, 11, 39, 45, _58_, 77, 78, 105, 107, 231, 240
Shoulder rolls, in Mindful Movement meditation, _123_
Showering, paying attention to, _77_
Sleep, 1, 116
Sleepiness, during meditation, 64
Sounds
  likened to thoughts, 143–45
  receiving and noticing, 145
Sounds and Thoughts meditation, _59_, 142, 143–45, _146–47_, 148–53, _172_, 196

Sowing some seeds Habit Releaser, 183–84
Standing in stillness, in Mindful Movement meditation, _123_
Stone-down-a-well analogy, 246–47
Storm analogy, describing wandering mind, 86
Stream, thoughts as, 45, 87, 88, 101, 143, 149, 150, 152, 153, 159
Stress, 2, 3, 8, 12, 18, 22, 24, 26, 56, _59_, _60_, 71, 95, 118, 119, 156, 164, 212, 242
  affecting future plans, 42
  attempts to solve, 28
  case histories about, 15–16, 90–91, 94
  chronic, 115
  from Doing mode, 231
  effect of mindfulness meditation on, 5, _6_
  Exhaustion Funnel and, 213
  helplessness from, 226
  mindfulness for controlling, 5, _37_
  motivation and, 229
  from overloaded memory, 66
  preventing pleasure, 230
  realizations about, 236–37
  reduced sense of control from, 230
  self-feeding nature of, 19
  symptoms of, 217
  thoughts and, 40–41, 140–42
  Three-Minute Breathing Space meditation for, 130–34
Stretching, in Mindful Movement meditation, 118–19, _120–23_, 124–26
Suffering, primary vs. secondary, _155_
Suicide, 180
  attempted, 185–88
Supermarket line frustration, _154–55_
Suppression, 48, 71, 117, 169, 170, 194, 205, 231

Ten-finger gratitude exercise, _109_
Tension, 18, 19, 25, 28. _See also_ Stress

Thoughts. _See also_ Sounds and Thoughts meditation
  autopilot and, 71–72
  body influencing, 21, 91–92
  common negative, 140–42
  connected to emotions and body, 30
  disrupting sleep, 1
  in Doing vs. Being modes, 40–41
  effect on mood, 8, 19, 20
  interfering with senses, 78–79
  irreversibility of, 189, 194
  likened to rumors, 139–40
  likened to sounds, 143–45
  as mental events, 40–41, _59_, 60, 64, 86, _132_, _147_, 153, _244_
  observing, 148–50, 152–53
  Practice Interfering, 160
  receiving and noticing, 145
  self-attacking, 9–10
  as stream, 45, 87, 88, 101, 143, 149, 150, 152, 153, 159
  transient nature of, 5
Threats, fight-or-flight response to, 22, 27
Three-Minute Breathing Space meditation, 57, _118_, _143_. _See also_ Breathing Space meditation
  carrying on after, 159
  guidelines for, 130–31
  instructions for, _132–33_
  in Week Six, _197_
  in Week Seven, _227_, 228–34
Time
  changing outlook, 33–34
  spent on meditations, 56, 57, 61, 62, 96
Tinnitus, 149–50
Tiredness, 11, 15, 18, 27–28, 41, 48, 96, 104, 116, 162, 186, 191, _193_, 226, 229, 236, 241, _244_, _245_. _See also_ Exhaustion
Transcendental Meditation, _51_
Trapped feeling, 114–15

Traumatic events, effect on
    memory, 191–92
TV, valuing, as Habit
    Releaser, 134–35

Unexpected events,
    happiness from,
    159
Unhappiness, 3, 5, 9, 11, 12,
    18, 19, 26, 40, 42,
    44, 46, 56, <u>58</u>, 61,
    71, 91, 95, 111, 116,
    <u>192</u>, <u>193</u>, 212, 214,
    216, 226, 229, 242,
    <u>244</u>, 249
    attempts to solve, 28,
        29–30
    case history about, 15–16,
        18–19, 23–25
    common thoughts with,
        140–41
    Exhaustion Funnel and,
        213
    increase in, <u>17</u>
    moods creating, 8
    reduced sense of control
        from, 230

Walking
    as mindfulness bell, <u>236</u>
    as Week Two Habit
        Releaser, 106–7,
        109
Washing dishes, mindfulness
    during, <u>235</u>, <u>245</u>
Weather analogy, describing
    wandering mind,
    86, 87
Week One of Mindfulness
    Program
    practices in, <u>89</u>
        chair changing Habit
            Releaser, 88–89
        cultivating mindful
            awareness, 87–88
        mindful awareness of
            routine activities,
            <u>76–77</u>, 78
        Mindfulness Meditation
            of the Body and
            Breath, 80–82, <u>83–85</u>,
            86–87

Raisin meditation, 72,
    <u>73–75</u>, 76–79
    understanding autopilot,
        67–72
    realizations from, 94–95
    summary of, <u>58</u>
Week Two of Mindfulness
    Program
    practices in, <u>110</u>
        appreciative attention
            exercise, <u>108–9</u>
        Body Scan meditation,
            94–96, <u>97–100</u>,
            101–6
        learning to connect with
            body, 93–94
        understanding body's
            influence on mind,
            90–93
        walking Habit Releaser,
            106–7, 109
    summary of, <u>58</u>
Week Three of Mindfulness
    Program
    practices in, <u>118</u>
        Breath and Body
            meditation, 126,
            <u>127–29</u>
        Mindful Movement
            meditation, 118–19,
            <u>120–23</u>, 124–26
        Three-Minute Breathing
            Space meditation,
            130–31, <u>132–33</u>,
            133–34
        valuing the TV Habit
            Releaser, 134–35
    preparation for, 117–18
    summary of, <u>58–59</u>
Week Four of Mindfulness
    Program
    practices in, <u>143</u>
        going to the movies Habit
            Releaser, 159–60
        Sounds and Thoughts
            meditation, 142,
            143–45, <u>146–47</u>,
            148–53
        Three-Minute Breathing
            Space meditation,
            153–54, 156–59
    summary of, <u>59</u>, 142

Week Five of Mindfulness
    Program
    practices in, <u>170</u>
        Exploring Difficulty
            meditation, <u>59</u>, 167,
            169–81
        sowing some seeds
            or looking after a
            plant Habit Releaser,
            183–84
    summary of, <u>59</u>
Week Six of Mindfulness
    Program
    practices in, <u>197</u>
        Befriending meditation,
            <u>198–200</u>, 200–206
        extending Breathing
            Space to negative
            thoughts, 206–7
        random act of kindness
            Habit Releaser, 208–9
        reclaiming your life
            Habit Releaser, 207–8
    summary of, <u>59</u>
Week Seven of Mindfulness
    Program
    mindfulness bells in,
        <u>235–36</u>
    practices in, <u>227</u>
    rebalancing daily life in,
        221–26
    summary of, <u>59–60</u>
        Three-Minute Breathing
            Space plus concrete
            action in, 228–34
Week Eight of Mindfulness
    Program, 238–51
    summary of, <u>60</u>
Work. *See also* Job
    dissatisfaction
    Exhaustion Funnel and,
        213–14
Working memory, limitations
    of, 69
Worry, 1, 9, 22, 23, 26, 30,
    41, 42, 45, <u>60</u>, 66, 88,
    91, 94, <u>99</u>, 102, 109,
    114, 116, 125, <u>127</u>,
    <u>144</u>, 162, <u>173</u>, 178,
    188, 207, 247

Yoga, <u>58</u>, 94, 125, 176, 248